Governance, the State, Regulation and Industrial Relations

D0169144

This is an extremely impressive book, which draws upon an unusually broad range of academic research findings to produce a comprehensive treatment of the interplay of the state, capital and labour relations in the development of post-1945 British capitalism. The thesis advanced is bold and compelling. It is sure to become essential reading.

Peter Nolan,
Montague Burton Professor of Industrial Relations, University of Leeds,
and Director of the ESRC Future of Work Programme

This book examines the legacy of economic and political aims and objectives formulated by the British government during and immediately after the Second World War. By doing so, the author develops an innovative historically informed, yet contemporary, theory of the British state.

A significant proportion of post-war economic and political literature has highlighted the adverse effect of embedded patterns of industrial relations on British economic performance. It is argued in this book that this represents a superficial appraisal of post-war British political economy, and that it is instead necessary to look at the deeply ingrained causes particular to the UK's historical development. Equally, the book examines another neglected yet vital aspect of Britain's economic performance, the constraints and opportunities afforded by Britain's international relations.

This book makes an important contribution to the history and theory of British post-war economics. It will be of interest to anybody working in the areas of economic history, international relations or management policy.

Ian Clark is Principal Lecturer in Industrial Relations at De Montfort University. A leading authority on post-war industrial relations, he has written for the *Industrial Relations Journal, Business History, Historical Studies in Industrial Relations* and the *Human Resource Management Journal*. He is a member of a De Montfort University team currently examining American multinationals in Western Europe; the project is supported by a major ESRC award.

Routledge Explorations in Economic History

Governance, the State, Regulation and Industrial Relations

Ian Clark

London and New York

First published 2000
by Routledge
11 New Fetter Lane, London EC4P 4EE

Simultaneously published in the USA and Canada
by Routledge
29 West 35th Street, New York, NY 10001

Routledge is an imprint of the Taylor & Francis Group

© 2000 Ian Clark

Typeset in Garamond by
Prepress Projects, Perth, Scotland
Printed and bound in Great Britain by
St Edmundsbury Press, Bury St Edmunds, Suffolk

British Library Cataloguing in Publication Data
A catalogue record for this book is available
from the British Library

Library of Congress Cataloging in Publication Data
Clark, Ian, 1959–
    Governance, the state, regulation and industrial relations/Ian Clark.
        p. cm.
    Includes bibliographical references and index.
    ISBN 0–415–20263–9 (alk. paper)
    1. Industrial policy – Great Britain. 2. Industrial relations – Great
    Britain. 3. Corporate governance – Great Britain. 4. Reconstruction
    (1939–1951) – Great Britain. 5. Great Britain – Economic policy –
    1979–1997. 6. Great Britain – Economic policy – 1997–. 7. Great
    Britain – Foreign economic relations. I. Title
    HD4148.C54 2000
    338.941–dc21   99-059063
    CIP

Für meine Familie
Janet, Fabian, Max, Sheila, Gerda, Hans

Contents

Tables

Abbreviations

AACP	Anglo-American Council for Productivity
AEG	Allgemeine Elecktrizitäts Gesellschaft
AEEU	Amalgamated Engineering and Electricians' Union
BEC	British Employers' Confederation
BMW	Bayerisch Moteren Werke
BOT	Board of Trade
capex	capital expenditure on plant, equipment and machines
CBI	Confederation of British Industry
CEEC	Committee on European Economic Co-operation
CSO	Central Statistical Office
DfEE	Department for Education and Employment
DTI	Department of Trade and Industry
EC	European Community
ECA	Economic Co-operation Agency
ECU	European Currency Unit
EPU	European Payments Union
ERM	European Exchange Rate Mechanism
ERP	European Recovery Programme
EU	European Union
FBI	Federation of British Industry
GDP	gross domestic product
GNP	gross national product
GTFA	gross tangible assets per employee
HRM	human resource management
IMF	International Monetary Fund
ILO	International Labour Organization
IOD	Institute of Directors
IPD	Institute of Personnel and Development
MRC	Modern Records Centre at the University of Warwick
MLNS	Ministry of Labour and National Service
NATO	North Atlantic Treaty Organization
NIRC	National Industrial Relations Court
OECD	Organization for Economic Co-operation and Development

OEEC	Organization for European Economic Co-operation
OPEC	Organization of Petroleum Exporting Countries
quango	quasi-autonomous non-governmental organization
R & D	research and development
TEC	Training and Enterprise Council
TGWU	Transport and General Workers' Union
TQM	total quality management
TUC	Trades Union Congress
UIP	unfair industrial practice
UK	United Kingdom
UN	United Nations
USA	United States of America
WTO	World Trade Organization
YTS	Youth Training Scheme

Acknowledgements

I would like to acknowledge the helpful advice, comments and encouragement in the development of ideas that went into this book. The following tutors and colleagues have each provided critical feedback on chapter drafts or on conference, master's, doctoral and seminar presentations.

Martin Hoskins, Jack Spence, Mike Smith, Richard Hyman, Peter Nolan, Malcolm Sawyer, John Kelly, John Hillard, Jim Tomlinson, Anthony Carew, Alec Cairncross, Paul Smith, Damian O'Doherty, Margaret Spence, Tim Claydon, Trevor Colling, Sue Marlow, Ian Beardwell, Alan Ryan, David Buchanan, Anthony Ferner. All errors and omissions remain my responsibility.

1 Governance, regulation and industrial relations

Introduction – the aims and objectives of this book

This chapter summarizes the wider arguments developed in the main body of the book and suggests how an embedded pattern of governance constrains long-term economic performance and structures internal regulatory institutions, such as those in the industrial relations system. Moreover, although the book takes a critically informed approach, it seeks to draw out the consequences of decisions and processes that remain both historically significant and necessary.

The purpose of this book is to illustrate the conceptual and historical frailty of the period since 1979 as a contemporary transformation in economic performance, in the role of the state and in the industrial relations system. The argument of the book examines contemporary patterns of regulation by the state and also measures of economic performance and reform in the industrial relations system through historically embedded influences on the state. Contemporary patterns of regulation reflect historically embedded influences, although in many cases the contemporary period appears as a substantive break with the past. Formative influences structure historically significant processes, such as industrialization and the institutionalization and incorporation of the employed class into the state. For example, libertarian *laissez faire*, voluntary regulation, self-regulation and the virtues of short-termism remain key influences in the UK state. The relationship between each appears functional, yet it is contradictory. Moreover, the prevalence of short-termism further reinforces these tendencies. Hence, a formative influence only becomes historically embedded when it appears functional to practitioner groups to act as an autonomous yet contradictory part of the state. A preference for regulation by the voluntary agreement dominates not only in the industrial relations system but also in many other areas, e.g. the Police Complaints Authority, The Advertising Standards Authority and The Press Complaints Commission. Each institution regulates voluntary agreements and standards. In contrast to this, 'deregulation' of public transport and the public utilities, pension provision, training provision in Training and Enterprise Councils (TECs), etc. create pressure for voluntary codes of practice and complaints procedures, with few if any underpinned by statutory regulation.

To provide a historically informed yet contemporary theory of the UK state, it is necessary to emphasize the structural emergence and pervasive impact of formative influences throughout the institutional base of the economy and civil society. The immediate post-war era saw several strategic choices in the external and internal dimension of the state. Although some of these choices were historically necessary, each remains historically significant in the contemporary period. Hence, appreciation of the contemporary period must go beyond what Carr terms mere 'chronicle'.[1] The formulation of state policy in the contemporary period must proceed from an intellectual perspective that accepts the past and previous experience as relevant and significant. In contrast to this, the promotion of severance between 'now' and 'then' appears in terms such as 'new industrial relations', 'change management', economic transformation and the 'hollowed out state'. Carr also makes clear that the closer one is to the contemporary the easier ignorance becomes.[2] This is nowhere clearer than in the empirical – historically embedded – emergence of the UK's productivity gap that appears to have replaced the productivity miracle of the 1980s and early 1990s.

A blend of historical analysis with industrial relations, aspects of international relations and economic history creates the possibility of integrating different approaches. Each discipline highlights a particular causal process – the role of the industrial relations system in post-war decline. To address this argument, which often originates beyond the industrial relations literature, it is necessary to expose and take on some of the crass generalizations within other literature sets. For example, Fordism was 'flawed' in the UK by trade unions and collective bargaining, where resistance 'flawed' attempts by capital and the state to improve the potential of the UK manufacturing sector. More crucially than this, as an institution, workplace multi-unionism and associated restrictive practices in the early post-war period were directly responsible for low investment and low productivity in UK manufacturing until the emergence of Thatcherism reversed this tendency. Further, post-war governments made no attempt to restructure the UK economy because they were fearful of trade union resistance, etc.

Each argument appears significant and yet each is proximate. Moreover, causation, i.e. the why not the how, is often absent. A particular event or process may have several amalgamated causes – economic, political, ideological, short term and long term.[3] However, priority in causation may prove inconvenient or insignificant. As the remainder of this book demonstrates, arguments that position the industrial relations system as the central factor of explanation for the UK's post-war decline fail to constitute a hard core historical fact for two reasons. First, facts are a question of interpretation. Second, the argument, although influential, has failed to find universal acceptance – not all scholars accept it as valid and significant. The remainder of this opening chapter is divided into eight short subsections that outline the overall approach of the book.

Governance and industrial relations in the post-war period

Governance refers to the control and co-ordination of activities to attain a range of specified outcomes. In the main, this is the province of the state. In the domestic sphere, the state may delegate the control of economic and social activities to interest groups or figurehead groups that represent the interests of capital and labour. In the external arena, the individual nation state and its particularized pattern of governance confront international institutions and practices. The aims and operations of such institutions, for example the International Monetary Fund (IMF), the Marshall Plan and associated European Recovery Programme, the European Union, the North Atlantic Treaty Organization (Nato), the United Nations (UN) and the Organization for Economic Co-operation and Development (OECD), may be democratic and federal or hegemonic and unitary. Nation states create, participate within and sustain international institutions nationally; hence, the nation state remains the main governance structure in domestic and international political economy.

The term 'national pathway' contains an external and an internal dimension to the state. In the UK's case, empire and early industrialization have had a seminal impact on the UK's international relations and its position in the hierarchy of international political economy. Equally, and by association, both have influenced the UK's overseas markets, domestic production methods and related patterns of job regulation, an impact renewed in the immediate post-war period and further renewed during the 1980s.

The legacy of economic and political aims and objectives agreed and formulated by the UK government during and immediately after the Second World War is resonant in the contemporary period. In the immediate post-war era, securing the balance of payments and the viability of sterling as a reserve and settlement currency necessitated an all-out recovery of industrial output. The seriousness of the situation produced an output drive that eschewed any large-scale reconstruction of plant and machinery.

UK industry remained committed to non-standard production of goods for its highly diverse domestic and empire markets. As a result of this, craft-based methods of production, production management and patterns of craft control on the shop floor continued to operate in many sectors of manufacturing industry. Critics label this situation as a missed opportunity or as an outright failure by the state. This may be the case, but it explains very little – a proximate and isolated argument. If markets and production methods retained continuity with the pre-war era, it appears reasonable to assume that broadly defined patterns of industrial relations, including management interests, would also retain a similar continuity.

Throughout the post-war period, many scholarly contributions from economics and political science highlight the sclerotic effects of embedded patterns of industrial relations on UK economic performance. However, many such approaches position these patterns as a proximate cause of decline. As a result, they ignore the significance of more deeply ingrained causes that are particular to the UK's historical development. The overall theme generated by the arguments presented in this book suggests that 'popular' and proximate approaches to economic decline are dominant in economics and political science. In defining a prescribed role for industrial relations and the industrial relations system, these disciplines isolate one factor from critical aspects of the real economy, such as employment levels, management policy and employer interests. Equally, there is no consideration of *realpolitik* – the constraints and opportunities afforded by the UK's international relations.

The innovative approach of this book centres on the integration of historically significant decisions made by UK governments during the immediate post-war years within an emergent international order. The UK's pattern of power politics, governance in the economy and the institutional structure of civil society represent a series of interrelated continuities in a national pathway of sovereign regulation. This series of historically embedded relationships and the pursuit of independence and sovereignty they represent weaken the assertions of generalized regulation approaches to industrial capitalism in 'Atlanticist' states. 'Atlanticism' describes a conjunction of nationally regulated and interdependent policy innovations that created a coherent Atlanticist yet sovereign economic and political order. Equally, embedded independence and sovereignty illustrate a primacy of national pathways over integrative structures and institutions, termed Fordism, and wider hegemony in US foreign policy.

The UK state illuminates historically embedded and hence historically significant patterns of domination and accommodation within an individual nation state that limit the significance of generalized patterns of regulation in capitalist economies. Interaction between internal and external forces in the state reinforce these embedded aims, interests and patterns of behaviour. Moreover, an appreciation of the UK's contemporary relationship with the European Union and emergent patterns of pan-European regulation is likely to reflect a pattern of interests and power politics evidenced in the immediate post-war years.

The linkage between international relations and the UK's pattern of industrial relations is evident in initially hegemonic and in subsequently anarchistic attempts to maintain and reproduce a stable international order. Both designs aimed to develop an expanding world economy encompassing a coherent international division of labour centred on the import of foodstuffs and raw material in exchange for exports of manufactured goods. In this respect, US foreign policy played a key strategic yet unsuccessful role in galvanizing a 'Communist threat' countered only by the integrative export of US methods of management, work organization and industrial relations. To present this argument and retain a contemporary relevance, it is necessary to contain contemporary and recent economic performance within a framework that focuses on the whole of the period since 1945.

Contemporary views of the post-war period suggest that the UK system of industrial relations regulated managers and workers through institutions and mechanisms that operated beyond embedded patterns of regulation in the UK state. To challenge this view, it is necessary to establish that, although the UK is part of a sovereign and stable European state system, the UK state has retained a peculiarly national pathway in the related areas of international relations, economic management and its industrial relations system.

As a revisionist approach (some would say heretical) to the UK state in the period since 1945, it is necessary that the argument and its material be original yet useful. This raises a methodological issue of 'what does the book do'? But, in addition, 'where does it look'?

Methods and sources

To add value to the existing stock of knowledge, a particular 'research method' must deploy a system of investigation that is capable of underpinning theoretical analysis by informing research techniques which address specific scholarly or research problems or areas of inquiry. For example, what role does an industrial relations system have in the process of economic decline? How can a presumed link be examined? Why is a presumed link seen as significant? However, theory is only one means of organizing reality. A conceptual positioning of relationships between different spheres of activity, for example the relationship between international relations and its impact on economic management and industrial relations, necessarily oversimplifies, restricts and, in the process, distorts. All scholarly methods have strengths and weaknesses, so a combination of several approaches may yield a critical mass of different types of evidence.

This project uses theoretically informed primary archival and documentary research methods to complement the use of established secondary sources in established literature sets that provide its narrative and analysis. In addition, the reconstruction of historical evidence through a relativistic approach positions the contemporary in an unending dialogue with the past. This further complements the theoretical approach to create a triangulation of methods in the examination of the state and patterns of governance.

The first priority for any state is survival. In the external dimension, this brings a nation into contact and conflict with other nations to create a pattern of inter*nation*al relations. In the internal dimension, state survival necessitates an effective yet acceptable organization of political institutions and economic resources to position a particular nation state in the hierarchy of the international political economy. In the political sphere, this requires sovereignty and territorial integrity, whereas economic ranking is subject to competitive economic performance that is in turn dependent on comparative productivity growth and control of unit labour costs. Both factors assume the effective regulation of labour power by the state at the workplace. However, the process of particularization peculiar to the individual nation state limits and weakens the abstract functionalism of generalized approaches to regulation that prescribe a structured role for the capitalist state.

An individual state, although sovereign, is subject to the regulatory dynamics of international political economy. Hence, in economic relations, the nation state is subject to political constraints. It is necessary to manage and maintain its comparative position in the international monetary system, e.g. under either floating or fixed exchange rate systems nations must regulate and defend the value of their currency. Politically, this has an impact upon the domestic economy and civil society, e.g. the state may have to legitimize unacceptable levels of wages, unemployment or inflation as necessary to contain unit labour costs and thereby position competitive productivity growth internationally.

The 'hegemonic' model of regulation, sometimes referred to as 'Fordism', initiated during the post-war years and recently (since the late 1980s) consolidated as 'post-Fordism' remains elusive and remote in the UK economy. In addition to looking beyond the expected areas, it is necessary to justify how and why this approach adds value to the existing stock of knowledge.

A legacy of connections

Single-state analysis is for some commentators and publishers redundant in an era dominated by the growth of comparative studies or internationalized approaches imbued with a new hegemony 'globalization'. However, comparative analysis can only build on single-state analyses that contribute to a cumulative comparative analysis. Before embarking on comparative analysis, particularly in a period of presumed and inexorable convergence, it is necessary to establish a series of thematically connected arguments particular to one nation state. As a precursor to subsequent comparative analysis, it is necessary to establish the historically distinctive features and processes that particularize an individual nation state – defining what makes it individual. Comparative studies that either pre-empt nationally embedded patterns of regulation or ignore references to it may result in haphazard comparative research which acquires only transient significance. Such studies may be able to highlight contemporary differences between states yet may be unable to provide historically significant yet contemporary relevant explanations for them.

The legacy of an unconstructed industrialization and empire has contributed directly to an internally consistent set of institutional ideologies that create an embedded pattern of governance which constitutes the UK state. The effect of political institutions on the political economy provide revealing explanations of the UK's deteriorating economic performance since 1945. Equally, a historically positioned approach offers a multidisciplinary triangulation of methods that addresses the role of the state in the decline of the UK economy. Triangulation highlights a consistently particularized pattern of regulation in several areas crucial to explaining the position of the UK economy in the 1990s.

Contemporary analysis can only proceed by appreciating the past. This requires the use of a theoretically informed empirical, yet historically underpinned, methodology. The identification of causation in the success and the failures of the post-war UK state, in particular economic performance, necessitates an integrated analysis of internal and external aspects in state policy. This will enable an assessment of individual causes – proximate causes –

identified with and significant to a particular literature set in relation to a bigger whole. For example, Kaldor has consistently argued that the UK's post-war economic performance was no worse than its potential when examined in relation to wider political objectives that constrained the state.[4] Equally, Kaldor identifies the qualitative significance of institutional inclusiveness. Pluralism and collective bargaining in the industrial relations system are good cases in point. Each played a role in cushioning the process of long-term comparative economic decline by contributing to the UK's good economic performance in terms of output relative to the recent past. In addition to this, beyond the marginal, over the longer term, neither pluralism nor collective bargaining undermined the aims of economic management in the post-war period. In the contemporary period, this position appears completely reversed, whereby the promotion and isolation of individual causes from the bigger picture appear as a strategic focus in state policy.

However, movement from the post-war period to the contemporary period retained many continuities in the state but exhibited three significant differences. First, economic policy and surrounding institutional inclusiveness during the post-war period cushioned decline, whereas in the contemporary period economic policy became procyclical and accelerated economic decline. Second, institutional exclusion increasingly separated the interests of the state and capital from civil society. Third, comparative economic performance during the 1980s and early 1990s appeared insignificant. Economic performance relative to the recent past became the central measure of political success. For example, a low taxation culture, privatization, deregulation and the exclusion of trade unions from the state each created short-term gains – property booms, greater consumption, the productivity miracle – yet each has generated significant longer-term costs.

Institutional inclusiveness retains historical significance and relevance to the contemporary period. Although it is perhaps less popular as a methodology than previously, a focus on historically embedded processes prefigure the contemporary. Equally, they challenge proximate explanations of decline and transformation, such as external shocks, globalization, Thatcherism or Blairism. Historically informed political economy reveals crucial insights into the contemporary: (history is) a living entity given contemporary life by its unending dialogue with the past. Economic history and industrial relations are subject to periodic rewriting and revision, yet revisionism often displays a consistent pattern of arguments. Themes and issues retain significance in particular disciplines because they are not subject to falsification, whereas other arguments acquire significance that remains only transient. For example, Chapter 3 illustrates that the proposition of economic transformation from decline in the UK economy during the 1980s is (was) open to clear falsification. The political rhetoric of this claim runs counter to the arguments of the multivoluminous declinist literature and official data sets prepared by the OECD and the UK Central Statistical Office (CSO). Equally, claims of a singular cause for decline – fixed exchange rates, the effects of public sector crowding out or a lack of entrepreneurial spirit or the effects of the industrial relations system on productivity and unit labour costs – have all at varying times acquired a profound significance. However, each singular cause was subject to falsification because it was possible to specify both intellectually and empirically an argument or data that could dislodge, disprove or limit its significance.

The political and economic structure of a particularized nation state may buoy, distort or impair the pursuit of the generalized functions sustained by the capitalist state. This variety of possibilities prevails because the structure of a state, the historically embedded process of particularization, predominates over and limits functionalism in the state. The distillation of this process appears to pronounce that the historically significant aims and objectives of a state remain so where continuity in the state is in evidence, e.g. those announced and agreed to by the UK government in 1941, 1947, 1956, 1973, 1987 and 1999. The Atlantic Charter secured the remnants of empire, whereas successful resistance to the pan-European aims of the Marshall Plan prefigured a decision to pass on membership of the European Community (EC). In contrast to this pass, the subsequent decision to join the EC aimed to secure continued national greatness and avoid political integration at the pan-European level. Opt-outs from the European Social Charter and a decision to eschew commitment to the Euroland area echo earlier short-term decisions designed to secure national sovereignty

UK aims and objectives in the post-war world

The wartime and post-war aims and objectives of the UK state remain historically significant in the contemporary period. They reflect a continuous and conservative development whereby the effects of industrialization and empire have created a particularized approach to governance in the state. This pattern permeates international relations, domestic economic management and the industrial relations system. By positioning the industrial relations system and embedded patterns of job regulation within this wider framework, it is possible to arrive at a more significant explanation of decline beyond proximate explanations of economic decline.

For the UK state, victory in and recovery from the Second World War was both an opportunity and a problem. It was an opportunity to sustain the UK's sovereign polity and its economic management. Equally, in the context of wartime agreements between the UK and US governments, post-war continuity in UK export markets and the introduction of a comprehensive welfare state programme both looked doubtful. A series of agreements running from the 1941 Atlantic Charter, through Lend Lease agreements in 1942 to the 1944 Bretton Woods agreement on a post-war international monetary and trade system committed the UK to ending preferential trade arrangements such as Imperial Preference and the maintenance of unconvertible sterling balances. In summary, the agreements committed the state to multilateral free trade and a fully convertible currency. As Chapter 2 details, the disastrous consequences of these commitments became all too evident in 1947.

A two-month flirtation with convertibility and free trade in 1947 contributed to the emergence of a more substantial and contrary framework for post-war recovery. The Marshall Plan and subsequent European Recovery Programme (ERP) further consolidated the UK's problematic post-war recovery. The pan-European aims of the programme threatened UK sovereignty in the requirement for a major overhaul of manufacturing industry. The effects of this would seriously inhibit national greatness, particularly the reserve currency status of sterling, the sterling area and export markets therein.

From the outset, the UK government mounted a series of campaigns designed to ensure that the Marshall Plan and the ERP oversaw national pathways to post-war recovery. For the UK, this was absolutely necessary to maintain the external dimension of the state, its domestic modernization and recovery plans. In short, throughout and beyond the Marshall Plan era, the formulation of the UK's domestic and foreign policy aimed to maintain the UK as a (residual) great power – a *European* great power. The consequences and effects of this remain far reaching, if in some areas unintended. A strong, if short term (i.e. at a given scale of plant), production effort sustained an embedded framework of management interests and management practice in the manufacturing sector. Chapter 6 demonstrates that the wider aspirations of state policy are an appropriate context to examine the implications for the industrial relations system and organized labour over the whole of the post-war period.

The UK government secured (residual) great power status, i.e. autonomy of action and independence in an emergent European state system. This situation prevailed, although two external *(super)*powers managed and stabilized the European states system. UK autonomy was manifest in three areas. First, in return for the USA guaranteeing the reserve status of sterling, the UK played a major role in internationalizing the Cold War throughout Western Europe. Second, the UK secured atomic and nuclear status in a US-dominated Nato. Third, the UK government committed to instigating a productivity programme centred around US 'best practice' in management and job regulation techniques.

As subsequent chapters illustrate, the UK's necessary national aims and objectives were short term. Post-war recovery was an output-dominated effort that had insignificant effects on the scale of plant and operations, yet had a considerable impact on labour productivity. However, the necessity of output prevented employers and management at workplace level from taking US proposals for industrial renewal and restructuring with any seriousness. The political dimension to post-war recovery flowed through international relations and embedded patterns of domestic state policy. The flows interlocked in a framework of delegated institutions that constituted the particularized methods of governance in the UK state. Chapter 4 amplifies and details this argument, whereas the following section briefly specifies its approach.

Governance and the nation state

Embedded relationships between and within capital, labour and the wider state apparatus of political and institutional arrangements, for example voluntarism in the industrial relations system, structure a pattern of governance – a national pathway to capitalist regulation. Particularized structures, although not determinist, may affect the position of a nation state in the international political economy – its economic performance – negatively or positively.

An embedded pattern of governance may reflect particular determinants of historical formation, such as the UK's continuous unity, its unconstructed and early industrialization and the absence of a centrally regulated constitution. Equally, the relatively peaceful transition from absolutist monarchy to partial democracy is significant. The aristocracy found common cause with the industrial class to lobby against active state intervention in industrial capitalism, particularly in the embryonic employment relationship. An embedded pattern of governance may reflect strategic choices in the military and political sphere, e.g. acquiring, developing and maintaining an empire. This contributed to the maintenance of a large but small-scale and diverse manufacturing sector. Equally significant and reflecting continuity with the previous point was the post-war impact of Atlanticist and empire and then commonwealth approaches to trade and markets rather than one geared towards Western Europe.

The sovereignty of a nation state demonstrates the process of particularization, both domestically and in international relations. In the domestic arena, distinctive historically embedded processes provide the basis for institutional regulation, however poorly institutionalized and regulated by the state. In contrast to this, in international relations nation states deploy economic and military power and power seeking – invasion, territorial and border disputes, empire building and war – to retain and strengthen sovereignty. Power and power seeking create an anarchical (international) society of nations to complement the anarchy of the market. In both spheres, accumulated views and perceptions held by institutional actors are difficult to dislodge even in the face of emergent hegemonic patterns of regulation. Indeed, in the immediate post-war years, US hegemony became legitimate in the UK state only by deviation from a strategized pattern of integrative regulation in production, defence and international trade and payments. The incorporation of empire areas into the Marshall Plan, US support for sterling beyond multilateralism, Marshall Plan support for national pathways and the relative and comparative failure of the management and productivity programme each serve as examples of US deviation from initial strategies.

The immediate post-war years saw established – historically embedded – aims and objectives in the state necessarily renewed and legitimized to underscore the UK's strategic position in the emergent Cold War. A political determination to maintain national sovereignty sustained established markets and the reserve status of sterling and empire to provide short-term opportunities for the state and economy, yet maintaining both created consequential longer-term constraints for state and economy. For example, the primary research in Chapter 6 demonstrates that in the immediate post-war years continuities in markets, production methods and established patterns of management practice breathed new life into comparatively uncompetitive production systems and the industrial relations system, particularly the tradition of workplace regulation.

The consequences of national distinctiveness

The necessity of gearing the UK's post-war production effort to the domestic market and empire markets reveals three emergent consequences for the UK state. First, as the buoy of Marshall Aid declined in the late 1950s, a now 'bloced' Western European economy began to challenge the UK's competitive position. Western European markets, particularly intra-European trade in manufactured goods, grew much faster than those markets in which UK manufacturing industry concentrated its efforts. Second, Marshall Aid effectively suspended the convertibility of sterling until 1958. The absence of convertibility until this date shielded the comparative weakness of the UK's manufacturing sector, in particular poor management techniques in established patterns of job regulation. The restoration of convertibility exposed balance of payments difficulties and the comparatively weak performance of productivity and unit labour costs in the UK manufacturing industry. By the early 1960s, the growth of UK markets, both domestic and overseas, and the competitiveness of UK industry within each sector was open to direct competition from Western European states. This period saw the emergence of unfavourable comparative analysis in the UK's economic performance. Equally, the period witnessed the beginning of the UK's post-war economic decline, concern about measures of economic performance and the role of the industrial relations system within both. Third, the period 1957–73 saw the 'external shock' (Suez, convertibility, the Cuban missile crisis, commodity and oil crises) and domestic stereotype (militant trade unions, especially shop stewards, 'strikes' and pickets) emerge as significant factors in weakening economic performance. External shocks and trade union activity had some effects on the state and economy, the former more than the latter, but both exposed problems rather than creating them. However, each category proved a convenient beacon for blame that shielded more significant problems that domestic and international institutions failed to regulate.

The regulation school, post-war economic recovery and boom

The regulation school has developed a varied but highly influential approach to explaining post-war economic growth in Western European and Atlanticist economies. As Chapter 2 demonstrates, the regulation approach is diverse and includes Marxist political economists and sociologists, institutional economists and some political scientists, who focus on post-war international relations and US foreign policy. The common ground between these groups is a shared approach to explaining the stability and growth of post-war capitalism.

The most common explanation for post-war political stability and economic boom is the successful deployment of mass production and consumption – *Atlanticist Fordism* may describe the integrationist (convergent) effects of institutional regulation. In this, fixed exchange rates disciplined Keynesian welfare states to successfully minimize balance of payments deficits, align wages and productivity and peg both to inflation rates. In contrast to this view, both realist and revisionist approaches suggest that US foreign policymakers aimed to create an 'Americanized' Western economic system. Initially, the base for Americanization was the export of domestic patterns in economic and corporate management – Fordism. Fordism retained ideological significance throughout the post-war period, yet after 1947 military and political interests in the deepening Cold War became the substantive focus for Americanization.

Sovereign nation states within a bloced Western Europe, including the UK and 'West' Germany, represented a US sphere of influence. Equally, the emergent independent nation states in eastern Europe, with the exception of Yugoslavia, constituted a Soviet sphere of influence. Anglo-American economic aggression combined with a fear of Communism to 'bloc' the economic and military interests of Western Europe with those of the USA. This provided a mode of regulation that internationalized a superpower Cold War by economic, ideological, industrial and political means, each regulated by individual nation states.

Particularized patterns of regulation

Qualitative and contrary counterfactual arguments demonstrate the particularized effects of historically embedded patterns of regulation in an individual nation state. This approach disputes generally accepted arguments as influential and rhetorical yet proximate and not always borne out intellectually or empirically, e.g. the significance of Keynesian demand management in maintaining conditions of economic boom throughout the post-war period or the pivotal effect of the industrial relations system on economic decline during the post-war period. Both arguments may hold some truth, but they are proximate explanations of boom and decline. This is the case because the effects of demand management on economic boom and the industrial relations system on decline explain little. Equally, each argument may be significant but cannot clearly identify causation, hence they are not necessarily historically significant explanations as both propositions are open to dispute.

In contrast to highlighting proximate causes of economic decline, the approach deployed in this book positions the contemporary as the result of an embedded historical process. A particularized theory of the UK state specifies four integrative and challenging components. First, as this chapter argues and as Chapter 4 consolidates, the individual nation state is subject to a series of formative influences. These influences particularize regulation in the framework of industrial capitalism described in generalized theories of regulation and the state. Historical formation within a particular nation state particularizes regulatory behaviour, the processes of coercion and accommodation in and between capital, labour and the state in government. Libertarian *laissez faire* is the formative ideological and coercive influence over the UK state and its institutional structure. Its effects are permanent yet unfolding.

Second, Chapters 2 and 4 develop an argument that establishes the permanent yet unfolding effects of formative influences in a nation state – the primacy of national over generalized modes of capitalist regulation. Chapter 3 demonstrates the significance of historically embedded aims and objectives in the UK state. These interests legitimized the UK's post-war political economy and its economic performance as the necessary aims of and constraints on a great power. The imperative of this framework necessarily legitimized the output drive that sustained an extensive deployment of capital and labour, in turn legitimizing embedded management approaches to production and job regulation.

Third, Chapters 5 and 6 demonstrate that the industrial relations system was of marginal significance in explaining the UK's post-war economic decline. Last, Chapter 7 develops this argument to illustrate that industrial relations reform during the 1980s had an equally marginal impact in improving the UK's trend pattern of economic performance.

Chapter 8 follows on from the theoretically informed and empirically underpinned arguments developed in the previous chapters. The chapter asserts that the state and embedded patterns of national regulation retain significance, wherein the nation state remains the significant actor in domestic and international political economy beyond supranational mechanisms and pan-European modes of regulation. External power seeking and internal coercion and accommodation in the state combine to sustain the primary objective of the UK state – the maintenance of free will and independence, the literal meaning of libertarian *laissez faire*.

The following chapter outlines and examines three approaches that prescribe mechanisms and systems of international regulation. Each approach presents an interpretation of economic reconstruction and military and political stability in the post-war Atlanticist order.

2 Regulation and the post-war order

Introduction

The post-war period from the late 1940s until the mid-1970s was an era of remarkable economic success. The USA, the UK and war-ravaged nations in continental Europe all experienced high rates of economic growth. Full employment became the norm as did relative exchange rate and balance of payments stability, with only moderate or creeping inflation. However, the UK experience of the last appeared persistent and problematic.

The regulation approach has developed as a highly influential and all-encompassing explanation of the capitalist boom during the 1950s and 1960s, subsequent instability in the 1970s and restructuring during the 1980s. This approach fuses institutional economics with systems of work organization commonly referred to as 'Fordism' and 'post-Fordism'. The analytical limitations of the regulation approach are the concern of this chapter. In particular, it focuses on the neglect of historical material covering international relations and *realpolitik* during the immediate post-war period. By drawing on historical material and *realpolitik*, it is possible to develop an 'Atlanticist' approach to post-war regulation that is more plausible and robust as a means of interpreting the post-war order. *Realpolitik* describes a dominant pattern of politics – Altanticism – in which political realities define material needs rather than a pattern of politics based on morals or ideals.[1] The chapter focuses on neither political hegemony of Fordist production techniques nor on Fordism's economic imperative, but on the presence of *historically embedded national pathways* in the political economy of sovereign nation states. Equally, the historical material on the post-war aims and objectives of the UK state demonstrates that, within the wider context of the Cold War, US economic and political interests were not mutually reinforcing. To secure US political interests in Western Europe, the USA provided economic support for Western Europe that either consolidated or recreated national pathways. Paradoxically, economic and political action that shored up nationally distinctive systems of regulation was the only way to diffuse an international order for regulation. A historical specification of regulation in the post-war order suggests that the export of Fordism appeared successful by recognizing variety in the depth and scope of its take-up in national pathways.

'Atlanticism' refers to an amalgamation of economic, military and political ideologies that came to dominate US and Western European international relations during the post-war period. More particularly, Atlanticism created an alliance of interests that consolidated a bloc of Western European nation states, later formalized in the OECD. Within this bloc, national pathways formed a basis for European accommodation to and internalization of the dominant ideologies that created and sustained the Atlanticist bloc. Although US foreign economic policy on convertibility, exchange rates, trade, production and managerial systems was initially hegemonic, deviation from and dilution of its component parts was necessary to create an alliance of sovereign nation states in the Marshall Plan and Nato. This chapter is divided into three sections. The first section examines the concepts of Fordism and institutional regulation, whereas the second section develops the analytical category of Altanticism as an alternative mode of regulation in the period since 1945. The third section examines how the Marshall Plan, rather than transforming the UK's national pathway, merely consolidated historically embedded interests and patterns of regulation in the state, in capital and in labour in a manner that complemented the wider structure of Altanticism.

Common purpose in historically embedded national pathways to industrial capitalism held together the 'Atlantic alliance'.[2] This 'state system' argument is in marked contrast to the 'production system' argument of more orthodox regulation approaches detailed in the following section.

What is the regulation approach?

The regulation approach contains little systematic unity, yet its variants contain common themes. First, the characterization of industrial capitalism moving in and between stable stages. In each stage, a series of economic structures referred to as a regime of accumulation regulate the crisis-prone nature of the capitalist system.[3] A Fordist regime of accumulation characterized the post-war period during which large-scale mass production and mass consumption dominated economic relations. A regime of accumulation can only sustain profitability, productivity and stable prices as long as its internal regulatory institutions – the mode of regulation – remain mutually consistent and retain the capacity to generate economic growth.[4] Fordism contained institutions such as collective bargaining linked directly to wage increases and labour productivity, a welfare state and the use of Keynesian macroeconomic management to secure full employment. Each inclusion bolstered the legitimacy of post-war capitalism by consolidating the social wage. Once such institutions appear unable to regulate the economy and contain class struggle, economic crisis emerges to mark the breakdown of the Fordist regime. Thus, forms of work organization and wider institutions that regulate class conflict and economic distribution in civil society appear historically contingent, ending in structural crisis. Periodic crisis heralds a new regime of accumulation, often referred to as post-Fordism, in which a new mode of institutional regulation emerges, centred around monetarist economics and the natural rate of unemployment. In addition, measures to stimulate greater labour market segmentation and flexibility and the associated erosion of collective bargaining creates what some commentators term a 'hollowed out' state. In the UK, the primary concerns of the hollowed out state are deregulating the social wage and the public sector and the control of inflation in a low tax flexible economy increasingly attractive to foreign direct investors.[5]

Adherents to the regulation approach see the period between 1973 and 1975 as that of breakdown and stagnation of the Fordist mode of regulation. Other scholars, for example Marglin,[6] emphasize the gradual breakdown of the structured international economic order between 1968 and 1971. This period saw the suspension of convertibility between the US dollar and gold, followed by the downward float of the dollar, i.e. the end of fixed exchange rates. For Marglin, breakdown in the regulatory capacity of fixed exchange rates and the Bretton Woods international monetary and reserve system represented a proximate cause of crisis in international regulation. This breakdown triggered a series of independent crises – the depth and scope of which reflect nationally embedded relations among capital, labour and the state. Although tangential to the main regulation variants, this approach opens the possibility to a more Atlanticist explanation of stability and crisis grounded in national pathways. Table 2.1 reviews and summarizes the variants of the regulation approach.

The regulation approach as Fordism

Advocates of this variant to the regulation approach, for example Jessop[7] and Aglietta[8], argue that Fordism is the central institution in the post-war period. An era of intensive accumulation with a mode of regulation consciously developed as a response to the failings and limitations of extensive accumulation during the inter-war period. The production of capital goods, often referred to as 'department 1', was the basis of extensive accumulation. In contrast, the extensive regime left the production of consumer goods, 'department 2', unchanged. Economic growth – accumulation – resulted from increases in the level of capital stock in department 1, where there were few technical changes in methods and cycles of production. Competitive advantage was basically one of scale, in which growth in the size of capital stock brought additional labour into the manufacturing sector. The use of overtime and long hours of work supplemented increases in the stock of labour.[9]

In contrast to the scale emphasis of extensive accumulation, productivity and value added strategies dominate within intensive accumulation regimes. Here, the social and technical organization of work assumes a key significance. By combining a growth in the level of capital stock per employee, intensive accumulation demonstrates the importance of scientific management techniques first introduced in the US economy during the period of extensive accumulation. Scientific management techniques aim to remove (craft) skills from the shop floor, thereby separating the conception of work from its execution.[10]

Table 2.1 Variants of the regulation approach

	Fordism	Institutional regulation	Hegemonic US foreign policy
Main drivers	Standardized mass production Specialised equipment Mass consumption Intensive production techniques	Institutionalized and indexed collective bargaining Productivity bargaining Social democracy in state (welfare state and distributional management) Confinement of wage disputes to nominal wage	Realists → Power and security → Soviet threat to Western Europe; Revisionists → US national interests → Linkage → Political system / Economic aid
Assumed presence	Effective management prerogative Effective management take-up Subordination and incorporation of trade unions and institutionalized collective bargaining Integrated circuit of capital	Fordist economics and management drivers	Blocking Western Europe Material superiority of West US domination in Nato Incorporation of West Germany into Atlantic block
Measures of success	High productivity, high profits, high investment, diffusion of new production techniques under management control	Party political consensus, mixed economy, full employment, rising living standards, improved distribution	
Sources of instability	Diminishing returns to investment Global Fordism – lower labour costs Multinationals investing beyond Atlantic area	Cost of public sector, breakdown of political consensus, class conflict in industrial relations and wage disputes	Course of European integration Failure of Marshall Plan Reappraisal of US foreign policy German unification
Restructured as	Post-Fordism	Reform of collective bargaining Privatization and deregulation Non-accelerating inflation as policy priority	New Cold War under Reagan New focus of US foreign policy Iraq, Libya, international terrorism

Scientific management and an emphasis on the social and technical organization of work are the central drivers of increased labour productivity in departments 1 and 2. In addition, collective bargaining agreements regulate labour productivity. In turn, bargaining agreements sustain an agreed division of labour, work study and the use of specialized equipment to produce highly standardized components and final units.

Mass production during the inter-war period was unable to sustain mass consumption, creating a crisis of underconsumption that led to stagnation and world-wide recession during the early 1930s.[11] In contrast, intensive accumulation combined Taylorist scientific management with simplified and standardized production in both departments 1 and 2, generating continuous improvements in the regulation of work organization and labour productivity.[12] These measures generated the mass production of both capital goods and consumer goods. The mass consumption of consumer goods facilitated price reductions to sustain mass production, thus halting the tendency to underconsumption.

Fordism linked wages to productivity and gave management executive control of production and the deployment of new technology. Institutionalized collective bargaining legitimized management control of production. Further, improvements in workplace industrial relations (union recognition and collective bargaining) and the emergence of social democracy (the welfare state and distributional management through active fiscal and monetary policies) contained class conflict without reducing managerial prerogative. As a result, Fordism appears as a general system of production.[13]

Fordism legitimized intensive production and the subordination and incorporation of the employed class, materially through mass consumption and politically through social democracy in the state and industrial relations.[14] The Fordist production system stimulates labour productivity and improved wages and generates profit levels that secure high levels of capital investment per employee in the manufacturing sector. This leads to high labour productivity and high wages in an integrated circuit of capital.

By the early 1970s, however, the structural limitations of Fordism became evident as the law of diminishing returns saw successive additions to the capital stock yielding smaller improvements in labour productivity.[15] In addition, full employment and social democracy improved and legitimized the bargaining position of trade unions, denting management ability to speed up production or introduce new technology.[16] The result was a profits crisis and failure of institutions to contain and regulate class conflict and legitimize inequality in distribution.

An underlying strand within the Fordist approach suggests that intransigent trade unions frustrated the introduction and deployment of intensive accumulation by the state and employers. This assumption characterizes an analytical diagnosis of UK economic performance termed 'flawed Fordism'.

Flawed Fordism?

> The British case shows that Fordism is not always an inevitability which imposes itself due to its superior economic efficiency. A strong labour movement, defending precise skills, tasks and job rules, can block most of the productive potential associated with modern management methods. This can be termed *Flawed Fordism.*[17]

Prominent advocates of the regulation approach argue that the UK reached the technical limits of Fordism comparatively early. This was the case because the state failed to effectively institutionalize collective bargaining.[18] By the mid-1950s, this created a pattern of industrial relations dominated by lay activists in the workplace. This prevented job reorganization and created inflationary pressure in the economy, often termed wage drift. Successive governments regulated inflation by stop–go fiscal policy. As a result, the UK workplace generated productivity gains that were small in comparison to Western European competitors. In turn, poor labour productivity deferred investment in research and development and the diffusion of new technologies, a pattern reinforced by stop–go economic policies.

As demonstrated in Chapter 6, by the mid-1950s the capacity of many units in the UK's manufacturing sector was small and exhibited poor standardization of output. The UK's manufacturing sector was efficient enough to secure levels of investment, productivity and profitability that generated rates of economic growth that were very favourable relative to the recent past. However, investment, productivity and profitability all grew faster in Western Europe. This was the case not only because of a superior regulatory capacity in other national pathways but also because of higher levels of trade and demand in the intra-European market.

The prefixes flexible, flawed and genuine appear to establish national pathways in Fordism. However, a causal relationship between prefix and economic performance is not proven. Development of this argument will facilitate a national pathway approach to economic decline beyond the category flawed Fordism. However, before developing the detail of this argument, the second variant to the regulation approach is reviewed.

Institutional regulation

This variant concentrates less on Fordist methods of work organization and regime of accumulation but more on the wider institutional infrastructure associated with Fordism. Boyer, the central advocate of this approach, has argued that institutionalized industrial relations are the basis of industrial stability and the source of economic crisis.[19] In the post-war period, trade union recognition and institutionalized collective bargaining created a wage dynamic that institutionalized standard cost of living increases plus productivity increases. Institutionalists argue that this dynamic eroded profit levels in UK manufacturing before the sector reached the technical limits of Fordism. Equally, the scope and depth of trade union interests created inertia and inflexibility in employer objectives, patterns of training and industrial relations management.

In periods of stability, the institutional regulation of the employed class through collective bargaining, the welfare state and social democracy helps to sustain high investment by employers. Hence, the components that constitute a mode of regulation appear mutually reinforcing. Labour and trade unions accept modernization, whereas employers and management in the workplace promote modernization to confine labour disputes to the nominal wage. High investment stimulates a diffusion of new technology in the workplace, which in turn helps to sustain productivity growth. Management is firmly in control of production, with organized labour sharing in its regulation through collective bargaining.

The domestic institutions that regulate Fordism represent a particularized version of a wider set of global institutions centred around Keynesian demand management and fixed exchange rates. However, institutionalists argue that the sources of economic crisis are at least partly endogenous to national Fordisms. The failure of institutions to contain class conflict exposes crisis. However, the primary cause of this is economic – the failure to generate sufficient levels of productivity increase to confine distributional disputes to the level of increase in the nominal wage. The UK experienced periodic crises over the period 1974–84, e.g. the IMF crisis in 1976 and procyclical recession between 1979 and 1981.[20] Poor institutionalization of the Fordist regime sustained and repeated crises, not the emergence of external shocks.[21] Institutionalists argue that the scope and depth of regulation within individual nation states contributes directly to the relative success they experience in crisis management in the international system, e.g. the end of fixed exchange rates in 1971 and the Organization of Petroleum Exporting Countries (OPEC) crises in 1973 and 1978.

Although institutionalists emphasize national specificity in institutional regulation, the theoretical specification is 'top down'. This suggests that the theory is sound, yet institutionalism and institutional regulation failed because within national pathways the state failed to institutionalize regulation. Glyn *et al.* and Kindleberger both argue that Fordism was a historical aberration, a conjunction of independent yet interactive institutional and policy innovations ranging from fixed exchange rates to Taylorist work organization in the workplace.[22] In relation to the UK, this top-down specification echoes the notion of a flawed Fordism. In the UK, the narrow scope and shallow depth of institutional regulation created defensive responses in the labour movement often expressed as a lack of flexibility. Only a movement to neo-liberalism in the state and a rejection of social democracy brought these defensive responses under control.[23] Thus, successive failures by the UK state to effectively institutionalize industrial relations appear as the flaw in the UK's version of Fordism. It is this that creates the top-down nature of this variant to the regulation approach.

The central difficulty with the concept of institutional regulation is twofold.

First, the presumed presence of a Fordist accumulation regime. Second, the matching of institutional regulation with the *de facto* presence of Fordism, a *non sequitur* that assumes the wider institutional framework of Fordism can generate Fordist work systems. Hyman argues that if a connection exists between regime of accumulation and mode of regulation it is difficult to explain why.[24] It would appear that the only explanation is to accept the conceptual pattern of the regulation approach and 'fit' economies into it. This creates a peculiar determinism which suggests that the model is correct but the pattern of institutionalization was good or bad. Lane illustrates that advocates of the regulation approach are astute at parrying charges of determinism, functionalism or bad and overstretched theory.[25] However, the categories 'post', 'neo' or 'national' each appears to sustain the approach of stability, crisis and institutional and economic restructuring (see Figure 2.1).[26]

The notion of economic and political regulation requires more thorough multidisciplinary grounding that incorporates the effects of historical patterns in international relations in a particular nation state. The UK's historical record illustrates that wider aspects in post-war foreign policy consolidated deeply embedded employer interests. Equally, the notion of flawed Fordism in the UK fails to acknowledge the historical significance of strategic choices made by employers and management in the immediate post-war years. These choices cast doubt on the argument that employers promoted the use of new systems of work organization and associated patterns of job and work regulation, only to be thwarted by worker resistance in the workplace.[27]

Atlanticism – national pathways to post-war regulation

The Atlanticist approach demonstrates that European nations were, in the immediate post-war years, economically, politically and socially incapable of institutionalizing Fordism. The export of model Fordism was not the basis of regulation in the Atlantic region during the post-war period. Rather, it was the power and power-seeking capacity that the technical supremacy of large-scale mass production created. From 1947 until the early 1970s, the Cold War provided the substantive context for the Western economic and political order. The Marshall Plan, followed by rearmament in the wake of the Korean conflict, suspended narrow economic regulation and with it the crisis-prone nature and deflationary bias of industrial capitalism. By switching focus to the capacity of power seeking and away from international economic regulation, the US government and foreign policymakers created the space for the continuation of national pathways to post-war reconstruction.

The role of US foreign policy in the consolidation of national pathways in post-war regulation

In the power politics of international relations, the objective of any state is survival; power and power seeking in an anarchical society of sovereign nation

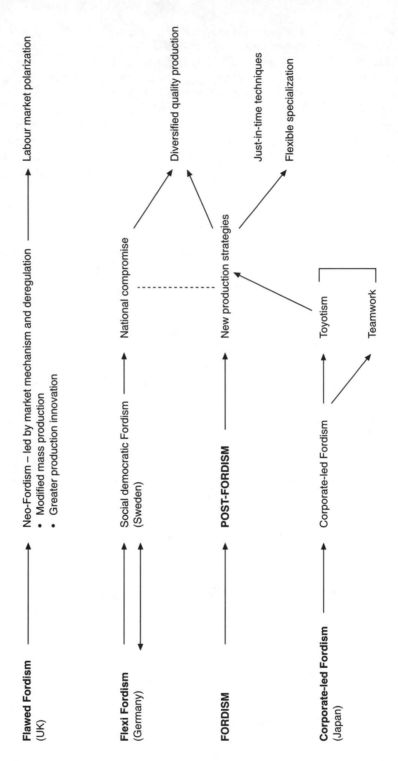

Figure 2.1 Deviations from 'ideal' or model Fordism

states.[28] Dominant states may act unilaterally in accepted spheres of influence or operate through alliance systems to create a balance of power and legitimize their hegemonic interests in a wider community.[29]

In the twentieth century, both world wars resulted from alliance systems in which an individual nation sought to unilaterally challenge an established balance of power and create a hegemonic pattern of relations.[30]

Before the conclusion of the Second World War, the UK, the Soviet Union, France, China and the USA sought to create a universal system of post-war security based on the United Nations and the five permanent members of its security council. However, the rapid termination of the wartime alliance saw the reversal of this ideal. New alliance systems in Nato and the Warsaw Pact created a new European balance of power. Each alliance stablized Western and Eastern Europe as blocs under the tutelage of outside superpowers, creating a new Western European state system.[31]

The realism of alliance systems remains dominant in the power politics of international relations – they create a balance of power. However, the authority of realism is open to challenge. Other approaches emphasize planned and instrumental linkage between economic and social strategies as the underlying approach of US foreign policy. Anglo-American and US/pan-European relations in the immediate post-war period represent the height of instrumental linkage in US foreign policy.[32] The effects of this remain significant in the contemporary period.[33]

In the immediate post-war years, the strategy of instrumental linkage between economic and social and between military and political institutions and structures had two roles. First was the suppression of European nationalism, while the second – the instrumental linkage – aimed to serve the hegemonic national interests of the USA. Initially, liberal economics were based on open markets, fixed exchange rates and a multilateral monetary and trading system; however, by 1947 narrowly prescribed economic regulation based in political isolationism proved a failure.[34]

The contradictory basis of US power politics and power seeking

In the immediate post-war period, the USA held unrivalled economic and military power. For example, the USA held 60 per cent of the world's gold and had the largest and most efficient manufacturing base. Equally, it held a balance of payments surplus on goods and services of $7 billion in 1946, rising to $11 billion in 1947. In contrast, in 1946, European dollar reserves were $6.7 billion; this was a time of dollar shortage but equally a time when the notion of dollar convertibility predominated in US economic thinking.

The Bretton Woods monetary and trading agreements ushered in arrangements that created a system of fixed exchange rates for Atlantic states. The US Treasury department and Morganthau, its head, in particular saw the Bretton Woods arrangements as a precursor to an inexorable movement to free trade multilateralism and convertible currencies. Multilateralism would terminate bilateral trading arrangements, specifically the UK's system of Imperial Preference whereby Empire nations exchanged dollar surpluses for inconvertible sterling balances. Here, sterling balances represented a form of forced reserve saving which allowed the UK to use Empire dollar surpluses to finance its own deficits. Wartime necessity saw the system greatly extended, with additions to sterling balances acting as the main method of financing overseas troop garrisons and imports of raw materials and foodstuffs.[35]

The Bretton Woods mechanism contained an in-built deflationary bias. In order to defend the value of a currency, it was necessary to make adjustments in the domestic economy. Fiscal or monetary deflation or reducing wage levels or improving labour productivity would theoretically reduce a balance of payments deficit, in turn reducing speculative pressures on a currency parity. However, the system had several flaws, and one in particular that undermined its theoretical rigor.

The Bretton Woods arrangements established a dollar system backed by US gold reserves. Therefore, international trade rested on the availability of dollars, yet in Western Europe it was a period of severe dollar shortage. This resulted from the deflationary bias of the system. For example, if states had a shortage of dollars, they must reduce domestic consumption of dollar goods and increase exports to the USA to secure enough dollars to trade internationally. However, in the post-war period, the USA was the primary source of necessary imports to secure an export-led domestic recovery. More significantly than this, a central contradiction in the system was not evident to US Treasury department internationalists. Domestic deflation in the UK would restrict US exports and percolate deflation and recession through the international economic system as the US economy reduced demand for European exports.

The objective of the Bretton Woods mechanism was to break up the system of Imperial Preference in the British Empire and usher in free trade multilateralism, dominated by US competitive advantage in manufacturing. However, in Anglo-American negotiations over the wartime Atlantic Charter, Lend Lease arrangements and Bretton Woods, the UK government secured the maintenance of Imperial Preference.[36] Retention of Imperial Preference, although it did secure UK export markets and Empire export markets into the UK, did not overcome the general dollar shortage.

In an effort to maintain industrial production and secure imports of raw materials and equipment only available from the USA, the UK government secured a $3.75 billion loan in December 1945, ratified by Congress in July 1946.[37] The ratification process contained several letters of intent that the UK had to adhere to, the most pressing of which was that in one year sterling balances would be made freely convertible to dollars. Clearly, US negotiators in the Treasury department aimed to break into the sterling area. The strategy of breaking Imperial Preference in bilateral trading proved impossible, hence breaking into bilateral sterling balances thereby allowing Empire nations to finance dollar imports independently of the UK became the basis of US action.

The result of sterling convertibility was disastrous, and within six weeks there was a convertibility crisis leading to its suspension. By September 1947, the UK government had virtually run out of dollars and had no supplies of convertible currency.[38] The US strategy could only fail; sterling balances were in the order of $14 billion, whereas the UK's gold reserves were in the region of $2 billion. The dollar convertibility of sterling balances led to the rapid liquidation of the loan and the use of gold reserves to finance the conversion of further sterling balances. This made the UK's dollar shortage worse, thereby reinforcing the deflationary bias of the Bretton Woods system. Hence, for the US national interest, the system was a regulatory failure because the dollar shortage stimulated deflation not reflation. Moreover, the pursuit of power politics was gradually moving away from an economic model to a geopolitical model based on spheres of interest and alliances. The inauguration of President Truman saw the State department eclipse the Treasury department in foreign policy formulation. Truman actively promoted the State department in this area, driving a brief dominated by traditional power politics rather than internationalist economics.[39]

In the wake of the apparent failure of liberal capitalism, the attractiveness and spread of Communism in Western Europe became the primary concern of the State department. This culminated in Kennan's 'X' article,[40] in which he outlined what eventually became the Truman Doctrine of Containment and the Marshall Plan. Kennan (X) argued that the Soviet Union and the Communist ideology thrived in the austerity and deprivation of post-war economic conditions, particularly in France, Germany and Italy. Equally, Communist agents successfully infiltrated trade unions and the European labour movement, particularly in the workplace. The X article suggested that a strategy to contain the source of discontent was necessary. Moreover, X argued that poor post-war economic conditions might sustain and recreate European nationalism, thereby undermining the multilateral free trade ideals of US foreign policy. The US first tried – unsuccessfully – to regulate the international economic framework on the basis of domestic adjustment to payments deficits, much like the gold standard. Second, and more successfully, US policy turned to a political strategy based on support to Western Europe to repel the threat of Communism. It is here that a movement away from economic regulation became evident in US foreign policy. The Marshall Plan and its subsequent European Recovery Programme followed by the inception of Nato in 1949 eventually suppressed nationalism in the European labour movement.

The linkage between the components of US foreign policy tied Western European interests to those of the USA to secure US economic and strategic interests – a large stable market for intra-European trade and US exports. However, this achievement had a considerable cost – an internationalized Cold War that necessitated the consolidation of national pathways to economic regulation.

The emergence of a Soviet threat in Europe became the primary concern of US foreign policy. Policymakers were highly instrumental in developing the Marshall Plan and the European Recovery Programme, both of which allowed nations to discriminate against US goods and the US dollar. This route secured the eventual acceptance of US demands for multilateralism and free trade. In addition, allowing the UK's medium-term retention of Imperial Preferences and bilateral trade and payments ensured economic dependence on the USA. However, these concessions gave the UK the material capability to prosecute the Cold War in Western Europe. The US Treasury underwrote the sterling area as a multilateral trading area.

The aim of US foreign policy was to secure markets and form Western Europe into an integrated economic and political bloc. The defence of the free market promoted the social and political benefits of greater material prosperity through a superpower Cold War, creating the *realpolitik* of the post-war period.[41] So instead of winding up the sterling area (the aim of the series of agreements culminating in the UK loan arrangements), US foreign policy actually sustained it. This was significant in the consolidation of the UK's national pathway, and its manufacturing sector in particular.

US hegemony in the international monetary and payments system failed to secure US power and security interests. Alternatively, US balance of payments deficits fulfilled this role. With 60 per cent of the world's gold supply backing the dollar in the Western economic system, the dollar was 'as good as gold'. This allowed the USA to run payments deficits without the domestic deflation that would have been necessary under the Bretton Woods system. Equally, this policy demonstrated the weakness of European economies.

The Marshall Plan followed by the inception of Nato in 1949 institutionalized the Cold War. Both served the US national interest, but equally they laid the foundations for a new European state system in which the international relations of containment overshadowed economic interests.[42] The predominance of *realpolitik* over economics was the strategy of the UK state, independently of US domination. This predominance undermined the export of model Fordism and some of its central economic elements, such as Fordist work organization and associated patterns of job regulation institutionalized and regulated in the workplace. To legitimize political domination, US foreign policymakers had to either tolerate or recreate national pathways to industrial capitalism, thereby reducing economic hegemony to domination. In the UK case, this tolerance eventually undermined hegemonic foreign economic policy.[43] In the case of West Germany, in contrast, the US policymakers, with strong UK support, recreated much of the pre-war economic structure of industry and civil society. Kolko, for example, illustrates how the US state department resisted attempts to nationalize industry in the Ruhr, instead placing it under the international control of private capitalists.[44] The eventual recreation of the Ruhr Iron and Steel company saw pre-war owners reallocated share ownership.[45] Further, Van der Pijl documents how Atlanticism pulled West Germany into the Atlantic institutional framework by its first post-war government led by the Liberal Free Democratic Party. Industrialists in German firms such as AEG and Dresdner Bank were active in regenerating a renaissance of industry in West Germany centred around such firms such as BMW and Siemens.[46]

The result, if not the original strategic aim of US policy, encouraged the (re-)emergence of national pathways. In the case of West Germany, it had two subsidiary aims. First, to channel US and UK investments into West Germany and, second, to avoid the socialization and nationalization of industry advocated by some UK occupation administrators and German trade unions such as IG Metall. Equally, the liberal bloc of industrial capital wanted to avoid the financial, industrial relations and political diversion of German unification, which the opposition party, the SPD, had made a central pledge for domestic policy.[46]

US support for national pathways aimed to illustrate the material superiority of liberal democracy in the free market system rather than the virtues of narrowly defined US capitalism and yet aimed to tie national pathways to it. The efforts to build an integrated Western Europe based on the US model proved unsuccessful, instead they merely consolidated national pathways in a loose European Union (EU), which over the last twenty years has become increasingly independent of the USA in economic and political matters if not in broadly defined defence interests.[47]

It is the permanence of national pathways and the embedded patterns of regulation they create which account for the differential impact of Fordist work organization and associated patterns of institutional regulation. In an attempt to internationalize the aims of US foreign policy, it became necessary to legitimize hegemony beyond narrow economic structures. However, this movement secured political domination but weakened economic hegemony based on free trade and Fordist production systems. For example, within the Marshall Plan, the UK secured sterling balances, the continuation of Imperial Preference and a national pathway to post-war recovery independent of Europe as a whole. In contrast, a substantial part of the German national pathway was reconstructed as West Germany. In Italy, US Marshall planners failed to introduce productivity bargaining or depoliticize industrial relations. Equally, during the 1950s high unemployment and Cold War politics sustained ideological opposition to Marshall Plan institutions. However, the Italian government and business had little interest or need to come to terms with poorly developed workplace industrial relations.[48]

The Marshall Plan: the consolidation of the UK's national pathway

In the UK, the effects of Marshall Aid were threefold. First, the retention of sterling balances and relatively guaranteed export markets for UK goods focused UK exports away from Europe towards empire markets and fledgling attempts to penetrate the US market.[49] Second, Marshall Aid suspended the Fordist logic behind the Bretton Woods mechanism and with it any strategic impetus to restructure and scale up manufacturing industry. In a system of multilateral free trade, such restructuring would have been necessary to promote high levels of capital and labour productivity and to ensure unit labour costs remained comparatively competitive in respect of the UK's exchange rate. Third, methods of work organization, managerial approaches and patterns of job regulation retained continuity with those established before the war. Chapter 6 develops these themes further. At this point, it is necessary to outline a series of significant strategic choices determined in the initial post-war period. These choices have been highly influential in shaping the economic performance of the UK's national pathway in Atlanticist regulation.

The UK's national pathway and the superstructure of regulation

The central weakness in the regulation approaches reviewed in the previous section centres on a failure to incorporate the impact of the post-war dollar shortage. The shortage was real but its effects were, as a result of Marshall Aid, only potential.[50] Industrial output rested on the availability of dollars to finance imports of food and raw materials. The imperative of output and the dollar shortage rendered the Fordist production systems, associated patterns of work organization and job regulation that Marshall planners aimed to transfer into Western Europe and the UK specifically insignificant.[51]

To develop this argument, it is necessary to outline the Marshall Plan and its subsequent effects on the UK state. An analysis of how the UK's national pathway of economic and political regulation superseded the superstructure of broader patterns of regulation in industrial capitalism follows this.

The Marshall Plan: an opportunity and a problem

United States Secretary of State George Marshall announced what became termed the Marshall Plan in a speech during a graduation ceremony at Harvard University in June 1947. At this time, there was no real plan, only a five-part condition to underwrite the idea.[52] First, Europe must administer and distribute US aid. Second, and related, the programme should be collective and integrated. Eventually, the Organization for European Economic Co-operation (OEEC) became the mechanism for joint US–European administration of the programme. Third, the programme should be costed on a pan-European basis. Fourth, US finance for the European programme must constitute a cure to the collective European dollar shortage. Hence, the conception of Marshall Aid was fundamentally different from earlier palliative loans, such as the Dawes and Young plans for German reparations during the inter-war period and the UK loan in the immediate post-war period.[53] Last, the USA would offer friendly aid and assistance in drafting and administering the European programme. Aid and assistance manifested themselves via the Economic Co-operation Agency and the Technical Assistance and Productivity programme.

The Marshall Plan served the US national interest in four ways. First, it furthered diplomatic and strategic interests first enunciated in the containment doctrine now dominated by the ideology of the Cold War. Second, and related, it further consolidated the *realpolitik* of the Cold War by blocing Western Europe within an US-dominated alliance system. Third, in the longer term, the injection of dollars into the European economic system actually saved the Bretton Woods mechanism for free trade and multilateral payments by suspending the mechanism. This was the case because Marshall Aid removed the necessity for a deflationary bias in the system of international trade. However, it retained the dollar as the driver in international economic regulation, a retention that grew in significance after the restoration of freer trade and multilateralism in the late 1950s. Last, the Marshall Plan solved the 'German problem' by incorporating the USA, UK and French occupation zones (which became West Germany) into its field of operations. Eventually, the US Senate and Congress allocated $13,500 million to the sixteen Marshall Aid nations and Trizonia after much isolationist wrangling.[54] Table 2.2 outlines the allocation and use of UK Marshall Aid.

A Marshall Plan conference held in Paris between July and September 1947 aimed at European agreement on the five-point conditions laid out by Marshall. As its title, the conference took 'The Committee of European Economic Co-operation'(CEEC). The conference culminated in the creation of the 'Organization for European Economic Co-operation'. Subsequently, the CEEC distributed aid funds through the European Recovery Programme (ERP) and the Economic Co-operation Agency (ECA), the administrative and executive branches of the Marshall Plan.

Both the CEEC and the OEEC were in large measure the creation of Ernest Bevin, UK Foreign Secretary. Bevin was a vehement anti-Communist and a hawkish Atlanticist.[55] Together, these qualities made him resistant to UK participation in European integration. He aimed to maintain the UK's great power status and associated sovereignty of action over economic and political decisions. Equally, he was the chief architect of Nato.

At the CEEC conference, Bevin used a strategy that aimed to create national but comparatively based technical and information-gathering committees on the particular economic and social needs of the sixteen Marshall Aid nations. The design of the committees aimed to maintain the sovereignty of national governments. The CEEC report reflected this position and fell a long way short

Table 2.2 Allocation and use of UK Marshall Aid

1948–1950:	UK receives $3,000 million through the ERP		
	$1,827 million	Direct grant	(68%)
	$531 million	Conditional aid	(20%)
	$337 million	Loan	(12%)

Marshall Aid paid for 12.5% of UK import, equivalent to 60% of Dollar area imports. The breakdown was:

	Food	40%
	Raw materials	40%
	Equipment	7%
	Oil	12%

Source: HM Treasury, *Recovery Record; The Story of Marshall Aid* (London, HMSO, 1951).

of US demands for an integrationist action plan to structure pan-European economic and political recovery. Significantly, the CEEC report and OEEC devised separate 'shopping lists'[56] for recovery based on the needs of established national pathways in individual nation states.

US Marshall planners accepted a commitment on the part of the European states to act collectively in terms of production targets, the removal of tariff barriers and a return to multilateralism as evidence of a future movement to political integration. Essentially, Bevin outmanoeuvred the Americans by firmly establishing the centrality of national pathways to recovery.[57] Latterly, the European Economic Community (EEC) that emerged in the mid-1950s was somewhat different in terms of aims and objectives from that which US Marshall planners had anticipated.[58]

The Marshall Plan amounted to very little in terms of Marshall's five-point plan. The main concrete development was the ERP and the OEEC, each of which had a state specific – national pathway – institutional structure. In the UK's case, the London office of the ECA controlled each institution. In addition to this, the technical assistance programme promoted the Anglo-American Council for Productivity (AACP) as a second prescriptive 'best practice' agency. Both bodies aimed to disseminate US 'best practice' production management systems and work organization and productivity-based management and job regulation techniques in the workplace. US Marshall planners in the AACP saw workplace productivity bargaining as a central mechanism to reducing the UK's productivity gap with the USA.

The UK opportunity and the US problem

For the UK government, the Marshall Plan was an opportunity and a problem. It was an opportunity to sustain continuity in UK sovereignty and its economic management. Equally, it was a problem because the US-inspired pan-European integrationist aims of the programme appeared to threaten the national sovereignty that the UK state had recently fought to maintain. The tension became manifest in the simultaneous pursuit of both national modernization and great power status. Modernization centred on domestic reforms in civil society, whereas 'greatness' entailed sustaining the sterling area and the export markets it represented. The sterling area was an outlet for exports of UK manufactured goods and a source of food and raw material imports. More significantly than this, the pooling arrangements for dollar surpluses earned by sterling area states provided the UK with an additional source of income to finance UK dollar area imports. In summary, revenues from sterling area trade and sterling balances supplemented Marshall Aid to fund the UK's dollar gap and breathe new life into sterling as a reserve currency. In short, throughout the Marshall Aid era and beyond, UK domestic policy operated within a wider foreign policy context that aimed to maintain the UK as a *European*-level great power.[59]

However, the UK's great power status became residual for several reasons.

First, the USA became the ultimate guarantor of the sterling area, in return for which the UK government played a major role in internationalizing a superpower Cold War.[60] Second, the UK secured atomic and nuclear status in a US-dominated Nato.[61] Third, the UK government undertook to carry out a detailed investigation into productivity improvement centred on US best practice management techniques and methods of job regulation in the workplace.[62] Fourth, the government had to accept, if ignore, significant criticism from the ECA, much of it bluntly delivered by its controller Paul Hoffman.[63] Hoffman was of the view that Europe must become a single market and a political union. He regularly criticized the lack of enthusiasm in UK policy in relation to the OEEC.[64] More specifically, Hoffman played a central role in the AACP, where he promoted a social engineering approach to production based on his experience in the Studebaker automobile corporation. The resistance of UK employers to these methods astonished him. Equally, the diversion of counterpart funds away from capital restructuring to debt retirement led Hoffman to argue that the UK was wasting Marshall Aid.[65] Last, the UK government retained its status as a great power in the context of an international political economy dominated by two superpowers. Economic independence from Europe and the creation of special economic and political relationships with the USA, the White dominions, empire and then commonwealth nations directed the domestic economy away from European economic and political integration. Hence, great power status was residual because it rested on reluctantly given US finance.

The UK government saw the Marshall Plan as a financial mechanism to underpin the sources through which the UK state earned income. There were five such sources. First, a disparate manufacturing base that served the domestic market and varied exports, the majority in the sterling area. Second, freight charges for transport in UK ships and, third, insurance premiums taken out in London on the cargo. The war effort diminished both of these sources, as did the associated losses in the commercial shipping fleet. Fourth, interest on money borrowed in London and, last, overseas investments.

Marshall Aid provided the hard currency that secured a pattern of post-war recovery based on continuity in the existing structure of capital and labour relations; wartime conditions had consolidated both areas. The programme eschewed reconstruction, raising output and production rather than the scrapping and replacing industrial plant and machinery necessary to raise the scale of plant. Equally, and directly related, employers and employees at the point of production had little interest in efforts to transform methods of production management, work organization and job regulation.[66] However, over the short term, the UK's output drive did have a considerable impact on labour productivity.

In contrast to the UK approach, the US view saw the Marshall Plan as facilitating a conclusive restructuring, if not transformation, of European capitalism on a pan-European integrationist model. Internationalists in the US Treasury department assumed post-war military and political conditions would promote co-operative free market capitalism.[67] However, Kennan (X) demonstrated that the opposite was the case: defensive national capitalism with a flawed social system. The deteriorating political situation in Europe and the eastern Mediterranean persuaded Truman that economic and military intervention was the only method by which the USA could secure its long-term economic goals.[68] As a consequence, the USA accepted the necessity of the UK's national pathway to post-war recovery and adopted similar approaches in Germany and Italy.[69]

Hence, a superpower Cold War underpinned the limits of US economic and political domination. This resulted in the development of an Atlanticist approach to economic recovery and political stability via the Marshall Plan. The empirical basis of this argument for the UK state is now detailed.

Post-war options for the UK state

Nations operate in the context of an international monetary order. In the inter-war period, the gold standard required automatic domestic adjustment in a period of payments deficit. This was necessary to maintain the international value of a currency against gold. In the post-war period, it would appear that the UK government had four available options for its participation in an international economic order. First, a dollar-based free trade Atlantic union among the USA, Canada and the UK. Clearly, the UK would have been by far the smallest country as well as being starved of supplies of raw materials and foodstuffs. A second option centred around an empire and sterling bloc to protect UK export markets and guarantee food and raw material producers access to the UK market. In addition, this option would retain sterling as a reserve currency and inconvertible or semiconvertible sterling balances. Third, the UK could join an EU based on a new currency denomination. Last, the UK could enter into fully fledged convertible multilateral free trade. Consideration of the first option was rejected; the effects of an Atlantic union on the sterling area and sources for food and raw materials supplies appeared prohibitive. The European option was not a consideration because of the UK's great power pretensions. Equally, free trade convertibility and multilateralism were unacceptable for the same reason. Further, the disaster of sterling convertibility in 1947 demonstrated that with approximately $14 billion in sterling balances convertibility would bankrupt the UK.[70]

A compromise agreement resulted in the UK government retaining Imperial Preferences and sterling area discrimination against dollar area goods. In return for underwriting sterling balances, the USA secured agreement that the UK would return to multilateral free trade and currency convertibility in the medium term. The international order that prevailed until the late 1950s was a fixed exchange rate mechanism that incorporated the sterling area. This system slowly moved from discrimination and bilateralism towards multilateralism through dollar pooling arrangements developed in the European Payments Union (EPU).[71] However, this did not secure Fordism in the UK or its integrated and coherent institutional regulation.

Strategically, state department planners realized that the USA could not entertain a collapse of the UK economy. The UK occupied a large area of Germany and sterling was the only European currency that could finance its own trade in the short term. Further, if the sterling area collapsed or at least suffered severe deflationary pressures, US exporters would experience a considerable decline in demand, threatening a domestic recession. Equally, the pressures on the UK economy might threaten political commitment to the UK occupation zone in Germany. A potential re-run of the Greek and Turkish problem that instigated the Truman doctrine, encouraging a deeper retreat into Empire trading.[72] The weakness of the UK state was clear. However, the UK received enough financial support to retain its international status as a great power.

Production and industrial relations

By August 1947, UK industrial production had reached a level that approximated to its pre-war level, whereas production in the USA was approximately 150 per cent of its immediate pre-war level. In contrast, production in the US and UK occupation zones of Germany, 85 per cent of the future West Germany, was running at 40 per cent of its pre-war level (Tables 2.3 and 2.4).

Thus, in terms of industrial output, the UK had recovered before the introduction of Marshall Aid. What was in doubt was the UK's ability to maintain its recovery in the face of a shortage of dollars to finance the purchase of necessary imports from the dollar area. Over its four-year life, Marshall Aid secured imports of food and raw materials, each accounting for 40 per cent of ERP imports with equipment accounting for only 7 per cent (see Table 2.1). The ERP allocated $3,000 million to the UK, representing 2.4 per cent of the UK's national income until the 1949 devaluation of sterling and 5.2 per cent

Table 2.3 Indices (%) of industrial production per capita in Western Europe, 1947, compared with pre-war selected Marshall Aid states (1937 = 100%)

Norway	114
UK	99
Sweden	98
France	96
Denmark	90
Belgium	87
The Netherlands	79
Italy	59
US zone, Germany	41
US zone, Germany	40
USA	147

Table 2.4 Indices (%) of industrial production in Western Europe, 1948–51 (1938 = 100%)

Country	1948	1949	1950	1951
Austria	85	114	134	148[a]
Belgium	122	122	124	143
Denmark	135	143	159	160
France	111	122	123	138
W. Germany	50	72	91	106
Greece	76	90	114	130
Ireland	135	154	170	176[b]
Italy	99	109	125	143
Luxembourg	139	132	139	168[a]
The Netherlands	114	127	140	147
Norway	125	135	146	153
Sweden	149	157	164	172
Turkey	154	162	165	163[a]
UK	120	129	140	145
All participating countries	99	112	124	135
All participating countries, exclusive of W. Germany	119	130	138	145

Sources: *First Report to Congress on the Mutual Security Program*, p. 75; I. Wexler, *The Marshall Plan Re-Visited* (Connecticut, Greenwood Press, 1983), p. 94.

Notes
a Average of first three quarters of 1951.
b Average of first two quarters of 1951.

of the gross national product (GNP) thereafter.[73] As an injection into the economy, this windfall was equal to the economic growth of between one and two and a half years.[74]

The UK's major economic problem was sustaining the recovery in post-war output that prevailed before the introduction of Marshall Aid. In this context, it is of little surprise that the vast majority of ERP aid financed dollar area imports of food and raw materials. The UK was a manufacturing economy that exported goods to pay for imports of food and materials. This was absolutely necessary to secure output, earn dollars and maintain the sterling area. As Tomlinson demonstrated, the UK's use of Marshall Aid for food imports did not starve the manufacturing sector of investment funds.[75] Profit levels were high and self-finance out of retained profits was a major source of investment funding during this period and remained so under Marshall Aid.

The success of the UK's recovery before Marshall Aid has led some to argue that the Marshall Plan was unnecessary and of marginal effect.[76] Alternative arguments suggest that the UK's use of Marshall Aid represented a (lost) opportunity. In particular, the failure to restructure the UK manufacturing sector along the lines of US industry, a failure integral to the 'lost victory' thesis on UK decline.[77]

The effect of the Marshall Plan on the UK economy and the scale of operations in the manufacturing sector was marginal, but it was not a failure. Any attempt to restructure the manufacturing sector along the lines of US industry would have significantly reduced industrial output. Equally, it would have denied sterling area and empire economies export markets for food and raw materials and stalled the domestic modernization programme. More significantly, in 1938 exports to the sterling area accounted for 45 per cent of total UK exports and 47 per cent in 1950, and until 1970 they exceeded exports to Western Europe (Table 2.5). It seems implausible that the UK could have replaced these export markets in the short term. Although the USA guaranteed sterling balances, it was necessary for the UK to trade with the sterling area in order to retain confidence in sterling as a reserve and settlement currency.

Equally implausible in this context was a transformation of patterns of work organization towards standardized mass assembly production and the associated deployment of US patterns of job regulation negotiated formally in the workplace. The process of hysteresis describes the economic effects of losing output and markets. A loss can be permanent or create a lag effect. The effects of permanently losing empire markets would have been considerable. The potential benefit of a smaller number of more integrated large-scale manufacturers operating in highly competitive markets in Western Europe, the commonwealth and the USA could not replace this loss. Although the decision to avoid any of these courses appeared necessary, as the following chapter argues and demonstrates, it held future consequence for the UK economy.

Table 2.5 Shares of UK exports to UK countries and EEC6 (%)

	UK countries	*EEC6*
1907	23.2	24.8
1912	36.0	22.7
1924	42.1	18.7
1930	43.5	18.3
1935	48.0	14.7
1948	52.7	9.8
1951	55.0	10.4
1954	53.0	13.0
1958	49.3	13.1
1963	37.5	20.3
1968	31.2	19.3
1970	25.1	21.7
1980	20.1	34.6
1990	16.7	41.3

Source: HM Customs and Excise (various issues), *Annual Statement of the Trade of the United Kingdom* (London, HMSO); S. Broadberry, *The Productivity Race* (Cambridge, Cambridge University Press, 1997), p. 96.

Note
'UK countries' includes the Irish Free State/Republic and the Republic of South Africa, as well as the Commonwealth.

A more immediate constraint on the economy during the Marshall Plan years and throughout the 1950s and early 1960s was the presence of full employment. The UK's rapid return to full employment after the war was in many respects a testament to the prudence of the Labour governments post-war economic management. The retention of spending controls and consumer rationing in combination with the export drive removed much anticipated inflationary pressure in the domestic economy.

However, the presence of full employment and the equally rapid rise in industrial output removed any likelihood of an intensive Fordist regime of accumulation. First, the spheres of interest approach to the Cold War further marginalized the significance of agencies of US economic reconstruction and transformation; the technical assistance programme and the AACP were of minor technical importance while retaining considerable propaganda value.[78]

Second, the UK's initial recovery of output continued into the 1960s, however less by intensive and more by extensive means. Tables 2.6 and 2.7 illustrate that the UK's comparatively low level of investment in new plant and machinery (which regulation accounts of the period present as essential) to produce standardized final goods appeared of little significance. This was the case because of the initial windfall in the recovery of output. Tables 2.3 and 2.4 illustrate that the UK's immediate post-war economic performance was well ahead of other European states. However, Tables 2.8 and 2.9 illustrate that to achieve the recovery of output a considerable use of overtime working was necessary, otherwise termed extensive means.

In the UK, the empirical depth of Fordism was quite shallow. The UK's immediate post-war recovery made its adoption less pressing, therefore making its introduction economically and politically destructive. Moreover, data demonstrate that, since 1870, the UK economy has been comparatively less competitive than Germany and the United States. Economic decline reinforced the deployment of established techniques in sectors such as iron and steel, textiles and car production. In each case, established methods assumed a necessary priority over new methods that may have stalled production in the short-term, required new forms of training that were costly and appeared ill-suited to established markets.[79] The state's necessary approach to international relations in the immediate post-war period reinforced the inertia resulting from each pressure. The embedded nature of the UK's established accumulation regime was, before Marshall Aid, reinforced in an effort to reduce the dollar gap. Marshall Aid further reinforced the UK's established regimes and patterns of regulation, making the utility of a new pattern of institutional regulation in the workplace marginal. The series of strategic choices made by the UK government during this period illustrates that the strategy behind US foreign policy may have been dominant, but it was not omnipotent.

Table 2.6 Investment ratios and growth of output in industry in selected Western European countries, 1953–60

	W. Germany	Italy	UK
All industry			
Gross investment, % of GNP	16.6	16.3	14.5
Net investment, % of GNP	14.6	14.7	8.9
Annual growth of output, %	8.0	8.9	3.5
Annual growth of output per head, %	5.0	4.0	2.6
Manufacturing industry only			
Gross investment, % of GNP	13.3	13.8	10.7
Net investment, % of GNP	11.0	11.6	5.9
Annual growth of output, %	8.5	9.0	3.8
Annual growth of output per head, %	4.8	3.9	2.7

Source: A. Lamfalussy, *The United Kingdom and the Six* (1963), pp. 92 and 94.

Table 2.7 Investment and output ratios in selected Western European countries

	Gross investment ratio (% of GNP)		Growth of output (% p.a.)	Gross marginal capital–output ratio
	National prices	Adjusted prices		
W. Germany	22.0	21.9	7.0	3.1
Italy	20.5	20.5	0.1	3.4
France	17.7	17.6	4.5	3.9
UK	15.0	15.0	2.8	5.4

Source: A. Lamfalussy, *The United Kingdom and the Six* (London, Macmillan, 1963), p. 72.

Table 2.8 Actual amounts of overtime and short-time working by operatives in manufacturing 1956–92 (workers on full-time adult rates)

Years	% on overtime	Average hours	% on short time	Hours lost
1952–8	a	11.7	a	7.7
1959	25.7	7.5	1.4	13
1960–9	33	8.2	.8	9.3
1970–9	35	8.5	1.2	14.5
1980–9	33	8.8	1.9	9.4
1989–92	35	9.4	1.3	13.9

Source: Calculated from *Department of Employment Gazette*.

Note

a Before 1959, percentage figures for numbers involved in overtime working were not given, instead actual figures were cited. Calculations suggest that between 1952 and 1958 the percentage of operatives involved in overtime was 22– 26%.

Table 2.9   Actual hours worked 1948–92 for manufacturing (M) and all industry (M+) (full-time workers on adult rates)

Years		Men	Women	Length of normal week[a]
1938	47.7	43.5	48	
1948	46.7	41.6	44	
1948	46.8	41.7	44	
1950–9				
	M	47.9	41.7	44
	M+	48.1	41.6	44
1960–9				
	M	46.2	38.8	44/40
	M+	46.9	39	44/40
1970–9				
	M	44	38.8	40
	M+	44.8	37.3	40
1980–9				
	M	44.1	39.4	<40
	M+	44.3	39.8	<40
1990–2				
	M	44.2	39.8	<40
	M+	44.2	39.4	<40

Source: Department of Employment Gazette; figures calculated and cross-referenced with figures and averages calculated in *British Labour Statistics Yearbook* and *British Labour Statistics Historical Abstracts 1968–1968* (London, HMSO).

Note
a As defined in the *Department of Employment Gazette*.

Particularized national pathways

In the immediate post-war period, the UK government made a series of inter-related strategic choices. Each choice consolidated the domestic economy, reinforced sterling as a reserve currency and encouraged a structured modernization in civil society through the creation of a welfare state and a nationalized public sector. Each choice left many regulatory institutions and mechanisms unchanged, e.g. the UK's industrial relations system – an apparently flawed Fordism – without the supporting structures. Chapters 4–6 demonstrate that a conservative – historically embedded – state such as the UK necessarily displays institutional and organizational inertia. Take, for example, the UK's slow and still contested political realignment from Atlantic union to European Union.

A failure of accumulation and regulation alone cannot explain the UK's economic and political weakness domestically or internationally. The nation state maintains and organizes its political economy on the basis of power politics and power seeking, i.e. the maintenance of a particularized pattern of national governance.

The golden age of intensive regulation?

The term 'golden age' has been used by a variety of economists to summarize the period of post-war economic boom between 1947 and 1974.[80] This period represents the high point of Keynesian economic policy[81] and a historical epoch of interlocking domestic and international institutions.[82] In the parlance of the regulation approach, the golden age was a period of stabilization and prosperity. A period followed by the erosion and emergence of a new regime and appropriate mode of regulation. For most of the golden age, the UK had low unemployment and inflation, rising incomes and an approximate balance on the current account, yet comparative economic performance deteriorated[83] (Tables 2.10–2.12).

Conclusions

A leading UK commentator on the regulation method has recently argued that national economies are increasingly unable to regulate their national economic space because of the emergence of international economic trends often summarized as globalization.[84] Moreover, the argument further suggests that the national economic space no longer provides the best starting point for growth, innovation and competitiveness. The historical evidence suggests that this assertion is likely to prove partial. The global project launched by the USA in the post-war period appeared equally as powerful as the contemporary form of globalization. However, sovereign states contained and legitimized the strategy through accumulation regimes based in national pathways. The UK's experience of participation in the pan-European exchange rate mechanism is a guide to the limited capacity of integrationist regulation. For a comparatively uncompetitive economy, participation requires politically unacceptable levels of deflationary bias, resulting in high interest rates, recession and fiscal austerity particularly in the public sector. This points to the continuing, if reduced, centrality of the nation state.[85]

In addition, although regulation theory is highly influential, it is not without criticism. First, Marxists argue that the regulation approach is too functional and lacks theorization of class struggle. For example, state theorists who concentrate on the primacy of class struggle point to the emergence and failure of social democracy as a central objective of class struggle. In contrast to this, the regulation approach highlights the significance of historically contingent regulatory forms for the reproduction of wage labour in the employment relationship under industrial capitalism.[86] Also, institutional and post-Keynesian economists critically suggest that the inexorable movement from Fordism to post-Fordism including segmented and flexible labour markets merely provides a rationale for deregulation. For example, Hutton argues that the acceptance of segmented labour markets – what he terms the '30:30:40' society – and the pursuit of flexibility have created permanent insecurity for 30 per cent of the population and social exclusion for a further 30 per cent. Equally, flexibility in the labour market as a means of attracting foreign direct investment from

Table 2.10 Industrial Western Europe: output, employment and investment, 1950–70

	Output growth			Employment growth			Investment ratios	
	GDP	Manufacturing	Total	Manufacturing	Non-agricultural employment	Total economy	Excluding dwellings	Manufacturing
Austria	5.0	5.6	0.1	0.6	0.5	26.2	21.1	15.9[a]
Belgium	3.5	5.3	0.4	0.2	1.0	22.4	16.2	18.1
Denmark	4.0	4.6	1.1	1.2	2.0	21.0	17.1	8.5
Finland	4.4	5.7	0.9	1.5	3.2	27.3	21.2	19.6
France	5.0	5.8	0.4	0.5	1.6	23.7	17.8	21.1[b]
Germany	6.2	8.0	1.2	2.1	2.4	27.0	20.2	18.3[b]
Ireland	2.5	4.7	-0.7	1.0	0.4	21.9[c]	18.2[c]	19.8[c]
Italy	5.4	7.9	0.4	1.7	2.3	22.1	15.6	19.6
The Netherlands	5.0	6.3	1.1	1.0	1.4	26.0	20.8	20.3
Norway	4.1	4.7	0.3	0.7	1.4	32.0	26.7	18.5
Portugal	5.1	8.6	0.2	1.9	1.1	18.8	14.8	15.1
Spain	6.1	8.4	0.8	2.9	2.5	22.6	16.7	n.a.
Sweden	4.1	5.1	0.3	0.3	1.2	24.4	18.4	16.4
Switzerland	4.2	4.6	1.6	1.8	1.8	23.9	18.3	n.a.
UK	2.7	3.3	0.5	0.4	0.5	17.5	14.0	12.6

Sources: *United Nations, Economic Survey of Europe in 1971. Part I. The European Economy from the 1950s to the 1970s* (New York, United Nations, 1972), pp. 12–14; A. Maddison, *Economic Policy and Performance in Europe 1913–1970* (London, Collins/Fontana, 1973), p. 51; D. Aldcroft, *European Economy 1914–1990* (London, Routledge, 1993), p. 140.

Notes
a 1960–9, includes mining and construction.
b Includes construction.
c 1960–9, investment ratio for manufacturing includes construction.
n.a., not available.

Table 2.11 UK share in world trade in manufactures

Year	Per cent share
1950	25.4
1954	20.5
1959	17.7
1964	14.2
1969	11.2
1974	8.8
1979	9.1
1984	7.6

Source: M. Kirby, 'The economic record since 1945',
in T. Gourvish and A. O'Day (eds), *Britain Since
1945* (London, Macmillan, 1991), p.13.

beyond the EU creates cumulative pressures for job deregulation. Here, the UK is attempting to compete with economies whose labour costs it can never compete with; more critically, manufacturing industry in the UK is increasingly dominated by multinational employers.

The recent 'semiconductor' recession and BMW's sale of the Longbridge plant illustrate the power of multinational firms. Assembly plants and production plants appear as disposable cost centres governed by global economics and comparative productivity levels across the EU.[87] Evidently, much of the foreign direct investment into the UK results in greenfield assembly plants. In many cases, assembly plants support wage levels which by European standards are very low, creating a cycle of flexibility and low wages as the prerequisites for investment.[88] Finally, if post-Fordism represents the form of production for the next millennium, it requires the development of appropriate institutional arrangements – a mode of regulation – similar to social democracy during the post-war period. Equally, this mode of regulation, the elusive third way, requires acceptance and effective institutionalization. However, particularized patterns of regulation evolve over long periods, given that societal and institutional structures display inertia. The latter result from the historically embedded nature of institutions in a particular economy and civil society and not, as regulation advocates would argue, from friction between outmoded and emergent regimes of regulation as industrial capitalism moves between periods of stability.[89] Marxian and institutional advocates either brush over how the institutions themselves work or fail to explain what brought them into being.

The Bretton Woods mechanism prefigured regulation approaches to domestic economic management within the constraints of international economic regulation. Further, the Bretton Woods mechanism, cited by many advocates of the regulation approach as the backdrop to institutional regulation, was by 1947 a complete failure. The mechanism did not regulate Atlantic economies until the late 1950s (1958 in the UK's case), when in a few years its deflationary bias became a central regulatory mechanism over the UK economy.

Table 2.12 Comparative indicators of UK economic performance

	Growth in GDP (%)		Annual rates of inflation (%)			Unemployment (%)			UK in international table of income/head (UK = 100)			Real output/head in manufacturing (average % change)					
	1950/73	1973/84	1965/73	1974/81	1982/7	1965/73	1974/81	1982/7	1950	1973	1987	1960/84	1960/8	1968/73	1973/9	1979/84	1984/6
UK	3.0	1.1	5.9	16.0	5.3	3.1	5.7	11.3	100	100	100	2.9	5.7	4.6	0.8	2.7	5.4
USA	3.7	2.3	4.3	8.4	3.6	4.4	6.8	6.8	160.6	148.1	147.6	2.7	3.3	3.4	1.2	2.7	2.6
Germany	5.9	1.7	4.5	4.7	2.8	0.9	3.3	6.8	60.1	102.5	108.6	4.2	5.2	5.0	3.9	2.0	3.8
Japan	9.4	3.8	6.2	7.0	1.1	1.2	2.0	2.6	26.8	89.3	106.3	8.1	9.1	9.9	6.1	7.0	5.7
France	5.1	2.2	5.0	11.0	7.1	2.1	5.1	9.5	70.5	100.7	103.2	4.9	6.3	5.9	3.8	3.1	3.5

Sources: M. Kirby, 'The economic record since 1945', in T. Gourvish and A. O'Day (eds), *Britain Since 1945* (London, Macmillan, 1991), p.13; N. Crafts and N. Woodward (eds), *The British Economy Since 1945* (Oxford, Oxford University Press, 1991), p. 9; V. Rossi, J. Walker, D. Todd and K. Walker, 'Exchange rates, productivity and international competitiveness', *The Oxford Review of Economic Policy* (1986) 2(3), 56–73; D. Coates, *The Question of UK Decline* (London, Wheatsheaf, 1994), p. 6.

Moreover, the Marshall Plan dispensed with the necessity of the Bretton Woods economic discipline. To secure the legitimacy of US domination, national pathway geopolitics[90] superseded internationalist economics, removing any prospect of the Marshall Plan modernizing the UK economy in the image of the US economy.[91] Instead, Marshall Aid secured the UK state and continuity in its national pathway. In relation to the UK state, over the post-war period, the regulation approach is rhetorically compelling but historically flawed.

Regulation implies order and common purpose, a set of rules that explain orderly behaviour. Rules can have the status of law, morality or custom. Equally, Bull demonstrated, in a classic study of international relations, that rules and order go beyond economics and economics alone cannot regulate.[92]

The anarchy of power politics and power and security seeking by nation states create instruments and mechanisms imbued with the specific interests of dominant states, often termed great powers or, in the post-war period, superpowers.[93] The economic and political interests of the USA were from 1947 to 1971 secured in Cold War geopolitics. This approach focused beyond an all encompassing economic theory. Instead, it focused on the suppression of the left and Communists in the labour movement, incorporating the latter in the anti-Communist position of the Marshall Plan, its ECA in particular.

A historically informed Atlanticist perspective provides a useful counterweight to the tendency of the regulation approach to overemphasize the central significance of Fordism or the coherence of regulatory institutions. Atlanticism throws doubt on many aspects of the regulation approach in relation to the development and performance of the UK economy in the post-war period.

The Atlanticist perspective captures the approach of the UK government to post-war recovery. From the earliest Anglo-American wartime agreement, UK leaders sought to avoid complete subordination to US foreign policy and consequent incorporation within economic and political hegemony. The UK was successful, for example, in retaining a strong military capability and its empire. Equally, the government was successful in avoiding integration into a federal pan-European pattern of economic and political regulation.

The Atlanticist perspective on the UK state and Anglo-American–European relations demonstrates that the central difficulty for US hegemony was the contradiction between the simultaneous pursuit of hegemony in the economic and political areas. Subsequent chapters illustrate that the development of an independent post-war national pathway to economic recovery has not been without consequence.

A national study that integrates the *realpolitik* of international relations within a discussion of the domestic political economy can provide an explanation of the UK's comparative economic decline beyond the analytical limitations of '*flawed* Fordism'.

3 The UK's competitive decline during the golden age, 1945–79

The Problem…raises sociological and political issues that are outside my competence…I do not propose to consider it in any detail.[1]

Introduction

This quotation from Kaldor illustrates one of the central disputes in addressing the process of UK economic decline in the post-war period. Kaldor was referring to the use of incomes policies to regulate wage increases within a framework of internal demand management designed to maintain full employment and secure the UK's fixed exchange rate. Kaldor's recognition that economic problems have a sociological and political dimension illustrates that beyond economics as a discipline economic explanations of decline are partial. Specifically, economics can demonstrate factors in decline but cannot necessarily demonstrate why they are of central importance. Rational actor models of economics emphasize the centrality of the market mechanism and are able to side-step the presence of political and sociological factors by applying the rational actor model to such factors. This has the effect of sealing complex and interdependent material as a contiguity – a proximity of ideas and impressions. The principle of association creates categories of explanation such as the failure of technological evolution, the absence of the market mechanism, the presence and effects of multi-unionism and, lastly, the UK's flawed Fordism.[2]

This chapter presents a historically embedded approach to UK economic performance during the golden age. It aims to inform and reconcile the space between and within relative and comparative explanations of economic decline. To do this, the chapter is divided into three sections. The first section examines the economic effects of external constraints on the UK economy during the golden age. The second section details the process of economic decline during the golden age. The final section of the chapter attempts to reconcile the parallel but mutually separate discussions of relative economic success and comparative economic decline through a historically informed presentation of proximate and significant factors of explanation.

Measures of the UK's recent economic performance that compare the 1980s with the post-war period or the post-war golden age with the inter-war period reveal very little about the UK's comparative success or failure. Further, and of key significance to this chapter's argument, measures of the UK's relatively successful post-war economic performance but comparative economic decline appear reconciled by a reliance on proximate explanations. The absence of extra economic analysis, which as Kaldor points out is significant but beyond the terms of reference of economists, represents a crucial limitation in this regard.

A qualitative and multidisciplinary consideration of narrowly defined economic issues necessitates a critical consideration of historically embedded institutional factors that preceded and dominated the UK's economic decline during the golden age. A purely economic analysis is unable to capture this wider consideration of economic decline. In order to be efficient, consumer and capital goods markets need not necessarily clear, however they must facilitate the wider aims and objectives of the nation state. Hence, markets operate within an institutional framework that is likely to reflect and reinforce historically embedded patterns of relations between and within the state in government, capital and labour. In the immediate post-war years, the wider political economy of the state in government structured economic efficiency around three related aims. First, to maintain the UK's territorial sovereignty and national economic pathway by independent means and avoid supranational regulation and political integration within a pan-European state. Second, and related, an export-led output drive to secure sterling and finance necessary imports. Third, maintain domestic modernization in civil society, secure full employment and avoid post-war inflation. Successive post-war governments prosecuted these aims. As political and sociological factors, each structured a measure of economic efficiency defined by a combination of historically embedded political economy and post-war *realpolitik*.

The pattern of institutional or Fordist regulation considered in Chapter 2 failed to assume significant influence in the UK economy. In the early years of the golden age, the UK's central economic problem was securing resources to produce for export, it was not a problem of markets. As a consequence of this, the recovery of output eschewed structural and scale changes in terms of production capacity, a pattern that created a necessary second-best solution. Here, a distinctively national pattern of political governance surrounded and constrained the organization of economic efficiency. However, by the 1960s, UK economic performance appeared unable to support the wider political goals reflected in the conservatism and ambition of national governance. Moreover, before this, the arrival of sterling convertibility in 1958 demonstrated that privileged access to secure empire markets had generated an output boom which, relative to the inter-war period, was very good. However, the output boom shielded concern with the UK's comparative economic decline, particularly in terms of market share of exports, manufactured import penetration into the UK and comparative levels of investment and labour productivity in the manufacturing sector.

Both relative growth and comparative growth in manufacturing productivity are good indicators of international competitiveness. However, the former concentrates on measuring recent economic performance to that since the 1870s, or more recently that of the 1980s to the post-war period.[3] In contrast, measures of comparative growth possess the additional quality of positioning the (relatively successful) UK economy against its main industrial competitors. This approach often leads to a simple prescription that the UK economy and its pattern of job regulation should mimic that of its more successful competitors, for example follow a course of economic deregulation and human resource management (HRM) and non-unionism in job regulation. However, this approach is flawed in two ways. First, these contemporary patterns may or may not explain why the US economy remains comparatively successful. Second, labour productivity in the US manufacturing sector has fluctuated around twice the UK level, with labour productivity in German manufacturing fluctuating broadly in line with that of the UK. Thus, the comparative labour productivity gap between the USA and Germany and the UK remains. However, since 1870, when a broad Anglo-American equality of performance prevailed, the US economy has pulled far ahead of that of the UK. In contrast to this, the German economy has risen from 60 per cent of UK productivity to broad equality in the post-war period. Further, German productivity has developed a reasonable lead over the UK during the contemporary period.[4]

External constraints on the UK economy during the golden age

The sceptre of US hegemony loomed large over the UK state in the late 1940s; avoiding subordination to this represented the major extra economic constraint on the UK economy. The Atlanticism of UK foreign policy and, by implication, domestic economic management successfully parried complete US domination to secure the UK state as a national pathway independent of supranational regulation in a pan-European state. These extra economic constraints reflect a series of consequential if contradictory economic constraints. First, to maintain the UK as a sovereign pathway, it was necessary to meet sterling area debts – sterling area member reserves – by fiduciary means[5] (a microversion of US policy under the Bretton Woods agreement during the late 1960s). The utility of inconvertible sterling balances and sterling area dollar pooling arrangements for balances necessitated maintaining empire markets as the main outlet for UK exports. This maintained secure essential imports of food and raw materials, but more significantly it marginalized the European export market. A second and related contradictory constraint centred around the UK's crisis of production in 1947. The only viable way to meet the first constraint was to concentrate on what economists term short-run output, i.e. at the existing scale of capacity.

Kaldor demonstrates convincingly that post-war governments used Keynesian economic theory to manage full employment through fiscal and monetary policies that avoided significant change in the UK's institutional framework.[6] For example, in relation to pay and productivity, the government recognized the utility of continuing the existing pattern of joint regulation among government, employers and organized labour. Kaldor further argues that the pattern of internal demand management, eventually termed stop–go policy, succeeded because it was an exchange rate policy transmitted through fiscal policy.[7] The effect of this was to tie the level of economic growth, particularly productivity growth in the manufacturing sector, to the level of domestic consumption and not export growth. Here, Kaldor acknowledges the extra economic constraints he previously refers to and details the significance of their presence under the heading of second-best conditions. For example, the policy of maximizing output out of current capacity was necessary, if consequential. The policy secured a *certain* rate of growth in industrial capacity yet it failed to improve the adverse long-term decline in the UK's international competitiveness.[8]

Dow argues that the mechanism of internal demand management became destabilizing after 1958.[9] This situation prevailed as the economic constraint of maintaining sterling as a reserve, but convertible currency increased dramatically from this date. For example, convertibility reintroduced the deflationary bias of the Bretton Woods system, dormant since 1947. Attempts by the Wilson government to resist domestic deflation or consider an early devaluation of sterling reinforced the deflationary bias of the system. In addition, seeking to ride out the deflationary bias contributed to severe balance of payments pressures and speculative sterling crises between 1964 and eventual devaluation in 1967. The diagnosis laid out by Kaldor suggests that the deflation of domestic consumer demand was a second-best, if consequential, necessity. Consequential in that it further weakened the growth and productivity potential of the UK manufacturing sector, a necessity defined by the wider aims and objectives of the state in government.

The movement to floating exchange rates in the early 1970s appeared as a second proximate solution to this impasse. Advocates of floating exchange rates argued that removing the burden of maintaining an exchange parity would create the potential for independent fiscal and monetary policy, i.e. independent of the commitment to a fixed exchange rate that constrained the growth potential of the UK economy.[10] However, the expansionary Barber boom under the heading of competition, credit and control saw the rapid return of speculative pressures on sterling, followed by a period of sustained depreciation in the real value of sterling. Deporte and Hall both argued that the movement to floating exchange rates could not overcome the UK's economic difficulties.[11]

Theoretically, removing the constraint of the fixed exchange rate that anchored the UK's internal demand management further weakened the UK's comparative competitiveness because the exchange rate deteriorated. Without the external stimulus of Marshall Plan protection and fixed exchange rates, use of fiscal and monetary policy to actively manage the domestic economy (as opposed to the exchange rate) acquired only a transient independence. The fallacy of floating exchange rates is the idea that an exchange rate policy is not necessary.[12]

The international monetary system retains a deflationary bias. Under

Marshall Aid and before the restoration of sterling convertibility, the UK avoided this as the relatively successful post-war performance masked comparative decline. However, once positioned within a multilateral convertible system of international trade, avoiding the perils of deflationary bias rested on the comparative productivity performance of the UK economy. The central difficulty for the UK economy was the restriction of growth and productivity capacity in the manufacturing sector to domestic consumption demand followed by that of empire markets. In summary, to avoid deflationary bias, a state must have a strong currency. Strong currencies result from improved comparative economic performance, which in turn rests on comparative investment levels and labour productivity. For much of the golden age, the UK suffered from a weak, if sometimes surplus, balance of payments under fixed exchange rates and inflation under floating exchange rates. Both represent an external constraint on the domestic economy that reflects comparatively declining economic performance.

Comparative economic decline during the golden age

During the period 1947–73, particularly the years from 1958, the UK's relatively successful economic performance did not close or reverse an embedded pattern of declining comparative industrial competitiveness. Moreover, while appearing to represent domestic prosperity or golden age, this period of relative success merely consolidated comparative economic decline. A variety of arguments demonstrate this paradox. First, as Maddison argues, during the immediate post-war years the UK economy went through a period of recovery rather than reconstruction or internal transformation.[13] By association, several influential commentators argue that UK recovery from the Second World War was complete by 1950 when output surpassed pre-war levels.[14] Second, if more controversially, Matthews argues that the UK's level of investment in capital stock during the golden age was comparatively low and technologically slow.[15] As Tables 2.10–2.12 illustrate, whereas UK investment and additions to capital stock were relatively high during the period 1950–70, both were far less impressive when examined in a comparative context. Third, and less controversially, at full employment improvement in the rate of economic growth can only be secured by raising productivity.[16] However, although UK labour productivity was relatively good during the golden age, it appears to be one result of a series of strategic choices made by the post-war government. In particular, productivity improvement resulted from the necessary decision to stimulate output at the expense of longer-term investment that might transform the UK's manufacturing capacity. Essentially, productivity improvement resulted from increasing output through extensive means: a relatively high level of investment that institutionalized long working hours and overtime. In turn, over the short to medium term, this success removed the apparent necessity for management in manufacturing industry to modernize structures for work organization, job regulation or the scale and capacity of manufacturing plants. This reason for this was precisely because UK recovery appeared complete by

1950.[17] Deterioration in the comparative competitiveness of the UK economy represents the paradox of relative success. This paradox remains significant into the contemporary period, particularly the productivity miracle of the 1980s. Measures of investment and productivity are able to demonstrate this paradox.[18]

Investment

Armstrong *et al.* demonstrate that although the UK's stock of machine tools increased by 15 per cent during the war years the total stock of fixed capital (net additions minus war losses and scrapping) remained at the pre-war level.[19] In contrast to this, German capital stock was 20 per cent greater. In both cases, it is arguable that each state had the necessary economic capacity to sustain a post-war recovery, but that military and political factors intervened to create short-term problems. The UK's major problem in the immediate post-war years was securing the necessary imports to produce manufactured goods for export markets and the domestic market. In Germany's case, four-power occupation followed by its centrality to the superpower Cold War ensured that manufacturing capacity would not reach efficient scale until well after the creation of West Germany in 1949. The UK was able to move ahead of Germany in terms of output and exports, but as Broadberry demonstrates both the UK and Germany, over the long term, returned to trend in terms of productivity growth.[20] Relatedly, as Tables 2.6 and 2.7 illustrate, for the period 1953–60 West Germany secured a higher level of net investment as a percentage of GNP than the UK. Equally, the data illustrate that the marginal capital–output ratio – the measure of increased capital necessary to produce an extra unit of output – is greater at lower levels of investment. This suggests a cumulative effect from higher investment that may further widen gaps in comparative economic performance. To balance this point, it is not always the absolute level of investment that is the key factor but the efficiency of its use. Data on comparative value added labour productivity tend to reinforce this point. Moreover, OECD data in Table 3.1 covering the period 1960–79 confirm that a higher investment ratio tends to a higher growth rate. Further, Table 3.2 suggests that states that have a higher investment ratio have superior investment productivity than lower investment states, i.e. the effect of a small change in investment has a greater effect on growth.

Productivity

Material in the previous chapter established that the UK's recovery of output was in the initial post-war period both comparatively and relatively good, whereas labour productivity was relatively good. In this respect, Tables 3.3–3.6 are revealing. Table 3.3 illustrates that although the UK's growth of output per capita for the period 1950–73 was respectable it was of a comparatively low order. Tables 3.4 and 3.5 are more revealing in two ways. First, the data illustrate that German, French, Japanese and Italian growth levels of output

Table 3.1 Investment ratios and % growth performance (excluding residential construction)

	1960–73		1973–9	
	Investment ratio	*Growth rate*	*Investment ratio*	*Growth rate*
Australia	20.2	5.2	18.0	2.8
Austria	19.3	4.9	19.3	3.0
Belgium	16.5	4.9	15.6	2.3
Canada	16.7	5.4	15.5	4.2
Denmark	16.5	4.3	15.3	1.9
France	16.3	5.4	15.6	2.7
Germany	17.3	4.3	14.4	2.4
Italy	16.6	5.3	17.0	3.5
Japan	26.5	9.7	24.2	3.5
The Netherlands	19.8	4.8	15.7	2.6
Sweden	16.8	4.1	15.9	1.8
UK	14.6	3.1	15.3	1.5
USA	13.5	4.0	14.4	2.6

Source: *OECD Historical Statistics, 1960–1995* (Paris, OECD, 1997).

Table 3.2 Effect on growth of a 1% change in the investment ratio[a]

Country	1960–73	1973–9
Australia	0.26	0.15
Austria	0.25	0.15
Belgium	0.29	0.15
Canada	0.32	0.27
Denmark	0.26	0.12
France	0.33	0.17
Germany	0.25	0.17
Italy	0.32	0.20
Japan	0.37	0.14
The Netherlands	0.24	0.17
Sweden	0.24	0.11
UK	0.21	0.10
USA	0.29	0.18

Source: *OECD Historical Statistics 1960–95* (Paris, OECD, 1997).

Note
a Investment defined as gross fixed capital formation less residential.

per capita were well ahead of the UK rate during the golden age. Second, over the long period, European levels of productivity per man–hour relative to US levels remained below US levels. In 1979, European productivity per man–hour was approximately 75 per cent of the US level (69 per cent in 1973), with Japanese productivity per man–hour lower than that found in Europe. In addition, Table 3.6 further illustrates the relative comparative issue. UK economic performance over the whole of the post-war period until 1979 appeared to be relatively good compared with the period since 1870, the inter-

Table 3.3   Growth of output (GDP at constant prices) per head of population, 1950–73

Country	% Annual average compound growth rate
Japan	8.4
Germany	5.0
Italy	4.8
France	4.2
Canada	3.0
UK	2.5
USA	2.2

Source: A. Cairncross and F. Cairncross (eds), *The Legacy of the Golden Age* (London, Routledge, 1992).

Table 3.4 Productivity levels per man–hour relative to USA (USA = 100%)

	1870	1913	1950	1973	1979
USA	100	100	100	100	100
UK	114	81	56	64	66
France	60	54	44	76	86
Germany	61	57	33	71	84
Italy	63	43	32	66	70
Japan	24	22	14	46	53

Source: A. Maddison, *Phases of Capitalist Development* (Oxford University Press, 1982).

Table 3.5 Real GDP per man–hour

	1950–73	1973–81
USA	2.6	1.1
UK	3.1	2.9
France	5.1	3.0
Germany	6.0	3.7
Italy	5.8	2.5*
Japan	8.0	3.1

Source: A. Maddison, *Phases of Capitalist Development* (Oxford,Oxford University Press, 1982); A. Maddison (1984); *OECD Historical Statistics 1985* (Paris, OECD, 1985); R. Matthews, C. Feinstein and J. Olding-Smee, *British Economic Growth 1850–1973* (Oxford, Oxford University Press,1982).

war period in particular. However, the data in Table 3.7 demonstrate the UK's comparative post-war decline in terms of output per person–hour in the manufacturing sector quite clearly. For example, in 1951, output per person–hour in French manufacturing was 71 per cent of the UK level, by 1973 it was 101 per cent, and in 1988 it stood at 122 per cent of the UK level. Equally, in 1951, output per person–hour in German manufacturing stood at 68 per cent of the UK figure, by 1979 the level stood at 163 per cent, falling back to 138 per cent of the UK level in 1988.

Table 3.6 Growth of UK output (GDP at constant prices)
per head of population 1700–1987

Period	% Annual average compound growth rate
1700–1820	0.4
1820–70	1.5
1870–1913	1.0
1913–50	0.9
1950–73	2.5
1973–9	1.3
1979–87	1.5

Source: A. Maddison, *Phases of Capitalist Development* (Oxford
University Press, 1982), p. 44, figures for 1973–87; A. Maddison,
The World Economy in the 20th Century (Paris, OECD, 1989).

Table 3.7 Output per person–hour in manufacturing, 1951–88: comparisons with the UK in
selected years

	UK	USA	France	Germany
1951	100	270	71	68
1964	100	268	90	117
1973	100	234	101	133
1979	100	243	129	163
1988	100	224	122	138

Source: B. Van Ark, 'Comparative levels of manufacturing productivity in post-war Europe: measurement
and comparison', *The Oxford Bulletin of Economics and Statistics* (1990) 52(4): 343–73.

These qualitative arguments and conclusions appear to be confirmed by an
influential econometric study. Davies and Caves examine measures of relatively
good or poor productivity performance in subsectors of UK manufacturing in
a comparative analysis with US equivalents.[21] The study suggests that economic
factors, such as underinvestment, create comparative shortfalls in capital per
employee, manifest in the size of plant and resources devoted to research and
development. The last represent significant factors in superior comparative
economic performance. However, capital per employee appears to be of greater
significance than disintegrated but dependent sociological factors such as
employee educational standards and trade union problems in the workplace,
yet both appear to be of some significance. The study appears to confirm the
link between higher investment and greater productivity of investment and
growth. However, it confines the treatment of sociological factors to the
workforce, the same tests are not applied to management or employer interests.
Hence, the study lacks a sociologically or historically informed analysis of
comparatively deficient economic factors. Matthews *et al.* provide such an
approach to the UK's comparatively poor level of labour productivity during
the period 1951–64.[22]

Matthews *et al*. argue that during the low unemployment years of the post-war period UK employers preferred to see labour and labour costs as an overhead; this was particularly the case for skilled labour. Employers began to hoard labour, even in economic downturns, reducing working hours rather than laying off workers. It is likely that this ploy backfired as the labour market tightened and loosened to create a sustained and cumulative source of overmanning. It is arguable that employers tended to hoard and use overtime because of the extensive nature of the UK's post-war recovery. Overtime etc. was necessary because of the comparatively small scale of UK plant. The small scale of plant sustained lower levels of capital per employee and low research and development expenditure.

In 'the golden age', the UK's macroeconomy and its management through internal demand management appeared as a technical success, particularly before 1973. However, relatively successful economic performance masked comparative economic decline. Regulation approaches suggest that the absence of supporting structures in civil society designed to align output, productivity and wages increases created a flawed Fordism. The following section demonstrates that the strategic choices made by the post-war government consolidated a pattern of international trade and comparative economic decline set in train much earlier. The decision to position sterling area nations as primary export markets reprised what has been described as a 'retreat to Empire'.[23] This represented a continuity in the UK's great power aims[24] and the aims and interests of representatives of UK employers.[25] Equally, this choice was a major factor in returning the UK to a long-term productivity trend during the period 1870–1990.[26] A failure to modernize describes these interrelated factors. Key issues in this are the rationality of the alleged failure to modernize and its dating.

The car industry, iron and steel and textiles

Dintenfass has produced a short study of UK industrial decline that focuses general themes through specific arguments based in these three industries.[27] Dintenfass concludes that the UK's comparative industrial decline since 1870 results from a failure to produce and distribute a range of goods and services with a level of economic efficiency similar to its main industrial competitors.

Dintenfass traces the pattern of causation to business decisions made by UK employers and managers, in particular a persistent rejection of formal and systematic training on the shop floor and in management. A reliance on informal techniques generated a pattern of inertia in production methods and a failure to consider alternatives. This represents a very significant factor in the UK's failure to modernize at a rate similar to its main competitors. Dintenfass describes this as the continued employment of established techniques.[28]

In the case of a new industry – motor manufacturing – standardized units produced from interchangeable components manufactured over long runs by semiskilled workers operating a moving assembly line has the potential to make low cost (Fordist) construction efficient. However, during the inter-war period, craft labour dominated the UK car industry that lacked interchangeable tooling, making the manufacture of standardized units problematic. Several intervening factors explain the continued use of established techniques. Lewchuk argues that the strength of trade unionism at the workplace in the inter-war car industry prevented UK employers from moving to Fordist production strategies.[29] However, Lewchuk may have overstated the presence and effect of trade unionism in the car industry during this period.[30] In contrast to Lewchuk, Bowden argues that mistaken perceptions of consumer demand together with aspects of the taxation policy constrained the production and marketing strategies used by UK car producers during this period. The perceptions of demand and taxation policy assumed only a small market for cars. Here, the emphasis was on quality over cost, this reinforced the tendency to extreme product differentiation, the opposite of Fordism. For example, in 1938, the UK's top six car firms produced forty engine types and even more body and chassis types.[31]

In the cases of iron and steel and the textile industry, there is clear evidence of failure on the part of UK producers to adopt new production methods.[32] In textiles, UK persistence with the mule when ring spindles and automatic looms became available was a precursor to the UK's post-war and contemporary low-cost low-productivity trajectory. Both innovations enabled producers to substitute semiskilled for skilled workers. However, in the UK, skilled labour was comparatively cheap, whereas the capital cost of the new machinery was prohibitive. For example, more formalized systems of training and development that follow from the use of new machinery often raise unit labour costs and result in the slowing down of production. Equally, for textiles, Walsh argued that the industry was in decline in terms of market share during the 1920s, this further reduced the incentive to invest in costly new machinery.[33] Moreover, in the immediate post-war years, the industry conformed to the wider export-oriented output drive that further reduced incentives to re-equip and scrap, even in the face of legislation – the 1948 Cotton Spinning Industry (Re-Equipment Subsidy) Act. By the early 1950s, comparative decline in terms of output and employment was evident and from 1954 import penetration became significant.

In the steel industry, attachment to acid steel-making had the effect of making UK plant comparatively smaller than US and German plant. Dintenfass positions the iron and steel industry as a primary example of resistance to technical change in UK manufacturing.[34] Resistance to change led to a low use of metal-based appliances in the home and the slow manufacture of machine tools and equipment for industry and, therefore, even slower diffusion of their take-up.

In the immediate post-war years, the AACP found antiquated systems of work organization, training and job regulation in many steel plants. Some systems were so informal that the AACP was unable to calculate labour productivity with any accuracy, preferring instead to rely on Rostas's 1948 calculations suggesting a US/UK differential of 2.5:1.[35] More interestingly, the AACP Iron and Steel report suggested that the higher unit labour costs of smaller UK plants did not necessarily make it economically rational to build large plants. Over comparatively small production runs, larger plants may fail to reduce unit costs by significant measures that would be sufficient to provide an adequate return on the necessary capital investment.[36] The report also indicated that steel producers in the UK submitted to this argument.[37]

It appears that in providing a rational explanation for the UK's comparative competitive decline Dintenfass leans towards a historically embedded sociological explanation. However, Dintenfass is unable to provide a specific explanation for the motives of employers and managers.[38] To provide this, it is necessary to link the failure to modernize theses of the late nineteenth century, the inter-war period and the immediate post-war years to the issue of markets and international competitiveness. It appears that the retreat into empire markets in the Sudan, Egypt, India, South Africa and Kenya among many others extended markets for late nineteenth-century UK industry in railways, textiles, small arms and bicycles. Equally, Australia, Canada and New Zealand proved to be secure markets for exports of machinery, tools and bridges. Broadberry argues and demonstrates that before 1914 this pattern of trade was a rational response to the rise in competition from Europe and the USA.[39]

Moreover, Broadberry establishes that the UK retained a measure of comparative competitiveness in craft-based industries where Fordist systems appeared inapplicable, such as shipbuilding. In these cases, the source of the UK's competitiveness was comparatively low labour costs. However, for the post-war period, Broadberry is more assertive in his suggestion that the failure to introduce mass assembly *Fordism* represented irrational behaviour on the part of employers and trade unions.[40] For both the pre-1914 period and the post-war period, it appears that this type of argument may demonstrate declining comparative competitiveness, but cannot necessarily provide a satisfactory explanation for it. This is the case because during the nineteenth century and in 1945 the UK was one of the world's greatest imperial powers. In the post-war years, the UK retained a residual great power status that facilitated a relatively good economic performance over the whole period. In this context, it proved difficult for industry to recognize the need for change, particularly where the short-term rational self-interest of established markets generated good economic performance relative to the recent past. More specifically, in the post-war period, these actions directly reflected the political economy of the state in government. Rather than lose an opportunity, the government in its domestic and foreign policy actions took an opportunity. A significant consequence of this appears to be not the failure to adopt US mass production methods but the continuation of established production and management techniques. Explanations of this that fail to provide a historical dimension fall back on the category of *flawed* Fordism. An associated consequence – the UK's comparative economic decline – is more difficult to position.

Reconciling the UK's comparative economic decline and historically relatively good performance in the golden age

In the main, this is a question of how to interpret UK economic performance since 1945. Second, it is a question of depth in answers, for as this section illustrates there are many proximate answers to which economists and economic historians turn in order to rationalize measures of success or decline. Superficially (and perhaps substantively), they are plausible to convincing. However, to move beyond the superficial, i.e. to proceed beyond the demonstrative, it is necessary to explain factors by surpassing categories or generalization. It is here that historically embedded institutional factors in the political economy of a nation state are likely to retain significance beyond transient proximity.

Three points summarize the position of the UK state and economy during the golden age. First, in the post-war period, the UK's investment ratio was significantly higher than that during the inter-war period and the period since 1870, but in a comparative context investment levels were of a low order (see Tables 2.10–2.12). Second, the productivity of investment in other states was greater than that in the UK (see Tables 2.6 and 2.7). Third, the deployment of Marshall Aid funds aimed to secure the UK as a sovereign national pathway and therefore maintain disparate (non-standard) production in domestic and overseas markets, particularly in the sterling area. Each point reflects the *realpolitik* in the political economy of the state, wherein the UK's historically relatively good economic performance continued well into the golden age.

The predication of *realpolitik* was avoiding subordination to US hegemony and incorporation into a pattern of pan-European federalism. Both aims combined in the output-based recovery that necessarily limited the adoption of new techniques for work organization and job regulation based on assembly line production methods. The adoption of such methods would, in a period of high export demand, stall output and in some cases raise unit costs. The latter was the case because, although existing UK plant was comparatively less efficient than that of US industry and subsequently became less efficient than that of European competitors, UK plant was sufficiently efficient to meet the productivity requirements of the markets served. This in turn met the immediate goals of the state and the historically embedded interests, aims and objectives of employers, which in turn structured the interests of organized labour.

Historically embedded institutional factors such as those referred to by Kaldor structured internal demand management in two ways. First, as a mechanism to maintain the UK's fixed exchange rate. Second, and related, as measures to maintain the fixed exchange rate became more severe, restraint of the domestic economy, principally consumer demand, became equally severe.[41] In combination, both mechanisms represented an appropriate second-best solution. Each contributed to relative success but comparative decline by limiting growth capacity to the necessarily constrained growth of consumer demand. As a result, the growth of export demand became insufficient to secure the UK's full growth potential, particularly as sterling area markets appeared less dynamic than those in Europe and those in the domestic economy. The aims and objectives of the post-war state in government were necessary, but reinforced a longer-term downward trajectory in the UK's comparative economic performance. In summary, Kaldor's analysis suggests that internal demand management could not secure export markets but could merely structure the UK's relatively good economic performance until the early 1970s.

The restrictive nature of internal demand management intensified after the restoration of sterling convertibility in 1958 when the deflationary measures associated with stop–go policy became more pronounced. For example, the use of incomes policies and taxation had the effect of restricting domestic output, which tended to be met in go periods by sucking in imports. In addition to this deflationary effect, higher taxation and incomes policies had the effect of reducing consumer demand and therefore the growth capacity of the domestic economy. Further, from the late 1960s, defiance of incomes policies represented significant workplace conflict. As a remedy, many employers followed the recommendations of the Donovan Commission and repositioned industrial relations management at plant level and attempted to introduce productivity bargaining.[42] In an attempt to arrest the UK's now evident comparative economic decline, the state and employers aimed to raise the efficiency of the manufacturing sector by using management control systems designed to *intensify* extensive labour performance.

The last years of the golden age saw the emergence of the first proximate (although it remains ideologically, at least, very intransigent) explanation for the UK's post-war decline, variously termed the UK worker problem, the UK disease or the inefficiency of restrictive practices. The attractiveness of proximate explanations requires specific consideration in order to reveal the necessity for more significant supporting analysis to underpin generalized patterns of association.

Various approaches within different literature sets that demonstrate and explain economic decline during the golden age have created a series of proximate and significant reasons for the process of decline. Proximate explanations appear and may be convincing but are often transitory. For example, the human resource management literature has proffered numerous such explanations – disorderly workplace employee relations, the absence of productivity bargaining in the workplace, personnel management, the absence of integrated human resource management, poor performance and quality management, low performance workplace systems, etc. Each has assumed, prescriptively and journalistically at least, significance as a factor of explanation in either the golden age or the contemporary period. Equally, the economics literature focuses on sealed 'black box' explanations of economic decline. For example, industrial relations and a failure to adopt US production and managerial methods, each explanation, however convincing, requires further explanation.

The limitations of proximate explanations

In addition to the factors described above, low investment, slow adoption and diffusion of new production techniques and poor work organization find frequent citation in the literature as influential in the UK's economic decline. However, each factor requires further explanation, i.e. the direction of or even the presence of causation is not proven. Moreover, significant qualitative factors derived from these demonstrations such as comparatively poor production systems and poor design and marketing appear as disintegrated factors that are necessary to generate high productivity and low unit labour costs. Unfortunately, whatever the significance attached to these factors, in isolation the qualitative or counterfactual nature of their impact appears as an effect of comparative decline and not a cause of decline. Hence, proximate demonstration does not equate to significant specific explanation.

Economic historians, economists and those who subscribe to variants of the regulation approach often cite the significance of external shocks to the Western economic systems. The reintroduction of sterling convertibility in 1958 and the OPEC crises in the 1970s are two frequently cited external shocks. However, neither created internal economic difficulties beyond the short term, yet each exposed other embedded but shielded difficulties. However, the weight of argument beyond the regulation approach suggests that external shocks expose the presence of structural economic crises within national pathways but do not actually cause them.[43]

More particular difficulties arise when economic historians or advocates of the regulation approach develop historically based explanations that lean too heavily on economics rather than on history. For example, the premature nature of the UK's industrialization and the subsequent absence of a bourgeoisie revolution appear influential and significant factors. As explanations for comparatively poor post-war economic performance, conservatism and *laissez faire* in all branches of management suggest a historical specificity for the absence of more strategic management of the economy and in the employment relationship.[44] There are two difficulties with these arguments. First, it is curious to describe a historical process – the UK's industrialization – as premature. Historians agree that the UK was the first industrial nation and that in very general terms the process was organic as opposed to instrumental and integrated as in Germany and the USA.[45] However, UK industrialization was only premature in the sense that chronologically it occurred before that of the other states. The state could neither induce nor forestall the organic process of industrialization. The second difficulty relates to the issue of bourgeois revolution. There was a bourgeois revolution in the UK, but in contrast to that which occurred in other states it was relatively peaceful. As Perkin explains, by the early 1800s the industrial bourgeois had established that the productive base of the UK economy was manufacturing and not agriculture. This was the case even though the UK remained dominated by pillars of 'old society' – the Monarchy and the landed aristocracy.[46] In summary, this movement required the reconstitution of labour away from the land as free individuals subject to market conditions. Hence, the patronage interests of the old society required conversion to private property on a contractual model.

The emergence of private property with labour as its substance created citizenship for property-less labour. Equally, the mobilization of emergent class interests against an apparently arbitrary monarchy and landed aristocracy was of great concern. The emergent industrial capitalist class appeared to fear this too; but equally, the industrial class opposed central regulation by Parliament. The significance of *laissez faire* was the creation of a common cause for monarchy, aristocracy and the industrial class, an apparently material but, in substance, rhetorical pursuit of freedom from centralized regulation by Parliament.[47] The Reform Acts of 1832 and 1867, with the latter enfranchising a majority of the urban working class, assured parliamentary domination over that of the Monarchy. The Monarchy and the landed aristocracy conceded the decline of landed patronage, but sought to secure their property interests through paternalism. This move meshed with the wider movement to regulation by employment, contract and private property. As Barrington-Moore demonstrates and explains in a comparative historical study, this movement represented a peaceful bourgeois revolution – the beginning of a democratic route to liberal industrial capitalism based on free but incorporated labour.[48] Thus, as proximate explanations, chronology appears insignificant when described as premature, whereas reference to historical work casts doubt on the claim that no bourgeois revolution occurred.

From 1958, inflation became a serious enough problem to structure the application of deflationary fiscal and monetary policy, otherwise termed stop–go policy.[49] A key point often allied to this is the cumulatively negative effect of stop–go policy on the expansion of industrial output and investment.[50] However, equally significant was the source of the inflation problem. As Kaldor demonstrated, external constraints imposed by the state structured internal demand management, which after the introduction of sterling convertibility became more restrictive on the domestic economy. By the mid-1960s, the cost of imports and wage inflation combined to create the notion of cost push inflation, which necessitated more severe stops in the stop–go cycle. As a consequence of stop–go economic management, many investment decisions in private sector manufacturing often appeared marginal. The longer-term effect of comparative decline in investment levels led to cumulative losses in output and output capacity.[51] More significantly, during this period the problem of sustaining relatively good economic performance focused on the effects of wage leadership, localized collective bargaining and wage drift. However, each development appeared somehow independent of the UK's relative success but comparative economic decline.[52] In contrast to this disintegrated explanation, a more integrated interpretation is revealing. The sustained boom in output, relative labour shortage and comparatively low level of investment in leading edge (as opposed to replacement) plant increased the bargaining strength of labour. Equally, the combined effects of these factors reduced the impact of established and authoritarian management control techniques which employers preferred to deploy.

Some advocates of the regulation approach have further positioned the emergence of strong trade unionism in the workplace.[53] The UK's rapid post-war recovery (in relation to output levels in 1937–8) enabled trade unions to consolidate low effort, comparatively low output and wages by successful resistance to dismissal and the prevention of job speed-up. Further, this process became significant in sustaining low productivity levels and poor comparative competitiveness during the golden age. The difficulty with the proximate nature of this argument is twofold. First, it isolates industrial relations from employer and managerial aims and objectives and the position of both within the UK's wider recovery from the war. Second, it is a further variant to the flawed Fordism argument.

A further limitation confronts proximate arguments that explain the UK's comparative economic decline through the process of convergence, sometimes referred to as 'catch-up'.[54] This argument suggests that the Marshall Plan structured the incorporation of Western European economies within Atlanticism through the diffusion of US capital and production strategies. Here, US capital grants reconstructed national economies, some, notably West Germany, without the burden of military and defence expenditure but with access to and the necessity for new investment in manufacturing capacity. In addition, theoretically implicit within this argument, unrestricted access to new methods should, rationally at least, lead to equal dissemination and take-up of best practice and use of new methods.

The previous section of this chapter established that in textiles, cars and iron and steel the interests of UK producers appeared best served by avoiding the take-up of new methods of production. This evidence illustrates that rationally informed economic explanations may be historically flawed. Equally, measures of productivity for the whole economy indicate that since 1870 when the UK stood in broad equality with the USA the latter has pulled substantially ahead of the UK. Also, Germany, which was at least 40 per cent less productive than the UK in 1870, now has a respectable if small productivity advantage over the UK.[55] The position of the German economy is significant because in the immediate post-war years only 40 per cent of its pre-war industrial capacity was useable. This pattern suggests that there has been little convergence between the UK and German economies since 1945 but, on the contrary, that there has been a continuation of trends in national pathways, i.e. comparative improvement and comparative decline.

Last, for some the comparative economic decline of the UK's manufacturing sector occurred primarily during in the period 1950–79, thereafter successive Thatcher governments reversed this process.[56] Broadberry demonstrated this point through substantial econometric data sector by sector and concluded that during the post-war period, in comparison with US plants, UK plants were small and failed to introduce mass standardized production techniques. The intransigence of trade unions and established interests in defined markets among employers appear as the primary factors of explanation in this failure. However, as disintegrated proximate explanations, plant size, production techniques and industrial relations are unable to specify why *economically* the strategic choice to continue with what Broadberry describes as 'flexible' production prevailed.[57]

In summary, whereas proximate explanations may appear convincing and may be convincing, contemporary significance requires historical specification in order to establish historically embedded significance within a particular national pathway. Such an approach is likely to demonstrate and to explain the embedded nature of interests and institutional processes that either inhibit or sustain economic performance.

The significance of historically embedded explanations

A failure to position demonstrative yet significant explanations within historically embedded patterns and processes represents a critical limitation of proximate explanations of economic decline. There are three historically significant explanations for the UK's declining international economic competitiveness. First, the historical legacy of employer organization and management preferences, particularly over the issues of control strategies and production systems, both remain significant in the contemporary period. Second, and related, the types of markets served by UK manufacturing industry, particularly export markets. Third, the amalgamated long-term effects of the previous factors on the UK's comparative competitiveness and economic performance, particularly during the post-war period.

The prevalence of family-run or family-dominated U' form firms represents a significant historical legacy of the UK's early industrialization.[58] Further, the evidence suggests that from the inter-war period family-dominated U' form firms, if they amalgamated or merged to create a larger overall business unit, exercised a preference for loose amalgamations via disintegrated holding companies.[59] As a result of this, after the merger there would often be little rationalization in terms of markets served by a component firm and therefore its products. Equally, alterations in production practices would be unlikely. Moreover, poor rationalization resulting in large, but disintegrated, holding structures would inhibit economies of scale. Normally derived from larger firms, these economies were often absent because in effect individual component firms appeared to continue as before the merger.

In contrast to the above, there is some evidence that inter-war merger and rationalization aimed to prevent the entry of US and German firms into UK markets or their acquisition of UK firms.[60] Some such mergers did lead to rationalization and improved economies of scale, e.g. those which created Imperial Tobacco and that which involved Unilever. However, in motor manufacturing, iron and steel and textiles, for many firms considerable vertical disintegration remained the norm. Hence, generalization from particular successes is not necessarily plausible. Further, in the immediate post-war years, the majority of the top 200 UK firms retained some element of family control on the board.[61] Last, Aaronovitch and Sawyer demonstrate and explain that although the size of plants in the UK was smaller than those found in the USA during the post-war period, industrial concentration was similar. Further, the evidence suggests that UK productivity was significantly below the level found in the US economy. It appears likely that scale economies in production and resultant reduction in unit labour costs after merger were potential benefits for capital. However, both represented a lower priority than those resulting from more concentrated ownership and control.[62]

One result of the above was that during the golden age, particularly after 1968, UK employers and managers attempted to deploy intensive management control strategies in existing systems of production organization. However, intensive efficiencies derived in the main from scientifically inspired technical and social aspects in management engineering of production. Systems of management engineering concentrated on efforts to deskill workers, combined with technical innovations in work organization based on standardized assembly production. The retention of existing systems of production was necessary to serve the UK's dominant markets, secure sterling and to meet the government's wider aspirations in foreign policy. The aims and interests of many employers in the manufacturing sector meshed with these objectives precisely.[63]

The period from 1945 to 1958 was really a manufacturing sellers' market, and the movement to sterling convertibility did not, in the short term, intensify the pressures associated with the UK's external constraints. However, by 1967, higher levels of import penetration in manufacturing, much of it from Western Europe, exposed the consequential impact of gearing UK export trade to highly differentiated markets in former empire nations. By association, this positioned the same variety of non-standardized goods and methods of production on the domestic economy. Equally, these factors reinforced the tendency to loose merger and amalgamation that, as international competition stiffened, exposed the comparative inefficiency in management and production organization as a key factor in the UK's declining economic performance.

In the textile industry, an apparent preference for antiquated production methods was a rational response to low wages, informal training and lay shop floor organization of production. Equally, the potential labour cost savings derived from new technology appeared, in the UK, marginal. Further, more standardized production would require closer management supervision. In contrast to this prescription, the presence of skilled craft labour was a great advantage to the employer. First, it facilitated less investment expenditure on capital. Second, management was able to delegate tasks such as monitoring, training and development and some aspects of recruitment and selection. However, delegation of these tasks reduced management authority. The loss of management authority often appeared when management made subsequent attempts to speed up or reform the labour process.[64] However, although production costs were relatively low, unit costs were relatively low but comparatively high, whereas productivity was relatively good but comparatively low, all of which suited employers and the markets they served.

The slow diffusion of organizational change in the UK manufacturing sector appears to be one of the most significant factors of explanation for comparative decline in productivity and wider measures of competitiveness. In turn, the generalization of managerial preference for existing techniques in work organization appears historically embedded. Preference, organization and techniques relate directly to the UK's early industrialization and empire role; during the post-war period, the UK's role in the Cold War retained then replaced empire ambitions. Moreover, the UK's central role in the Cold War demonstrated a determination by the state to retain a national pathway to post-war recovery independent of US domination or European assimilation.

Output-driven post-war recovery appeared complete by 1950. In part, the rapid recovery of output reflected wartime dislocation in which output and employment were both artificially high. A continuation of this and an absence of large-scale capital renewal extended existing methods of production, work organization and job regulation in established markets both domestically and overseas. In the early post-war period, this gave the UK a temporary advantage over other European states.

The outbreak of the Korean conflict in 1950 further reduced the pressures for structural change in the manufacturing sector that were promoted by Marshall Aid institutions such as the technical assistance programme and the AACP. The intensification of the Cold War in Western Europe created general pressures for rearmament as the focus of US foreign policy moved away from economic reconstruction and transformation to geopolitics. One effect of this was a consolidation of the UK's output boom well into the early 1960s. The technical assistance programme, the AACP and its successor, the UK productivity council, appeared of minor significance beyond being centres for prescriptive best practice. However, the consolidation of boom further reinforced a reliance on traditional markets, established methods of production and patterns of job regulation.

Kaldor has convincingly established that for the UK export demand represented a considerable share in overall production during the post-war period. More significantly than this, Kaldor established that the comparative competitiveness of the UK economy in the wider international economy determined the level and rate of growth of export demand.[65] In turn, comparative competitiveness depends on industrial costs and labour productivity relative to competitors in international markets.

The fusion of static and dynamic factors causes increasing returns to scale in manufacturing plants to generate rising productivity the faster output expands. Kaldor referred to this as the learning curve down which an economy must travel, indicating the importance of non-price factors in productivity growth. Non-price factors such as technological innovations in production systems, improved work organization and the devotion of adequate resources to research and development appear significant for productivity growth, each contributing to a process termed cumulative causation.[66]

The effective combination of dynamic and static factors positions the rate of productivity growth as central to the overall competitiveness of manufacturing industry. The former has to be high enough to sustain not only relatively good economic performance in terms of the recent past but also sufficiently high enough to maintain comparative competitiveness. More specifically, a reliance on measures of relative success appeared confined by the presence of apparently non-negotiable external constraints related to the UK's residual great power role. This necessitated a pattern of internal demand management that had the effect of limiting growth capacity to consumption in the domestic economy. The effect of this limitation tied the competitiveness of exports to the growth trend in the domestic economy to inhibit significantly the capacity of UK manufacturing to retain comparative competitiveness. The key issue is that to retain international competitiveness it is necessary to continue to increase domestic productivity relative to competitors and not to the recent past.

From the late 1950s, stop–go policies were in part designed to reduce the 'drag effect' of excessive wage increases on the UK competitiveness. However, as Ray among others has established, by the 1960s UK labour costs were falling compared with those in major competitor states.[67] This suggests that unit labour costs in UK manufacturing were high, whereas total labour costs and labour productivity were falling by international comparison.

By the early 1960s, governments began to focus on the UK's declining competitiveness as import penetration in the manufacturing sector began to threaten the viability of the fixed exchange rate. The Donovan Commission (1965–68) and eventual devaluation in 1967 both aimed to reduce excessive labour costs and reposition the UK's comparative competitiveness. The decentralization and proceduralization of collective bargaining in industrial relations management and the use of incomes policies associated with devaluation had a marginal effect on real wage levels but relatively little impact on productivity growth. As Hall argues, the central problem was one of falling productivity, which over the whole of the post-war period into the early 1970s had the effect of reducing the UK's competitiveness in world markets.[68] Ray and Hall demonstrate the limitations of relying on measures of relative economic performance; they provide little purchase on comparative competitiveness.

Low productivity in the UK's manufacturing sector was an effect of low investment. Moreover, comparatively low productivity is an effect not a cause of comparatively poor economic performance. Explanation of this argument requires reference to long-term trends in total factor productivity. This measure of productivity refers to the combined increase in the productivity of capital and labour. The productivity of investment and value added to labour productivity determine these measures. The last appear significant and derive from investment in training and development and the deployment and effective management of up-to-date capital and production systems, sometimes referred to as the social capability of labour.[69] However, the social capability of labour is not a disintegrated factor. Investment in human capital and labour capability operate within a wider system of production, hence the key issue for consideration is the series of factors that inhibit the social capability of labour.[70]

Long-term measures of comparative total factor productivity indicate that the UK's level and efficiency in use of capital and labour grew less rapidly over the period 1870–1984 than the majority of the UK's industrial competitors.[71] The UK's role in the Cold War and the role of sterling in the international economy acted as a wider structure for domestic demand management and the efficiency of capital and labour. Demand management policies did restrict the manufacturing sector while meeting other objectives of the state. By confining the potential of the manufacturing sector to domestic consumption demand, demand management techniques restricted not only the level but also the efficiency of investment and labour productivity. Equally, demand management restricted the growth potential of sectors where export demand was significant. However, this approach cushioned comparative economic decline, yet secured relatively good economic performance and maintained great power status.

Kaldor outlined a position which establishes that post-war policy was not necessarily a mistake. This is the case because in Kaldor's formulation post-war economic policy represented not the ideal which economists prefer but the second-best situation that actually prevailed.[72] Kaldor identified demand management as a necessary structure to maintain the UK's wider role in the international political economy and positions comparative economic decline as a potential result. This extends the authority of the Kaldorian argument beyond economic theory. By highlighting the role and significance of political and institutional factors as historically embedded, this argument produces an explanation of UK economic decline that combines institutional, economic and international factors. Further, it has the effect of clearly positioning regulation approaches which highlight the central significance of flawed Fordism as a proximate explanation. This is the case because under intensive production relations the social and technical organization of work represents a central driver for productivity increases. The evidence clearly suggests that, in large measure, the achievement of post-war recovery resulted from extensive methods of production that accorded with the prevailing, if mutually exclusive, interests of the state, capital and labour.

The comparative rate of growth in manufacturing productivity is an authoritative indicator of an economy's international competitiveness. The authority of significant explanations for decline over proximate demonstrations of decline lies in different starting points for analysis of the issue. For example, the former are able to demonstrate decline by highlighting and isolating particular issues that may be of significance. However, more significant explanations take as a starting point the historical process of decline and the role of proximate factors in the process of decline. This inevitably draws in factors beyond economic analysis.

The presentation of industrial relations as a serious problem for post-war government policy acquires a greater significance than that demonstrated by approaches that isolate issues in job regulation without explanation. In contrast to this, it is more likely that the problematic nature of post-war industrial relations reflected wider historically embedded issues within employer and management preferences.

Moreover, the *failure* of UK producers to exploit markets that became more productive than those in the sterling area markets, thereby creating a flawed Fordism, is not necessarily the case. Wider measures of the UK's profile in the international political economy were of equal or greater significance. More particularly, the chosen course was necessary but consequential. The UK's relatively good economic performance over the whole of the period since 1945 reflects a longer-term trend dating from 1870.[73]

Successive governments since 1945 have retained significant strategic choices made in the early post-war period. The maintenance of a sovereign national economic pathway combined with great power status to sustain sterling as a residual reserve currency, whereas established production techniques for established markets became the backbone of the manufacturing sector. Each factor encapsulates the historical legacy of the UK state. It suggests that patterns of industrial relations and the industrial relations system are of only marginal significance in relation to other factors that have inhibited productivity growth in the manufacturing sector and the whole economy.

Institutional, political and sociological factors combine to precede economic explanations of post-war economic decline. They create a mode of particularization that is historically distinct within national pathways. A pattern of governance within the institutional ensemble that constitutes the state. This pattern of governance structures the relationship between the state in government, capital and labour – the UK state and its particularization.

The UK's relatively organic pattern of industrialization was national in coverage but localized in terms of size of firm and markets served. As a pattern, this served the immediate and medium-term needs of the UK economy, however the absence of vertical or horizontal integration was manifest in a large number of efficient but highly localized firms. Once UK firms became subject to more structured overseas competition, particularly during the 1960s, the significance of this became more transparent, creating a comparative diseconomy of scale especially against vertically integrated competitors in manufacturing. The process of industrialization in the UK and the position of the state in government within it was unique, but it was small in scale compared with that in the USA and Germany. In the late nineteenth century, industrialization was refuelled and consolidated by the emergence of empire. A process repeated during the inter-war period under the label of Imperial Preference. Similarly, during the immediate post-war period, the strategic choice to retain the UK economy as a sovereign national pathway independent of US domination or Europeanization continued this process.

The retention of Imperial Preference and protected markets in the sterling area until 1958 and devaluations in 1949 and 1967 delayed economic and political adjustments by the state; this was the belated movement to European union, in which the economic and institutional interests in and between capital and labour appear to be more European than Atlanticist, although this remains a contested issue. In contrast to this, the UK's role in the international political economy appears to be that of a great power. A position maintained and reproduced over and above the logic of economics and the constraints of economic performance. The movement to European union is a recognition of economic decline, a mechanism by which the UK state attempts to sustain its position as a *European* great power.

Conclusions

Nation states organize political power both domestically and externally to maintain highly particularized patterns of national governance. Particularization is a historically embedded process. It creates a 'national distinctiveness' which reflects historically informed sociological and institutional factors that preserve a sovereign identity. The national pathway in economic interests and economic management is only one of these and as the contemporary period illustrates sovereignty does not always result in economic efficiency. However, sacrificing the second best of the former for the benefits of the latter remains controversial and contested.

The comparative deficiencies in the UK pattern of capital formation during the post-war period reflect the *laissez faire* legacy of the industrialization process and the subsequent effects of empire. The structure of empire trading in the post-war period was necessary if consequential. Unfortunately, the UK's post-war economic performance has been unable to support the wider empire-inspired goals of the UK state in *realpolitik* and international relations. However, remnants of the latter remain – nuclear power, UN security council member and *Great Power* actor in the Berlin crisis of 1948, the German occupation from 1945 until 1990, the Korean police action in 1950, the Iraq war in 1991 and in the Kosovan crises in 1999. The surges of great power action appeared marginal in a superpower Cold War and disproportionately expensive for a European great power in the contemporary period.

In contrast to the structural importance of institutions and political factors, misconduct in the management of economic policy and poor industrial relations often appear as the most significant factor of explanation in the UK's poor post-war economic performance. What is remarkable about this is the success with which consideration of the period since 1945 appears deleted from consideration of the contemporary period since 1979. It is as if the contemporary economic interests of the state, capital and labour were somehow significantly different from those which preceded and followed the Second World War. The convincing nature of proximate explanations – flawed Fordism, the failure to adopt US production techniques, disorderly workplace industrial relations or the 'wasted victory' thesis – is part of the problem.[74] Each factor does play a marginal role, yet each appears to be a significant scale factor.

A historically positioned examination of these explanations exposes the issue of prior significance. This leads to an explanation which suggests that differences in the performance of national pathways appear directly influenced by factors beyond mechanisms for domestic economic management or the functional aims of policymakers. This suggests that the component elements in improving or declining relative or comparative economic performance are not, beyond the marginal, automatically or technically transferable or reversible. This is the case because contemporary results reflect historically embedded factors.[75]

As Kaldor suggests, economists and the economics literature have been and remain reluctant to consider institutional explanations that lean too heavily on qualitative – historical, political or sociological methods, however significant –

rather than quantitative methods. The reason why Kaldor's position is unusual and significant is twofold. First, it does not visualize the observed developments in policy and process, what economists term the second best, as a failure. Second, Kaldor outlines the centrally significant, but necessary, role of internal demand management in cushioning UK economic decline. This points to a constructive engagement with the limitations of economic theory. Equally, isolation from the second-best conditions of political economy belies the complexity of economic management. For example, the determination of institutional and political factors that govern and particularize the economy lies beyond the market mechanism.

Competitiveness in dynamic markets governs comparative economic performance. International comparisons of labour productivity, unit labour costs and total labour costs are reliable measures of comparative economic performance. In the UK's post-war pattern of internal demand management and associated external constraints, restriction of domestic consumption was the significant variable in economic management. In an effort to peg wage costs to productivity, stop–go policies aimed to cheapen the cost of labour. The central difficulty with this policy was that while it sustained the UK's relative economic performance (cushioned decline) it had virtually no effects on improving comparative economic performance. In this context, attempts to reduce wages at a given rate of growth had insignificant effects on labour productivity or total factor productivity other than extending the life of capital, equipment and extensive labour use strategies.

As the opening quotation suggests, the institutional representation of political and sociological factors creates the reality of second-best conditions and within this framework internal demand management during the post-war period was not a failure. Relative to the inter-war period, there was a higher level of employment, investment and economic growth, such that during the period 1870–1990 overall UK economic performance appears loosely similar to that of Germany. However, Germany pulled ahead during the inter-war period and during the last years of the post-war period, whereas compared with overall US economic performance the UK remains some distance behind.[76]

A significant factor in explaining the UK's comparative economic decline is that the comparative method entered the language of economic analysis too late. Even once significant explanations are available, proximate explanations often retain contemporary utility.[77] Thus, to develop further a historically embedded explanation of economic decline in a particularized national pathway, Chapter 4 positions the foregoing economic analysis within political and sociological antecedents which in amalgamation are the UK state.

4   A particularized theory of the UK state

Nation states exhibit a domestic and external framework of political power that structure and sustain highly particularized and historically embedded patterns of governance, a pattern of institutional distinctiveness that signals sovereign identity. An institutional examination of historically embedded political and sociological constraints in the UK state can illustrate the significance of second-best conditions outlined by Kaldor, which are so often ignored by economic analysis.

This chapter examines the political and sociological frameworks that are amalgamated in the UK state, in particular the relationship between historically embedded patterns which structure political power in the state and the economic power of the state. The central theme relates to strategic antecedents in and between economic and political interests that constrain UK economic performance but which secure political and sociological distinctiveness that is the UK state. The first section develops a series of qualitative arguments that establish the historically distinctive features of the UK state, the embedded nature of which particularize the nation state to make it individual. The second section reviews theories of the state to illustrate how the institutional structure of a state may buoy, distort or impair the pursuit of generalized functions undertaken by the state. The third section draws on this material to develop a particularized theory of the UK state, underpinned empirically by the political dimension to post-war economic recovery outlined in Chapters 2 and 3.

Historically distinctive features of the UK as a nation state

The organizational basis of economic activity under conditions of liberal democracy revolves around enterprise, employment and profit, whereas political activity is governed by an institutional framework termed the capitalist state. As a centralized institutional authority, the state is able to enforce rules over a defined geographical area and compel the population to obey by consent or, if necessary, by coercion. The rise of industrial capitalism in Western Europe since the UK industrial revolution has witnessed the parallel rise of a centralized ensemble of sovereign institutions that structure and dominate the *modus operandi* of the nation state.

The UK state has three historically distinct features that directly structure its institutional make-up and shape in the twentieth century. First, the UK was the first industrial nation; second, the process of industrialization was, in general terms, achieved peacefully through a bourgeois revolution in the state; and third, the UK has experienced continuous sovereign integrity and authority over its territory since the industrial revolution.

Within the contemporary UK conscious, these features appear deeply embedded, both historically and ideologically.

Early industrialization

The UK's distinctive status as the first industrial nation has shaped and constrained the interventionist role of the state, especially in its economic dimension. Theoretically, the institutional structure that shapes the framework in the state fulfils the functions of the state. This specification of the state is a crude reductionism – the state is what the state does; however, it does have a particular resonance in the UK's case. The UK's premier status as an industrialized nation prevailed without active industrial policies on the part the state.[1] The term 'liberalism' encapsulates the movement from feudalism to capitalism economically and politically but, moreover, ideologically. As a philosophy, liberalism accepts the structure of Western society as given, while prescribing structural reform to improve economic and social conditions and the liberty of the individual. In the seventeenth century, the English civil war challenged feudalism as the natural order in the state, necessitating a reconstitution of the state in an emergent liberal capitalism.[2]

Under feudalism, exploitation was open and undisguised but cushioned by an ideology of paternal hierarchy. Feudalism was dependent on the countryside, where a dominant class of lords monopolized economic and political power in localized areas. The erosion of feudalism was secured by the emergence of militarily successful monarchs, the rise of empire and the development of town centres as trading, workshop and, subsequently, manufacturing areas.[3] The town and, later, the city sustained the economic dynamic of industrialization, structuring the emergence of a new economic – working – class apparently excluded from the reins of feudal hierarchy.[4]

The movement to capitalism sustained but reconstituted exploitation and hierarchy, disguising both through the ideology of freedom and equality – freedom from the (local) state and equality before the state. Ideologically, the bourgeoisie and the aristocracy presented these reforms as primarily concerned with individual liberty. However, both measures sustained industrialization and improved the machinery of an emergent capitalist, but not yet fully democratic, state. In summary, liberty and equality gelled with the organic process of industrialization often captured in the term *laissez faire* state, where economic activity and political control are formally separate. The embedded nature of this process in the UK has generated an ideology which suggests that active state intervention in economic activity should provide only a legal framework and institutional structure to regulate the economy and govern civil society; Cannadine has described this as retaining the hierarchy of the past, whereas Perkin sees it as the origin of modern English society.[5] It is impossible to underestimate the formative impact of libertarian *laissez faire* on the UK state and its subsequent institutional development. For example, the framework of civil law (contract and tort) and the common law exclude inalienable constitutional rights. The last might represent an active intervention by the state to promote freedom and equality.

The movement to capitalism in the UK was not fully democratic, with the majority of the working class excluded from the franchise until the late nineteenth century. Equally, the movement was relatively peaceful compared with France and the USA. The movement took the form of a bourgeois revolution, whereby the English aristocracy retained control of the political machinery until the nineteenth century.[6]

The movement from agriculture to manufacturing broke the economic hegemony of the feudal class, however it did not necessarily break its political hegemony. This it secured by promoting common cause with the emergent bourgeoisie to embrace commercial activity in the countryside. As Barrington Moore demonstrated in the UK, the landed feudal class helped to make the bourgeois revolution by embracing its economic dynamic to sustain their political hierarchy.[7]

A peaceful transition to capitalism? A bourgeois revolution

Struggle within the state to establish the conditions for capitalist accumulation and growth characterizes much of the seventeenth century. The struggle for Parliamentary dominance over the Monarchy followed by the English civil war culminated in the 1832 Reform Act.[8] This legislation provided for the registration of electors and widened the franchise by amending the property provisions to include short and long leaseholders and tenants, where the rental value was at least £50 per annum. In addition, the Reform Act disenfranchised fifty rotten boroughs and transferred over 140 seats to large northern towns. These reforms confirmed the succession of the middle classes over the landowning aristocracy as the central economic power in the state.[9] However, the Act enfranchised only 5 per cent of the population, a limitation that severely circumscribes its democratic and reform credentials. Hence, many, including the vast majority of the working class, remained excluded from the institutional structure of the state.

By the eighteenth century, UK urbanization – the emergence of industrial towns – consolidated the organic process of industrialization on a localized and regional basis. The early twentieth century saw 75 per cent of the population living in towns, with 75 per cent of the working population employed in manual occupations, making the UK the most industrially concentrated state in the world. Moreover, the state had become more democratic as a result of extensions to the franchise in 1867 and 1884 that established single-member single-vote constituencies. However, women remained disenfranchised until 1918, and twenty-two towns and several university constituencies retained two members, with double-member constituencies, until 1950.

The emergence of independent town classes – the bourgeoisie and the working class – showed them to be indispensable to the growth of liberal democracy; as Barrington Moore argues and demonstrates, 'no bourgeoisie no democracy'.[10] The peaceful if bourgeois revolution was a gradual economic and sociological process, whereby the feudal landed aristocracy found common cause with the town-based industrial class to resist an arbitrary and centralized Monarchy. In addition, both groups wanted to control the emergent working class and did so, gradually, by admitting them into the hierarchy of the state, first by a gradual extension of the franchise and second by the gradual acceptance of collective organization in the workplace between 1871 and 1906. Workplace collectivism exhibited a respect for craft and guild skill and time-served apprenticeships, a respect that revolved around continuity and common cause to reproduce the hierarchical nature of the UK state.

The UK's continuous sovereign development has created a libertarian reforming but strangely conservative ideology in the state. It is obsessed with the past and improving on it and yet reluctant to move forward on a fully fledged constitutional and democratic model. As a result, the UK state and its class dynamic appear hierarchical in structure.[11] More significantly, the bourgeois revolution generated two formative ideological and structural effects, both of which continue to reinforce a relatively *laissez faire* institutional structure in the state. First, the state stimulated industrialization and later technological modernization by providing only a politically supportive institutional structure independent of an active industrial policy; a framework for dynamic and organic entrepreneurship. Second, and related, the bourgeois revolution created an ideology of the state which promoted libertarianism as the basis of its activity. The modern parliamentary, not necessarily fully democratic, state freed the bourgeoisie and later the working classes from a tied relationship to the feudal state.

A conservative and sovereign continuous development

The UK's passage from feudalism to industrial capitalism prevailed without the military defeat of the landed aristocracy in a transformational political revolution. The common cause that held the bourgeois revolution together saw the national state withdraw the rights of the local feudal state to intervene actively and regulate economic activity. This created a position in which the centralized parliamentary state provided a peripheral legal and institutional framework, promoting an ideology of libertarian *laissez faire* to regulate economic activity. More substantively, beyond the ideological rhetoric, this framework provided a system to enforce private property on a contractual basis that is the foundation of historical development in the UK state.

Hence, a *laissez faire* institutional structure with executive powers delegated from a parliamentary legislature is the formative influence over the development of the UK state. Delegated power in the institutional structure of the state has created a voluntary pattern of regulation in many areas of economic and social activity, e.g. a voluntary industrial relations system. The formative organizational framework within a nation state becomes embedded to create a national consciousness and particularized identity. In turn, consciousness and particularization generate a cultural and sociological image that marks distinctiveness in the nation state, e.g. 'the free born Englishman'.[12] National images are a consequence of the nation state and, as a result, centralized institutions may easily manipulate national images to secure commitment to them.

The UK's unique historical circumstances have shaped its institutional framework. Significantly, the latter retains its formative influences. This remained the case during the post-war period, which for many secured working-class representation in the hierarchy of the state.[13] Social democracy, a contextual influence on the state, appeared to challenge the formative influence of libertarian *laissez faire*. However, the 1980s exposed the fragility of social democracy as (the more formative) libertarian *laissez faire* swept it aside to become the central contextual influence on the UK state.

This brief summary of the historically distinctive features in the UK state does not, as presented, provide a theory of the state. The task of particularized theories of the state is to establish a determinate, i.e. a definite, but not determinist (denying particularized free will) or reductionist (state is what state does) relationship between embedded formative influences and emergent contextual influences on the state.[14] The first constitutes 'relative autonomy' in the political economy of the UK state and its contradictory reproduction in the structure of more democratic contextual influences.

The formative influences that run through the UK state have created a particularized institutional structure that jars with the capacity of the state to accommodate more active and democratic interventions in the economy and civil society. The third section structures this assertion historically and theoretically, whereas the second section reviews more generalized theories of the capitalist state and evaluates them against the arguments developed in this section.

Generalized theories of the state

Generalized theories of the state present a framework of analysis centred around the emergence and dominance of a set of institutions separate from capitalism which in amalgamation constitute a sovereign law-making body in a given territory. This section presents a summary review of these theories; it is followed by a brief evaluation in terms of developing a particularized theory of the UK state.

Theories of the state

In broad terms, general state theories are divisible into four broad categories: pluralism, contemporary new right theories, contemporary elite theory and Marxian approaches. None of the approaches is completely successful in explaining how a disproportionate amount of wealth controlled by a minority is functional. Moreover, some approaches appear to present this as a natural phenomenon without a detailed explanation of how an embedded ideology in a state sustains and structures this as an established order. Others, in particular the Marxian approach, contain internal debates that necessarily lengthen any review. However, in order to develop a particularized theory, it is necessary to build on the full range of alternatives within generalized approaches.

Pluralism presents a theory of political power that emphasizes its more or less equal distribution between institutions and representative groups, hence pluralists present a variety of roles for representative government in the liberal democratic state. Here, the role of the state is conflict resolution and rule making, roles that create the necessity of legislative and economic intervention to arrest private sector market failure. As a result of this abstract specification, pluralist theory presents the state as a neutral broker which in the face of dominant institutional interests seeks to ensure fair play for minority groups that lack the support of institutional representation. Equally, pluralist theory presents the state as a 'weathervane' or passive cypher which processes ideas and interests.[15] This dimension suggests that freedom and sovereignty is relative but not absolute, reflecting a model of civil society that is stable but not static, one that arrives at new settlements by negotiation, co-operation and continuous compromise.[16] Extensions to the franchise, the post-war extension and subsequent legislative restriction of UK nationality in 1981 and the termination of national sovereignty in the European Communities Act 1972 are all representative of this process.

Pluralism rationalizes the emergence of Thatcherism as a realignment of the dominant political ideology in the UK which eroded liberal collectivism in the mixed economy to create liberal individualism in a market economy. The ejection from the state of collectivist institutions, such as a voluntary industrial relations system, is one manifestation of this. However, critics of pluralism, both generally and in relation to industrial relations, argue that an acceptance of the principles and assumptions that support the political social *status quo* presents the realignment of civil society as unproblematic. This is the case because the *status quo* is visualized as legitimate and empirically inevitable; however, pluralists counterargue that changes in the dominant ideology of the state have only a marginal effect on stability and broader institutional mediation of industrial capitalism in national pathways.[17] For example, the ejection of voluntary industrial relations from the state during the 1980s had only a marginal effect on the UK's economic performance.[18]

New right theories of the state come from a wide range of groups that, although diverse, share a rejection of social democracy as a contextual and orthodox influence on the UK state since 1945. The political programmes associated with the new right advocate a rejection of state involvement in the economy and a collectivist approach to the public sector. At the extreme are those who see social democracy and state intervention as a threat to the authority and legitimacy of the libertarian state, which left unchecked may lead to the emergence of an antidemocratic state socialism.[18] This version presents the market mechanism as more democratic than the political process, hence the more markets the state can create the more open and democratic it becomes. This ideology provided much of the rationale for privatization and deregulation of state-controlled industry and the public sector during the 1980s.

The new right rail against the post-war state to suggest that the UK's weak economic performance and the corruption of civil society by state control of industry require restoration through a contemporary reassertion of formative influences on the UK state. It is in this respect that the variety of approaches that constitute the new right amalgamate to create a hegemonic project based on an authoritarian populism. Thatcherism was hegemonic in that its rhetoric attacked all post-war governments – Conservative and Labour – as failures. This was the case because they embraced creeping socialism in the mixed economy to demonstrate the entrepreneurial failure of big government in nationalization and the public sector. More ideologically, post-war governments legitimized the presence and authority of unrepresentative and unaccountable institutions, such as trade unions.[20] Ironically, the central new right aims of rolling back the state, non-intervention, decentralization and deregulation required significant central legislative intervention in the political process. Presenting the erosion of social democracy as greater – *market* – democracy creates an increasingly centralized state, hence the term 'authoritarian populism'.

In economic management during the 1980s, the influence of new right thinking was paramount. An economic strategy that centred on sound money necessitated cutting public expenditure to secure a reduction in the tax burden on individuals and corporations. In turn, this justified a reduction in the size of the public sector through privatization and compulsory competitive tendering, both of which in turn justified further cuts in central and local taxation. The alliance of sound money with supply-side economics emphasized the importance of creating a successful capitalist economy by aggressive control of the money supply to cut inflation. In addition, public expenditure was criticized on efficiency grounds, the provision of public services is inefficient because of monopoly administration, here monopoly public services destroy choice, build dependency and inhibit enterprise.

In the political sphere, the new right attacked 'enemies without', such as the EU and international Communism to reassert the central significance of the Anglo-American special relationship and the necessity of a shared Cold War stance against the Soviet Union. Internally, the project attacked the 'enemy within', which in simple terms was any group that appeared to be against the project: 'wets' in the Cabinet, trade unions, the unemployed and the 'European' friendly. For many, the management of the 1984–5 miners strike and its 'non-interventionist' suppression by the government epitomized this approach. For the new right, a restructuring in the state is the only viable solution to the crisis of accumulation in the UK's 'flawed Fordism'. The failure of the social democratic state to secure sufficient levels of profitability and productivity during the 1970s sustained the crisis which reached such a depth that the necessary restructuring left no scope for a legitimate (*collective*) working-class voice.[21] This brings the new right perspective close to a regulation theory of the state that charts the erosion and defeat of the organized working class in Fordism and the distribution of surplus away from this group under an emergent post-Fordist regime.[22]

New right approaches defend a strong central state and a free economy, but it is questionable whether in the longer term either has improved the economic performance or the quality of civil society in the UK. However, some of its elitist aspects appear to have retained a utility under the 1997 Labour government For example, in the policies and pronouncements of primary and secondary schools inspector Chris Woodhead.

It is possible to understand elite theory as one strand to new right theory or as a theory in its own right.[23] In elite theory, executive control and regulation by a few is rational and empirically observable, e.g. international relations alliance systems between great powers or unilateral regulation by hegemonic powers constitute elite regulating groups. The realism of elite theory casts doubt on the effectiveness of liberal democratic forms of state organization, such as the regulatory role of the public sector. This leads to the suggestion that the scope and scale of democracy and democratically accountable institutions have limited future prospects. The growth of quasi-autonomous non-governmental organizations (quangos) and the privatization and deregulation of some elements in the public sector by the creation of 'government' agencies and regulators, for example those in secondary, further and higher education, in the child support agency, in the highways agency and in various public utility regulators, bear out this argument.

Elitism presents a view that a small ruling group state is desirable and effective. As an approach, it has well-established historical credentials in references to Plato's *Republic* and Machiavelli's *The Prince*. Its more modern form owes much to Weber and Schumpter.[24] For Weber, systems of logic and legally regulated administrative mechanisms in the government and corporation constitute systematic 'bureaucratic' control over the individual. Bureaucracy expresses legal equality before the state and state authority over arbitrary and unaccountable groups such as the aristocracy. In contrast to this, Schumpter regarded democracy as a mechanism that allows the elite to compete for authority over a population. Dunleavy and O'Learly suggest that the fusion of bureaucracy and democracy creates a control mechanism termed 'democratic elitism'.[25] This approach illustrates that power is not consensual because 'the ability to make people do things' rests on coercion exercised by force in which interests diverge and consent is not forthcoming. For example, the abolition of the poll tax was not retrospective, nor could it have been unless the central state agreed to underwrite all funding in the local state. Hence, after abolition, community charge bills remained recoverable, if necessary with the support of coercive mechanisms such as court orders, bailiffs or imprisonment were available. Hence, for elite theory, the state organizes and maintains domination by consent and coercion. In the contemporary period, this approach appears to legitimize a less democratic and unaccountable method of domination which, in some aspects, reprises what Marxian approaches previously termed 'instrumentalism' in the state, e.g. the relegation of the local government service ethos below urban regeneration, revenue collection and cost reduction in the provision of local services.

Marxian theories of the state are broadly divisible into two categories. Those which concentrate on the primacy of class struggle and those which emphasize state theorizing. The class struggle approach follows the dictate of the *Communist Manifesto* to suggest that class struggle between the bourgeoisie and the proletariat is the dominant antagonistic relationship in liberal democracies. However, once the aristocracy followed by the industrial bourgeoisie began to accommodate the working class in the hierarchy of the state, a simple class dichotomy appeared less clear cut. The franchise is universal and there are more working-class voters than any other group. This suggests class dealignment in voting behaviour or a narrow instrumentalism on the part of some voters; both suggestions illustrate the incorporation of the working class into the authoritarian populism of state projects such as Thatcherism during the 1980s.

To continue with an approach that concentrates on the primacy of class struggle, the category 'working class' has been extended to include groups of workers who are nominally middle class but subject to proletarianization in employment.[26] This occurs through standardized deskilling in the labour process that results from technological advance. Many white collar employees have been overtly subject to this process, e.g. bank employees, supermarket workers, teachers and public sector professionals such as social workers, local government workers and civil servants. In addition, the structures of some contemporary forms of employment overtly maximize the monitoring benefits of technological control, e.g. call centres.

The class struggle approach remains significant, but appears to emphasize domination rather than overt exploitation. In order for the continuing fragmentation of the working class to be arrested, this approach suggests that the 'wider working-class' community has to act as a class.[27] However, although some conflicts appear class related, for example low pay, unemployment, poor housing and access to benefits, other areas of conflict do not, e.g. the environment, food safety, reform of the hereditary principle in the house of lords, transport policy, etc.[28] To arrest discontinuity between class and the expression of class struggle in civil society, some advocates position the class struggle approach at the multinational level. Here, class struggle is increasingly conceptualized through the pervasive impact of multinational corporations.[29]

A second Marxian category based on state theorizing has proved more enduring. However, the significance of a particularized and historically embedded theory of the state has the potential to counter what many critics see as the generality of some functionalist approaches in this category.

From the functionalist perspective, civil society constitutes a system. In addition, the state represents an institutional mechanism that maintains order in the system and, in consequence, the stability of the system. The state dominates by creating an ideology of shared values that legitimize a minority holding a disproportionate share of wealth. In turn, this prevents any serious challenges to the established order or hierarchy of interests. A key difference between Marxist theories that are 'functionalist' and more traditional theories of functionalism turns on the deployment of power and domination. Traditional functionalists such as Talcott Parsons present power and domination as a societal resource designed to maintain the order and stability of the system.[30] In contrast, Marxian approaches purport to explain how the use of power furthers either the general or sectional interests of the capitalist class in the state.

Miliband presents an instrumentalist theory of the state which argues that under conditions of liberal capitalism the dominant economic class exercises effective political domination. Membership of conservative and nationalistic governments and opposition parties and occupation of key positions in the wider institutional infrastructure of the state, such as in the judiciary etc., allow the capitalist class to use the state as an instrument.[31] The success of concessions to the working class is a measure of instrumentalism; effective concessions fragment the potential of any serious threat to the power base of the capitalist class, e.g. the extension of the franchise, a welfare state and a voluntary industrial relations system. Moreover, success will further legitimize the sectional interests of the capitalist class, as the national interest, maintenance of empire as the Commonwealth and rejection then membership of the EC illustrate this point.

A forerunner to Miliband's instrumentalist approach was the theory of state monopoly capitalism. This approach fuses the interests of large – monopoly – corporations and the development of the capitalist state to create a single instrument of economic and political domination.[32] In the post-war period, the centralization and concentration of capital required the state to operate in an apparently social democratic mode via nationalization, active fiscal and monetary policy and extension to the welfare state. This mode of operation was necessary to cushion economic crises and marginalize class struggle to issues such as the nominal wage.

State monopoly capitalism and instrumentalism are open to the theoretical criticisms of determinism and crude functionalism: 'The state is what the state does' and 'does it in a functional manner'. Here, the infrastructure of the capitalist base in civil society shapes the wider superstructure of society in an instrumental fashion. The instrumentalism provided by members of the capitalist class occupying key positions in the state to create a ruling class generates a direct capitalist class–ruling class functionalism. The base–superstructure approach dominated by personal relations in and between the capitalist ruling class remains influential, but has been superseded over the past twenty years by the emergence of more sophisticated theories that emphasize the concept of relative autonomy.[33]

Relative autonomy looks beyond ruling-class/capitalist-class relationships to suggest that under conditions of industrial capitalism the state is able to separate the institutions of political domination and economic domination. For example, the contract of employment ties free wage labour to an employer, yet the employment relationship separates but structures the role of the state in two ways. First, through the infrastructure of the market mechanism; here employees produce goods and services for an employer who exchanges them for profit. Second, the basis of employment relations is the private ownership of capital and the sale of labour. The sale of labour necessitates the utility of the market mechanism and is part of it. As a consequence, the state automatically represents the interests of capital, not instrumentally but with a relative autonomy structured by formative influences over the state.

The institutional separation of the mechanism of economic and political domination is necessary – functional – for the state to represent the general capitalist interest rather than the sectional interests of one subgroup of capital. More specifically, instrumental theories of the state fail to accommodate the effects of competitive short-termism and the self-interests of capital. For example, to secure free enterprise, it may be necessary to look to the longer term and make collective concessions to the employed class, which not all individual capitalists are willing to entertain for competitive reasons. The introduction of a welfare state to maintain the working class and the emergence of a voluntary industrial relations system are evidence of these contextual concessions. Institutional separation within the state creates a relative autonomy for the state in meeting the needs of capital. It is this that enables the governing party in state to claim that it represents the general public interest as distinct from the narrow sectional interests of capital. The ideology of the neutral and democratic state masks its shaping by the infrastructure that constrains the state to represent the interests of capital. The discussion now outlines the relationship between generalized theories and a particularized theory of the state.

The role of generalized theory in the formulation of a particularized theory of the state

Generalized theories of the state seek to explain how in industrial capitalism a minority – the capitalist class – control a disproportionate share of wealth. More especially, they illustrate how the state generates an ideology of shared values that prevents any serious questioning of implications that flow from the establishment of this order.

Pluralism, the new right, elite theories and Marxian state theorizing approaches all share a base in functionalism. Each of the alternative approaches theorizes the ruling-class ideology as the basis of functionalism, yet they differ in the conception of power and the ability of the dominant class to exploit the employed class. Pluralist theory positions the representation of all interests, but some less than others. In contrast, the new right and elite theory explain and justify the political and economic defeat of the working class during the 1980s. Both approaches reject the structural hierarchy in the post-war state, which is represented by the overt and uncompromising extension of contextual – social democratic – influences on the state. Moreover, elite theory justifies the explicit fragmentation and eradication of the working-class (as a class or wider community) interests on the grounds of functionalist economics. Here, widening wage differentials between high earners and low earners justifies the general dissemination of cost reduction and/or interest reduction strategies. For example, the erosion of collective terms and conditions of employment towards the low wages and poor working conditions associated with non-unionism in the private sector are generalized as beneficial, even though the economic evidence in support of this assertion is weak.[34] Both strategies operate in parallel with very high executive remuneration based on the overall performance of an organization.

Only the Marxian theories have sufficient intellectual scope to move beyond the crude reductionism of the state is what the state does; however, instrumentalism and relative autonomy are both open to the charge of functionalism. First, instrumentalism overestimates the significance of ruling class–governing class connections, and therefore excludes the possibility of any autonomy in the state. Second, relative autonomy may represent a social democratic theory of the state to justify functionalism plus autonomy. Third, the significance of relative autonomy in the state may be overestimated. If the infrastructure determines the state, this constrains relative autonomy in the state as the state must represent the interests of capital.[35]

Generalized theories of the state lay out a set of ideas about how the state works. This constrains them to be functional. As a set of ideas they claim to explain how the state organizes and stabilizes liberal democracy that must be functional. The role of a particularized theory of the state is to extend the generalized set of ideas by drawing out the contemporary significance of historically embedded material structures in one nation state. In the UK, the formative nature of *laissez faire* in the political economy of the UK state created relative autonomy in the state but, in addition, it has structured the mechanism of relative autonomy. The libertarian and voluntarist ideology of the state limits the functionalism of the state. For example, the UK's relatively peaceful bourgeoisie revolution left the hierarchy of the UK state intact. The aristocracy retained control of government until the end of the nineteenth century, whereas the bourgeoisie increasingly controlled the economy but in a *laissez faire* fashion. Institutional and functional separation in the state has proved very effective in dividing working-class resistance and struggle against capital and the state. This is the case because separation retains a continuity – the common cause – between dominant interests but expresses them separately, both politically and economically.[36] Political concessions made by the state have reduced to negligible any political challenge to capital. This remained the case with the formation of the Labour Party. The adoption of Labourism legitimized discrete and limited objectives in Parliamentary channels to represent working-class political interests.[37]

Economic and political separation in the UK state has generated only a limited economic and political challenge from the working class, but in addition separation has generated a severely circumscribed functionalism in the political economy of the state. This presents the organic process of industrialization and entrepreneurialism as a natural order. More significantly, functionalism positions the economic and political regulation of capital and labour as matters most appropriately delegated to the parties themselves and their peak organizations. This has created an embedded ideology in the state that secures the state as an impartial institution positioned neutrally outside the market and the circuit of capital. Hence, the UK state has a particularized structural and historically embedded logic that dilutes its functionalism.[38] The third section of this chapter builds on this argument to present a historically embedded and particularized theory of the UK state that stresses not the functionalism of the state but its structural weaknesses.

A particularized theory of the UK state

To derive the UK state as a particularized empirical example of the generalized capitalist state requires a historically informed structural theory. The specification illustrates the deeply embedded structural effects of formative influences in the UK state, more particularly how contextual influences on the state reproduce this form. The formative influence of libertarian *laissez faire* structures the state and is highly significant in the separation of its economic and political dimensions.

The historical impact of formative influences creates a conceptual space between reductionist functionalism and the constraining effects of the capitalist infrastructure – the relative autonomy – to particularize political management but in addition informs apparently distinct methods of economic management. By specifying the state to illustrate how the process of particularization operates, this approach avoids functionalism by stressing structural limitations in the UK state. This section will demonstrate that the UK state is a phenomenon of the past 'always with us', as long the formative structure of libertarian *laissez faire* is the central mechanism of national governance. The empirical specification of this argument follows its theoretical specification.

Theoretical specification

The political and sociological factors that structure the UK state need theoretical analysis to explain the origins and functionalism of the state and raise answers to questions about post-war, contemporary and future limitations in the state. A particularized theory of the capitalist state presents consistent ideas that claim to explain how a particular capitalist state functions. The theoretical specification of particularization moves from the implicit assumptions of general approaches to more explicit hypotheses that are open to dispute beyond the individual nation state

The predictive capacity of a particularized theory rests on articulating key elements within generalized theory in a specific situation. For example, the functionalism of relative autonomy creates the scope for a particularized theory that highlights the structural limitations of the UK state. Particularization sharpens predictive capacity beyond the instrumentalism of relative autonomy to provide a historically derived theoretical specification of functional structures. This approach demonstrates how embedded structures severely constrain and limit functionalism.

Particularization creates the possibility for national patterns of governance in the capitalist state structured by influences which were formative during the period of industrialization – libertarian *laissez faire* in the case of the UK. Formative influences structure the separate economic and political relationships between the state and social formation in civil society to create an ideology in the political economy of the state. In the UK, the focus of this ideology centres on freedom and equality in the state secured by economic and political freedom from the state. The latter is manifest in the common cause between the landed aristocracy and the industrial bourgeoisie in the late nineteenth century. Here, the aristocracy continued to dominate government but conceded economic domination to the bourgeoisie, thereby separating the state from the economy. This separation secured a peaceful revolution in the state but, more significantly, began the process of fragmenting the potential solidarity of the working class into narrowly defined and mutually separate economic and political claims on the state. The legalization of trade unions during the late nineteenth century followed by the emergence of collective bargaining in the workplace resulted from political agitation by the working class. Both developments represent functional, if disintegrated, concessions designed to secure the continued reproduction of *laissez faire* capitalism. However, although the delegation of regulation in industrial relations to capital and labour did secure this, more significantly it reproduced the structure of the formative influence on the state in the industrial relations system.

A particularized theory derives its specification of the state from generalized theory and to that extent it is functionalist as the economic base of industrial capitalism structures the state that therefore inherently serves the needs of capital. However, particularization departs from instrumentalist theory and develops the theoretical specification of relative autonomy by illustrating how formative influences become embedded. Formative influences retain significance because ideologically they express the political economy of the state beyond the crude functionalism of 'state is what the state does'.

The capitalist class in the UK retains a preference for minimal regulation in non-interventionist industrial policies. From the industrial revolution to the post-war period, industrial policies have supported the unconstructed needs of capital. This structural preference for established techniques in established if differentiated markets appeared necessary and broadly welcomed. However, the functionalism of this approach became dysfunctional. For example, Chapters 2 and 3 demonstrate why during the post-war period it was necessary for the

UK to maintain output in established markets by established methods of production. The pattern of UK commitments and the series of decisions that gave rise to this were politically and strategically necessary given the external role of the UK state; however, they had constricting and structural consequences for economic performance.

The exploitation of established markets has, in the post-war years, failed to secure accumulation for capital at a rate similar to the UK's main industrial competitors. The embeddedness of freedom from the state, i.e. voluntary and self-regulation, is of such a depth that even in the face of comparative economic decline the capitalist class remains wedded to its virtues. This suggests that structures formatively defined may inhibit functionalism in the longer term. The reactions of the Confederation of British Industry (CBI) and the Institute of Directors to the minimum wage and the statutory recognition procedure for trade unions provide contemporary evidence of this preference.[39]

The organic development of capitalism in the UK resulted in the emergence of structural problems that the ideology of libertarian *laissez faire* was ill-equipped to accommodate. To rectify the market failure of short-term competition, state intervention in the economy and civil society emerged. State intervention aims to provide for and represent collective interests on behalf of capital. The abolition of truck and barter as a means of payment in employment, the emergence of a welfare state and the development of a voluntary industrial relations system are indicative of this development. However, the functionalism of this specification belies the structural hegemony of formative influences in a state and the emergence of significant class struggle. The structure of libertarian *laissez faire* is hierarchical and voluntary: hierarchical to the extent that it recognizes the interests of collective groups or classes in a conservative manner, voluntary to the extent that it eschews specifying the regulation of due process in the representation of collective interests.[40]

State intervention in the economy and civil society is significant beyond the crude reductionism of meeting the needs of capital. Class struggle and the democratization of civil society produce contextual influences on the state, summarized as social democracy that are independent of formative influences. However, by structuring the form of intervention in contextual influences on the state, formative influences ensure that they are conservative and hierarchical. The effect of this is to exclude many collective interests from the state until a later date, e.g. the movement from a feudal aristocracy to a market- and contract-driven industrial bourgeoisie, a respect for craft unionism, votes for property owners and votes for women aged over thirty years. To groups excluded from the state, concessions such as these did represent reform in the state, yet in class terms each development reinforces the libertarian ideology of the UK state: the past time-served hierarchical entry into the state and common cause. Economic and political concessions are institutionally separate, with each reinforcing the hegemony of the other, fragmenting working-class challenges by partial access to the hierarchy of the state.

By theorizing contextual influences on the UK state as structural concessions, the functionalism of state intervention is developed into a particularized theory of the state. The hierarchical and collective yet conservative nature of entry into the state enhances its autonomy to represent the interests of capital through the framework of formative interests, mediated by peak and representative institutions. To ensure political success in a state, the institutional ensemble which dominates economy and society must establish, maintain and, if necessary, modify a dominant ideology; in many ways, the history of the UK state is the embedded history of formative influences that constitute this process.

The conservative hierarchy of libertarian *laissez faire* excludes the majority and represents a freedom to be unequal, in which entry into the state secures the rhetorical exercise of liberty and freedom. Entry into the dominant ideology – libertarian *laissez faire* – gives collective but voluntary self-regulation on the basis of tradition and its partial reform, e.g. collective *laissez faire* in the industrial relations system.

The institutional separation of economics and politics mediates the relative autonomy of state intervention, yet influences that were formative over the state during the process of industrialization structure this process. Hence, an embedded structure, although conceived of as functionalist, is inhibited by its particularized subjective development. Collective struggle prevails within the structure of formative influences in which the institutional separation of economics and politics creates the relative autonomy of the state. However, from the 1880s onwards, the political success of this separation has been a major factor in its economic limitation. Functionalism has two dimensions, economic and political, the embedded conservatism of libertarian *laissez faire* structures both as the dominant ideology in the state. However, libertarian *laissez faire* failed to secure the competitive reproduction of capital on a scale similar to the UK's industrial competitors. Structure and function are not necessarily mutually reinforcing.

Empirical specification

Since 1945, UK economic policy has cushioned economic decline. The retention of empire and sterling as a reserve currency was the pile in the cushion and in many respects they both represent the active aspects of the state's post-war relative autonomy. However, more significantly, the *laissez faire* structuralism of relative autonomy confined the progressive aspects of social democracy as a contextual influence on the state and demonstrates why the state chose to eschew specific options. The material contained in Chapter 2 charts the UK's great power role, whereas Chapter 3 documents and demonstrates the limited and inhibitive economic role of the state. Empirical material from both chapters underpins the theoretical specification of a particularized theory.

The immediate post-war period was the culmination in a process of economic and political retreat by the state, summarized as Atlanticism in previous chapters. The legal and institutional framework of the state confined the economic role of the state to maintaining disparate markets for UK producers at home and abroad. In large measure, the reintroduction of the sterling area and sterling as a reserve currency secured the maintenance of pre-war markets, which in turn reinforced the conservative hierarchy in the political dimension of the state. Maintenance of empire, great power status and the UK's central role in the emergent Cold War all went unchallenged politically, as such policies secured markets from European or US competition and Communist domination. Troop garrisons in empire outposts, although costly, precluded losing these areas to US multinationals; this was especially true in the Caribbean, where its legacy recently resurfaced in the 1999 EU/USA/ World Trade Organization (WTO) banana dispute. Great power status provided the UK defence and aerospace industry with a secure future as delivery systems for nuclear weapons became the mainstay of industrial research and development – the fleets of 'V' bombers, polaris and then trident nuclear submarines fulfilled these roles. Last, the UK's central Cold War role helped justify the suppression of German competition in airline design and ship building, leaving only the French as serious European rivals in competition against the USA. UK Marshall Plan 'levels of industry' agreements document how UK manufacturers secured armaments-related status for both sectors, prohibiting or restricting production.[41]

Levels of industry agreements were a form of reparation designed to restrict German manufacturing capacity under allied occupation and Marshall Aid. By preventing the renaissance of the German aircraft industry, these agreements secured one area where the UK remains dominant and well ahead of German competition. UK dominance in aerospace contrasts sharply with the car industry. Levels of industry agreements gave UK manufacturers a ten-year buoy over their German competitors; however, it was insufficient to prevent a comparative German advantage (measured by the export–completed cars ratio) by 1959.[42] Moreover, a policy of facilitating production for the sheltered domestic market and protected empire markets wrote off the European market, which was expanding much faster than either of these markets.[43]

In the domestic and the external sphere, the strategy of the UK state encapsulated the benefits and the limitation of relative autonomy. In foreign policy, Atlanticism provided relative autonomy from US hegemony by rejecting the utility of US management and production methods in the domestic economy.[44] As a result, the UK state maintained external markets, the sovereign management of UK industry and the sterling area. Each cushioned post-war decline by contributing to lengthening the process of decline over the long term and lessening its severity over the short term, as favoured by US-inspired mulitlateralism and proposed industrial restructuring.

However, by conceding economic leadership in Western Europe for the Atlanticism of Nato, nuclear status and permanent membership of the UN Security Council, the UK relinquished economic performance for national sovereignty. The contradiction of this policy has been twofold. First, politically, as the contemporary period illustrates, it failed to secure economically viable sovereignty. Second, it illustrates the limitations of relative autonomy where the market failures of capital run through the state because formative influences in the state structure its relative autonomy. Although relative autonomy separates the state from capital, it equally constrains the state to represent the interests of capital in an embedded political culture and institutional infrastructure. Here, formatively embedded influences and the limitations of short-termism are reproduced in the policy of the state. To illustrate this, the issue of sterling convertibility is briefly revisited.

On the basis that the currency of a great power occupies an international position as a reserve currency, successive UK governments saw sterling convertibility as a vehicle to maintain great power status.[45] As such, convertibility became the objective of policy rather than a means to promote greater trade. The arrival of the European Payments Union (EPU) in the early 1950s installed a multilateral clearing house designed to enable states to settle intra-European debts more effectively than bilateral arrangements, thereby promoting increased levels of international trade among manufacturing nations.[46] In contrast to this view, the UK government, Foreign Office officials, the sterling area manufacturing lobby and the City lobby all viewed the EPU with scepticism. As Milward documents, the UK view asserted that as a collective mechanism the EPU would restrict European economic performance by inhibiting the entry of individual European states into a 'one world' system of multilateral convertibility based on the dollar supported by sterling.[47]

The interests of capital, both industrial and finance, aimed to re-establish pre-war markets and roles. As Chapter 3 demonstrates, UK governments, both Labour and Conservative, successfully represented these interests by securing relative autonomy from US economic and political hegemony during the Cold War era. The relative autonomy of *laissez faire*, both domestically and internationally, did secure the political interests of capital – the security of established markets and world-wide role of finance capital. However, comparative analysis of productivity and competitiveness illustrates that this approach, although designed to secure the UK's long-term economic interests, failed to secure even the short-term interests of industrial capital.

The formative influence of libertarian *laissez faire* in the UK state structures its relative autonomy from capital, but reproduces the collective limitation of short-termism. The contradictory structure of relative autonomy in the UK state is the political and sociological problem referred to by Kaldor.[48] In addition, it demonstrates how the historically embedded structure of libertarian *laissez faire* prevents a state moving down the learning curve of productivity improvement that emphasizes the importance of non-price factors and the growth of trade in manufactured goods between manufacturing economies.[49] In the post-war period, the political hegemony of great power status and maintaining the sterling exchange rate necessitated the stop–go economic policies that cushioned economic decline but tied the UK economy to the US economy, the sterling area and former empire nations. The US economy, although significantly more efficient, exported its recessions to the UK by reduced demand for UK exports, whereas sterling area and empire markets grew at a rate significantly lower than the intra-European market.[50] The mechanism of stop–go was essential to cushion the UK's economic decline, yet it represented a series of political and sociological factors constituted in the formative generation of the UK state that limited the UK's growth of exports to the growth potential of the domestic economy and its relationship to former empire nations and the US economy and not to the comparative growth of competitiveness and productivity of Western European economies.[51]

The post-war period saw the restoration of pre-war economic and financial interests, which in turn reflected the embedded structures of industrialization and empire. Retreat into the restoration of these interests and their sociological and political representation by the state illustrates the interconnected and mutually reinforcing structure of libertarian *laissez faire* in the state and its relative autonomy from capital. A brief examination of Thatcherism will further demonstrate the structural bonding between the state and capital.

The Thatcher government elected in 1979 positioned social democracy in the state since 1945 as the primary factor of explanation for the UK's post-war economic decline.[52] The primacy object in the political economy of Thatcherism was to expel or to minimize all vestiges of social democracy as a contextual influence on the state. The privatization, commercialization and deregulation of the public sector, fiscal rationing in the welfare state and local government and a political-cum-ideological determination to destroy the organized working class are all evidence of this strategy. By fragmenting social democracy, the Thatcherite state sought to fragment the working class, rendering its collective interests illegitimate.

The Thatcher governments reformed the UK state to the extent that the fusion of monetarist doctrine and the ideology of Austrian economics – new right theory – positioned libertarian *laissez faire* as a formative and the contextual influence on the state. The process of reform redefined the hierarchy of the state through a process of expendable collective exclusion. Throughout the 1980s and early 1990s, new right economics secured the global interests – beyond the confines of an integrationist EU – of finance capital and multinational industrial capital.[53] Equally, Thatcherite economic policies appeared to secure the short-term interests of industrial capital by encouraging industrial restructuring on a post-Fordist model.[54] However, the short-term economic interests of industrial capital were in the main secured in an alternative, if negative, manner.

The emergence of recession, higher unemployment, legal restrictions on trade union activity and employee protection against redundancy and unfair dismissal in the workplace all combined to create an apparent productivity miracle.[55] However, the source of the miracle was twofold. First, recession and unemployment reduced industrial output to create work intensification for many who remained in employment. Second, recession, the emergence of Youth Training Scheme (YTS) trainees as cheap labour and the erosion of employee protection in the workplace all had the effect of lowering wage costs. In turn, this extended the marginal efficiency of comparatively obsolete industrial capital.[56]

In combination, these measures appeared to indicate that low labour costs in a free market economy could boost economic performance. However, comparative productivity and overall competitiveness measured through unit labour costs and wage levels indicate that the UK's productivity gap with EU competitors remained only to widen during the 1990s. The DTI White Paper 'Our Competitive Future' indicates a UK labour 'productivity gap' of between 20 per cent and 40 per cent compared with the USA, Germany and France. Further, the DTI-sponsored capital expenditure on plant, equipment and machines (capex) scoreboard of international comparisons in capital investment that compares the UK's top 500 capital investment spenders with the world's top 300 capital investment firms demonstrates a considerable comparative shortfall in capital expenditure per employee and assets per employee. An EU-wide study of mechanical engineering provides a sector survey confirming the general pattern established in both DTI studies – the UK is a comparatively low investment economy that leads to low labour productivity, especially in the manufacturing sector.[57]

The pattern of UK policy towards the EPU and the EU, empire markets and the sterling area and the post-war and contemporary global interests of UK capital is historically consistent. The consistency demonstrates a deeply embedded political structuralism in the state that defines economic interests, if not the security of domestic economic performance in the manufacturing sector.

The industrial revolution of the late eighteenth century and early nineteenth century structured the emergence of the capitalist state in the UK. Further, as Chapter 3 demonstrates, the libertarian structure in the capitalist state stimulated a conservative reaction to the emergence of new production technologies in the late nineteenth century. The emergence of large-scale manufacturing during the inter-war and post-war periods saw this pattern of behaviour repeated. Moreover, reform of the state since 1979 has been equally conservative. However, before 1979, the relative autonomy of the UK state accommodated divergent class interests by incorporating defined subgroups into its hierarchy. In contrast, the Thatcherite state expelled the contextual influence of social democracy from the state on a class basis through the mechanism of authoritarian populism which created a dichotomy between 'one of us' and the 'enemy within'. The effect of Thatcherism was to embed further libertarianism and legitimize more extreme short-termism in the relative autonomy of the state; this demonstrates the structural integrity of a historically informed particularized theory of the state.

Conclusions

The history of the UK's movement to industrial capitalism is highly distinctive – particularized to the point of being unique. The process of industrialization was highly organic and localized, containing little instrumental management by the state; in contrast, the process itself structured the state and its relative autonomy from capital. The movement from feudalism to liberal capitalism is distinctive among European nations because its sovereign integrity has remained uninterrupted since medieval times. This is in marked contrast to many German, Italian and French citizens, who have experienced border changes, claims and counterclaims to territorial integrity relatively frequently in the twentieth century. Territorial integrity creates a form of sovereign nationalism which during the twentieth century has replaced the economic and political protection secured by empire. In the post-war era, sovereignty became fused with influences that were formative during the process of industrialization to express the embedded structure of libertarian *laissez faire* and its ideological, if rhetorical, expression as freedom from an emergent *European* state.

Economic functionalism is central to the elite theory, new right theories, pluralism and Marxian theories of the state, but only Marxian approaches specify its contradictory nature. An embedded pattern of influences structures the institutional functionalism of the UK state, captured by the category relative autonomy; in combination, they create an opportunity to build a historically informed theory in a particular nation state.

Economic and political values that were formative during the process of industrialization become institutionalized politically and sociologically and therefore structure economic functionalism. This theme is the central theoretical argument of the chapter. It follows from this that the UK is a modern state that is simultaneously obsessed with the past. The objectives of economic management and the performance measures that assess them position economic policy not in terms of comparative economic competitiveness but to the degree to which they secure national sovereignty. By maintaining the latter, economic policy in the post-war period and more generally in the period since the 1880s has cushioned economic decline by maintaining formative continuity with the past.[58]

The pressures of economic, monetary and political integration within the EU during the contemporary period create a major political challenge for the UK state. To undo the formative influence of *laissez faire* and pool some aspects of national sovereignty to maintain the viability of the UK as a nation state is a major political challenge. Clearly, this will require a successor to the peaceful revolution of the eighteenth century; whether the Blairite vision of a 'third way' can achieve this goal remains an open question.

The historically embedded structure in the institutional ensemble that constitutes the state constrains UK economic performance while securing its national sovereignty. The economy and the influences that were formative during its creation structure the political activity of the state. The relationship of the UK to the emergent *European State* during the post-war and contemporary periods illustrates the difficulty faced by new forms of governance, in which deeply embedded structural influences in national economic and political governance remain dominant.

The journey of the post-war and contemporary UK state is a vehicle to specify further the relative autonomy thesis. The theoretical category of particularization illustrates the extent to which economic and political constraints combine to create the UK's distinctive pattern of libertarian *laissez faire*. These are the significant political and sociological factors referred to by Kaldor. The institutional expression of these factors prevents the economy moving down the learning curve of improved economic performance.[59]

A particularized theory of the state seeks to take generalized theories of the state a stage further by specifying a specific hypothesis that illustrates the contradictory course of economic functionalism. A historically informed structural theory appears the best way to appreciate the post-war and contemporary pathway of the UK state. The emergence of liberal capitalism created a hierarchical state that became gradually accessible to the working class through the impact of contextual influences from the late nineteenth century. However, although collectivism reached a highpoint during the post-war period, it fragmented working-class resistance to the capitalist interest into narrowly defined economic and political interests.[60] Equally, the expulsion of social democracy from the state during the 1980s further fragmented the working class while overtly resurrecting the interests of the capitalist class under the label of economic restructuring. The hierarchical nature of the UK state rejected accommodation with the working class in favour of an increasingly *ancien régime*, dominated by the aim of restoring unbridled libertarian *laissez faire*.[61]

To apply this theory of the UK state further, the following chapter examines the UK industrial relations system and its erosion in the period since 1945. The central argument of the chapter suggests that the sovereign decline of the UK system of industrial relations mirrors the decline of the UK state.

5 The industrial relations system in the UK state

There is not much to be gained by looking to economics for a theory of industrial relations if economists have to go outside economics to find an explanation for wage determination.[1]

Introduction

Reference in previous chapters to Kaldor demonstrates that only a few economists are able to avoid the tendency to rationalize political and social factors that are beyond the confines of economic theory.[2] Clegg's observation illustrates the importance of including institutional analysis within the framework of economic analysis. The design and motivation of institutions are functional because they further and sustain specific interests in the pursuit of general economic efficiency. However, design and motivation, while functional on a collective basis, may also be defensive. Moreover, economists appear able to rationalize all aspects of employer behaviour as rational and functional in the quest for improved economic efficiency. In contrast, neoclassical and Austrian economics readily rationalize similar institutional behaviour by trade unions as destructive and obstructive.

More peculiar than the above distinction between employer and employee behaviour is the position taken by many economists and new right state theorists on the UK system of industrial relations. The voluntary system of industrial relations appears as an aberration that has corroded the authority of the UK state and the efficiency of the economy. However, as the previous chapter demonstrates, the historical process of particularization in the state is reproduced in the structure of political and social institutions and the economy. This chapter further specifies this argument by examining the system of industrial relations since 1945. The first section specifies the particular relationship between the state and industrial relations system; following on from this the second section examines the key issues of order and reform in the system. The third section introduces a critical insight into the relationship between economic performance and the industrial relations system that facilitates a brief examination of the 'UK worker problem' in the fourth section. Chapters 6 and 7 further develop the insights and arguments of the third and fourth sections.

The central argument of the chapter contends that the UK's distinctive pattern of *laissez faire* has created political and sociological mechanisms and processes beyond economics that both Clegg and Kaldor acknowledge as historically significant.[3] The industrial relations system is a case in point. However, the system is not an aberration but an institutional expression of the contradictory nature of particularization in the UK state, where the decline of the latter and its economic performance are mirrored in the former.

The industrial relations system and the state

The historically embedded pattern of job regulation in the UK system of industrial relations has two distinct features. First, the limited role of law in the regulation of industrial relations that is in turn derived from the process of particularization in the state during its transition to industrial capitalism. Second, the reproduction of formative influences over the UK state in the industrial relations system, a process often referred to as collective *laissez faire*.[4] Before proceeding to the detail of these issues, industrial relations and the industrial relations system are briefly discussed.

Industrial relations and the industrial relations system

As an academic discipline, industrial relations is concerned with rules that govern the employment relationship. Rules develop historically through a process of custom and practice. The codification of rules in the workplace may occur by negotiation between an employer and a trade union through the process of collective bargaining. Equally, employers may unilaterally determine workplace rules over reward motivation, training and employer control, with or without formal codification. In contrast to this, legal codification operates beyond the confines of pure voluntarism in the employment relationship, e.g. contemporary rules on redundancy payments, unfair dismissal and sex and race discrimination.

A central characteristic of UK industrial relations is the extent to which institutions remain and reflect a historically embedded process of particularization that structures the UK state. Employer associations, trade unions and collective bargaining or unilateral employer regulation are institutional mechanisms that express the process of regulatory delegation from the state to the central parties in the employment relationship. The pattern of voluntary regulation was institutionalized in the nineteenth century and since 1945 it has been supplemented by an extensive range of auxiliary legislation.[5]

The pattern of voluntary regulation illustrates what the previous chapter termed 'freedom from the state' and partial access to the hierarchy of the state. In the case of industrial relations, the emergence of freedom from central regulation by the state allowed employers to regulate jobs as they saw fit. Similarly, trade unions, once legalized, acquired economic, political and sociological legitimacy to act collectively, but on a voluntary basis. Strikes were decriminalized in 1871, whereas employees who went on strike were freed from the charge of criminal conspiracy in 1875. Last, strikes and other forms of industrial action to support a trade dispute were freed from civil liability in tort and contract in 1906. This process confined the political legitimacy of trade unions to parliamentary means whereas it confined democratic and economic legitimacy to participation in managerial decisions and negotiation over the distribution of surplus in the workplace.

After 1980, the Thatcher and Major administrations confined and curtailed access to legally codified rules on industrial relations and attacked the economic and political legitimacy of trade unions. The last was achieved by a substantial tightening of the legal definition of a trade dispute and the subsequent introduction of further legal prerequisites, such as a correctly constituted and worded ballot, to secure immunity from civil liability in cases of industrial action. The relative ease of this achievement illustrates the regulatory frailty of auxiliary legislation and a voluntary system in the face of a determined programme of economic, institutional and political deregulation.

Job regulation within a particular industrial relations system is functional to the extent that it is democratic and motivates and rewards the performance and productivity of labour in employment. However, as the previous chapter demonstrates, the longer-term process of particularization in a state reflects the embedded nature of influences that were formative during the process of industrialization. This process may inhibit functionalism, e.g. the creation of collective *laissez faire* in the industrial relations system reflects the libertarian bias in the UK state that is manifest as delegated self or voluntary regulation.

The structural limitations of functionalism emerge in other dimensions of industrial relations. First, although the employment relationship exhibits asymmetrical power, many employers deployed this position to sustain and reinforce a portfolio of short-term interests that revolved around traditional methods of production in traditional markets. Chapter 3 demonstrates that UK dependence on traditional markets and methods of production structured the maintenance of craft methods in job regulation where investment in machinery and new technology was relatively low. In the post-war period, the inertia of these interests created a pattern of regulation in the industrial relations system that oscillated between extreme conflict and co-operation. Second, libertarian *laissez faire* has structured the UK system of industrial relations since the 1870s, and for sustained periods such as the post-war era it performed an effective role in the generation of historically favourable economic performance. However, its structural limitation lay in endemic short-termism for employers and trade unions and chronic sectionalism for trade unions. The short-term concern of trade unions with pay and conditions in the workplace has minimized the active political role of the wider union movement in counteracting the longer-term economic effects of employer short-termism. For example, the cumulative effects of low investment, poor training and a slow diffusion of new technology compared with the UK's main industrial competitors since 1945. More specifically, in the immediate post-war period, the Trades Union Congress (TUC) attempted, within the AACP, to secure a longer-term reconstruction of UK manufacturing industry. However, embedded employer interests combined with some workplace opposition from trade unions frustrated these attempts.[6] The long-term effects of short-termism are manifest in the UK's comparative economic decline and inferior terms and conditions of employment compared with other EU states.

The regulation and distribution of economic surplus generated in the employment relationship is a key function of an industrial relations system. However, it is not necessarily the only or paramount function of industrial relations. Regulation and participation necessitate some form of industrial democracy in the employment relationship. The extreme functionalism of most economists leads them to ignore institutional factors which structure wider measures of economic performance. For example, new right economists and state theorists argue that pluralism, institutionalized in processes and mechanisms such as the industrial relations system, damaged UK economic performance during the post-war period. Hence, institutional industrial relations were not functional in terms of economic performance, but were so in terms of cushioning economic decline. The legitimacy of institutional representation in collective bargaining prevented successive post-war governments from introducing economic policies and patterns of reform in the industrial relations system that when they were introduced during the 1980s failed to cushion decline but accelerated the process. As Kaldor suggests, during the post-war period what might be termed the 'extra functionalism' of many such factors helped cushion the UK's economic decline.[7]

Extreme and narrow functionalism in the application of economic theory to employment ignores or rationalizes away the indeterminate nature of labour performance in the employment relationship. For example, most approaches to economics fail to recognize that although the performance of labour is the primary concern of employers performance is not what is purchased in the employment relationship. The performance of labour in the employment relationship is indeterminate because the potential productivity of employees that is remunerated and regulated in employment has to be transformed into effective labour performance – the process is not automatic. Most approaches in economics fail to recognize that an industrial relations system is functional but likely to contain many contradictory elements independent of measures of industrial democracy. The failure to recognize a difference between the purchase of labour by an employer and the performance of labour in the employment relationship is a case in point. By ignoring the difference between the purchase of potential and the actual performance of an employee, narrow economic analysis sustains an image that trade unions are restrictive institutions which rely on obstructive processes such as collective bargaining. The obstructive and restrictive image assumes that collective bargaining damages potential efficiency and inhibits efficient performance by the firm. However, all aspects of employer and management action, including short-termism, that may have a similar effect appear as rational and competitive measures designed to improve performance.[8]

A central problem in attempts to test empirically generalized models of an industrial relations system mirrors those encountered in the application of generalized theories of the capitalist state. The process of particularization sustains structural mechanisms within an industrial relations system that reproduce limitations in the institutional structure of a particular state. Hence, patterns of regulation legitimize the centralized power of the capitalist class yet are likely to operate in a potentially contradictory manner. Partial access to the state through a voluntary system of industrial relations has, in the UK, sustained the historically embedded yet short-term interests of many employers. However, collective *laissez faire* and voluntarism has positioned trade unions and collective bargaining as easy targets in proximate explanations of poor post-war economic performance. Collective *laissez faire* appeared functional – it helped secure post-war recovery – yet contradictory; in the context of full employment, it appeared inflationary. More significantly, collective *laissez faire* is functional because it is an institutional embodiment of the process of particularization in the UK state. However, its libertarianism, which for employers continues in the contemporary period of improved auxiliary legislation, remains contradictory. Self-regulation by employers sustains short-term approaches to economic performance that in the main marginalize quality-enhancing processes such as training and development, investment and democratic participation.

In a comparative study of fifteen European states, Crouch demonstrates that institutions in an industrial relations system act in accordance with the structure of a particular nation state.[9] Crouch concludes that libertarian states such as the UK have weak market systems of industrial relations. These systems eschew constitutional or corporatist approaches to employment regulation, which elsewhere (Germany and Scandinavia) structure better economic performance than that experienced by libertarian states.[10] In the UK, the apparent freedom of the parties in industrial relations from central regulation by the state has fractionalized the political capacity of trade unions to challenge the hierarchy of interests in the state. In addition, the delegated entry of trade union interests into the hierarchy of the state has structured the economic capacity of trade unions in collective bargaining to respond in a short-term and sectional manner to employee interests. The structural limitations of the UK state are the processes of particularization, in which the pattern of delegation dominated by employer interests operates as a significant impediment to the organizational capacity of UK employers and, in turn, trade unions. This has been the case since the 1870s, but has become a critical factor in the UK's comparatively poor economic performance since 1945.

To address how a delegated industrial relations system appeared and remains functional to the UK state requires the application of historically positioned theory. The following subsections pursue this application by examining the limited role of law in UK industrial relations and how this reproduces formative influences on the state as collective *laissez faire* in the industrial relations system. Both sections aim to specify embedded patterns of governance that connect the state and the industrial relations system.

The state and law in the UK's industrial relations system

The voluntarist tradition in the UK industrial relations system centres on the assumption that the regulation of employment is largely *ultra vires* to law resting on the acceptance of legitimate conflict in an otherwise co-operative relationship. However, whereas the contemporary pattern of legal intervention in the system has been a long time in coming, hostility from the legal community to collective conflict and representation by trade unions has a long history. Judicial latitude in the 1901 Taff Vale case held that a trade union was responsible for civil liability as a result of strike activity by its members. More recently, in 1964, judicial intervention in an otherwise legitimate trade dispute created the tort of civil intimidation to establish trade union liability for strike action taken by its membership. The 1906 Trade Dispute Act set aside the Taff Vale judgment to give trade unions institutional immunity from civil liability if the action of its members was in support of a trade dispute relating to terms and conditions of employment. Equally, in 1964, the incoming Labour government legislated to set aside the Rookes case. Moreover, the Rookes case played a direct role in the creation of the Donovan Commission. Further, the Labour government's 1969 White Paper 'In Place of Strife' proposed legal regulation of industrial action in trade disputes but failed to win Cabinet, trade union or significant levels of employer support. Finally, the National Industrial Relations Court created by the 1971 Industrial Relations Act failed to win support beyond the judiciary.

In 1906 and 1964, the state acted to restore and maintain a voluntary industrial relations system based on the principle of collective *laissez faire*. Voluntarism and collective *laissez faire* rest on the assumption that co-operation within the employment relationship secures effective job regulation negotiated between the two parties in the collective bargaining process. However, in the absence of a negotiated agreement, either party may deploy social sanctions against the other in the form of employer lock-outs or industrial action on the part of employees.[11]

As an institutional reproduction of the UK's highly particularized state, this pattern of self-regulation between employers and employees serves the broad interests of employers and trade unions alike. Employers are able, subject to auxiliary legislation, to manage industrial relations as they see fit. Equally, release from the charge of criminal conspiracy and immunity from civil liability legitimized trade union activity beyond their role of job regulation in the workplace. The inter-war period saw trade unions campaign against fascism in Spain, whereas in the post-war period trade unions supported the campaign for nuclear disarmament and the anti-apartheid movement. In addition, some trade unions campaigned for improved auxiliary employment legislation over redundancy, unfair dismissal and race and sex discrimination. More recently, trade unions have campaigned over the mis-selling of personal pensions and the threatened privatization of the Post Office; in addition, public sector trade unions successfully lobbied for the introduction of a minimum wage.

Cannadine contends that in 1906 and 1964 most trade unions did not threaten the state and nor have they done so since 1964.[12] The promotion of voluntary self-regulation on a plural basis retains continuity with preindustrial patterns of regulation that were highly localized, centring on the manor and the guild. The majority of trade unions were and remain non-revolutionary in their aims. Hence, decriminalizing trade union activity and providing trade unions with civil immunity in tort and breach of contract has resulted in a partial access to the hierarchical nature of the UK state. However, partial access on a voluntary basis eschews representation of employee interests, either collectively or individually, on a constitutional basis. Moreover, collective *laissez faire* positions co-operation and negotiated agreements as the norm. The acceptance of conflict within negotiation at the workplace legitimizes the economic role of trade unions in collective bargaining. Equally, this separates conflict over job regulation and the distribution of surplus from centralized political representation in the state by either constitutional or corporatist mechanisms. Historically, the negotiation of workplace agreements and the acceptance of industrial action as a legitimate employee sanction does not appear to have threatened employer interests. As the third section argues and Chapter 6 demonstrates in more detail, rather than threatening employer interests, both workplace agreements and industrial action have furthered and legitimized employer interests.

The tradition of voluntarism does not exclude the state from a direct role in the rules of job regulation negotiated at the workplace. Alternatively, it describes a pattern of delegation by the central state. Voluntarism in collective *laissez faire* has structured and legitimized a functional approach to the industrial relations system through a division of economic and political interests on a class basis. Like the aristocracy, the industrial bourgeoisie has retained significant regulatory freedom from the state, whereas voluntarism has divided and fractured the economic and political interests of the employed class. Equally, voluntarism in the industrial relations system has retained the hierarchical nature of the UK state. A retention which has only recently been challenged as a result of 'pooling sovereignty' in the EU.[13] Examples of this challenge include the provisions of the Working Time Directive and amendments to domestic auxiliary legislation resulting from judgments in the European Court on maternity pay and absence from work related to confinement.[14]

The process of industrialization followed by urbanization threatened traditional patterns of local regulation based on feudal hierarchy in the aristocracy. Industrialization established the importance of the employment relationship and freedom from the land. Urbanization established the significance of collective interests in the employment relationship. A common cause between the aristocracy and the industrial bourgeoisie centred around the maintenance of traditional – voluntary – if hierarchical methods of regulation and freedom from an arbitrary monarchy. Social science scholars describe this as *laissez faire*, analysed in Chapter 4 as the formative influence over the UK state. As a functional mechanism, it is reproduced in many areas of institutional regulation. Collective *laissez faire* in the industrial relations system saw the rule of law in job regulation delegated to the principal parties. However, the voluntary tradition did not emerge accidentally or organically, neither is it an aberration. The limited role of law in the system is a direct consequence of highly particularized ruling-class interests and preferred patterns of regulation in the UK state. The legacy of formative influences, particularized during the period of industrialization in national pathways, remains in the contemporary period. National pathways in economic and political regulation are deeply embedded, they precede and structure contemporary developments and pressures in the international economy at regional level (EU) or global level (globalization).

Particularization in the UK system of industrial relations

General theories of the capitalist state specify the accumulation of capital and the legitimization of inequality within the capitalist system of production and distribution as the functional objectives of the capitalist state. Chapter 4 demonstrated that in industrial capitalism the state is able to separate the institutions of political and economic domination. Separation provides the state with a relative autonomy from capital. The analytical category particularization captures the historical and social processes that structure institutional separation from the state. The processes of particularization are subject to formative and contextual influences in the formation of an individual capitalist state. However, the determinism and logic of formative influences once enacted becomes historically and institutionally embedded to restrain – structure – policy choices in specific areas, e.g. the industrial relations system.

However, the formative influences of libertarianism expressed as freedom from central regulation has structured and reinforced the conservative and short-term interests of UK employers in self- or voluntary regulation. The process of particularization describes how an individual state maintains accumulation and legitimizes distributional inequality, to this extent it is functional. More critically, particularization demonstrates how the generalized functions of the capitalist state are contradictory where formative influences structure the process to limit functionalism. For example, as Chapter 6 demonstrates, throughout the post-war period the interests of manufacturing capital and the state structured the allegedly restrictive role of the craft union model in UK industrial relations. The process of particularization flows from the state through capital and into labour. More generally than this, Clegg demonstrates that employer policies within the wider context of post-war recovery structured the process and the internal dynamics of collective bargaining.[15] In addition, Crouch demonstrates that a historically embedded, yet complex, institutional interdependence flows from the state through employers to trade unions and collective bargaining.[16] Moreover, structural interdependence remains as the institutional and structural base of regulation in national industrial relations systems. The evidence suggests that the erosion of institutional industrial relations in the UK during the contemporary period, in particular the movement to imported patterns of regulation such as HRM and total quality management (TQM) is overstated. In 1999, 30 per cent of the labour force remained union members, with 45 per cent of all workplaces recognizing trade unions for purposes of collective bargaining.[17] Data presented by Crouch appear to demonstrate that over the whole of the post-war period these figures do not represent a rump remaining after a transformation from collective *laissez faire* to individualism. Alternatively, they demonstrate a reduction in membership and coverage of collective bargaining which over the whole of the post-war period was less extensive than the proponents of individualism suggest. Union membership as a percentage of the labour force remained at approximately 40–44 per cent from 1950 until the late 1970s, when it reached approximately 50 per cent. Membership then fell back to around 30 per cent in 1990, where it has remained for most of the decade.[18] More significantly than this, the evidence suggests that vogue imports are unable to transform historically embedded flows and patterns of relations among the state, employers and employees.[19]

The embedded tradition of voluntary regulation represents the process of delegation by the UK state. Contemporary erosion of voluntarism results from the effects of economic and political decline, legal intervention and the rhetorical presence of new managerial strategies. The transformational thesis is overstated precisely because legal intervention and the rhetorical or short-term presence of new managerial strategies has reinforced, not transformed, embedded managerial and employer interests. For example, Cully *et al.* demonstrate that although new managerial strategies such as HRM are poorly developed in the UK there is some movement to employee participation beyond collective bargaining. Equally, Gallie *et al.* suggest that whereas new managerial strategies have helped to restructure the employment relationship they have a positive effect on employee training and upskilling for only a minority, doing nothing for the majority.[20] Together, these findings suggest that a lower level of trade union membership in employment has done little to encourage employers to improve access to training and development. This evidence also suggests that a trade union presence does not prevent access to training but actually makes it more likely. By positioning contemporary developments historically, it is possible to establish the continued presence and significance of embedded employer interests and patterns of regulation which 'casual' or ahistorical studies do not consider.[21]

In the immediate post-war years, industrial relations in the workplace remained unreconstructed. Employers followed by trade unions insisted on self-regulation in areas such as work organization and wage bargaining without intervention by the state or state agencies such as the Board of Trade (BOT) or the AACP.[22] The BOT wanted more centralized regulation of collective bargaining, whereas the AACP proposed the introduction of workplace productivity bargaining. The Ministry of Labour and National Service found more support from employers and trade unions by advocating voluntary collective bargaining.[23]

As the industrial relations policy of successive post-war governments, collective *laissez faire* was relatively short-lived. By 1965, the Donovan Commission was examining the UK's industrial relations system with special reference to the use of law. Subsequent to the voluntary recommendations of Donovan, the Labour government proposed but shelved legislative intervention. It was later reconstituted and extended by the incoming Conservative government as the 1971 Industrial Relations Act. The mid-1970s saw a return to collective *laissez faire* through the Trade Union Labour Relations Act, which restored trade disputes to the status bestowed by the 1906 legislation.[24]

The Thatcher governments followed by those of John Major rejected the use of incomes policy to regulate industrial relations in the private sector, supporting free collective bargaining. The Conservative governments maintained collective *laissez faire*, yet deregulated and regulated it simultaneously. In contrast to the provisions of the 1971 Industrial Relations Act, the legislation in the 1980s retained the assumption of negotiated agreements supplemented by the use of social sanctions on the Kahn–Freund model. The design of that legislation aimed to limit and channel the use and availability of industrial action and strike activity with the objective of substantially increasing the managerial prerogative within any collective negotiations. For many, this has further embedded established management interests and constraints centred on short-termism in terms of training, productivity and economic performance.[25]

Before the election of the Labour government in 1997, state policy on industrial relations highlighted formative influences but directed them towards reforming the historically embedded institutional base – collective *laissez faire* in the industrial relations system. Labour market deregulation and tighter regulation of dispute resolution in the employment relationship created more freedom for employers from institutions and processes – trade unions and collective bargaining – previously supported by the state. However, deregulation and tighter regulation express both the functionalism and the contradictory nature of historically embedded and highly particularized influences in the UK state. Legal regulation of collective relations in employment and the deregulation of individual auxiliary legislation helped to improve the managerial prerogative in the short run but had only a marginal effect on the UK's comparative economic performance, training levels and employee participation.

Legal abstention and legal intervention since 1945 are a contemporary expression of a historical struggle to maintain the pre-eminence of formative influences that have particularized the UK state. McCarthy demonstrates that in the post-war period a reliance on the 1906 Trade Dispute Act followed by its amendment in the 1980s was designed to keep the state out of industrial relations.[26] Collective *laissez faire*, operative in either collectivist or individualist mode, represents a *de facto* delegation of responsibility, from the state to employers, for industrial relations in the workplace. The movement from collectivist to individualist mode witnessed a reinforcement of historically embedded management interests and a significant erosion of employee representation and regulation in the workplace.

This section demonstrates that the state and its particularized development is the central antecedent that structures the institutional base of the UK's industrial relations system. The incorporation of the industrial bourgeoisie and later the partial incorporation of the employed class into the UK state posed no challenge to the political interests of the ruling class or the economic interests of the industrial class. Alternatively, it merely reproduced the contradictory structure of the state. Collective *laissez faire* in the industrial relations system has fractionalized the economic and political interests of the employed class. This has reproduced a structure of short-termism and self-regulation similar to that secured and retained by employers. The next section examines order and reform in the industrial relations system in this (historically embedded) context.

Order and reform in the industrial relations system

The structural relationship between the state and the industrial relations system exhibits a pattern of reproductive delegation. The formative influence of *laissez faire* is reproduced as collective *laissez faire* in the industrial relations system. Collective *laissez faire* structures a pattern of short-termism and self-regulation in unilateral employer interests through the industrial relations system, thereby incorporating employee interests into the UK's historically embedded pattern of regulation in the state. However, periodic reform retains order that appears orderly because the most significant and enduring tranches of reform in the post-war period have maintained and further embedded the formative influences in the UK state. For example, the 1982 amendment to the 1906 Trade Dispute Act retains negative immunity from civil liability for trade unions as institutions. Neither does contemporary auxiliary legislation give employees or institutions positive individual or collective employment rights. This even extends to so-called 'day one rights' that might have the effect of a positive constitutional right.[27] Hence, the majority of job regulation remains with the employer in the employment relationship.

An industrial relations system is functional if the pattern of institutional regulation that surrounds the employment relationship structures the generation of economic surplus and a democratic pattern of job regulation in the workplace. Together, structural and procedural rules, whether they are formally codified or they remain customary, regulate conflict to arrive at consensus in the workplace. Within this process, collective bargaining provides a measure of symmetry in an otherwise asymmetrical relationship that the gentrification of unilateral employer power in new managerial strategies cannot provide.[28]

The indeterminate nature of performance in employment is subject to material and political dynamics that are much wider than the workplace. The creation of a post-war Western economic system during the Cold War, the weakening of the system between the late 1970s and early 1980s and subsequent efforts to regulate and restructure the system on a pan-European basis since the early 1990s represent these dynamics. Within each period, the state has attempted to reform the industrial relations system, the process has remained functional (securing surplus and managing conflict) yet contradictory. The processes of voluntary and statutory delegation by the state have, since 1945, facilitated and reinforced historically formed interests in and between employers and trade unions, although sometimes beyond their functional confines.

Historically, the imbalance between reform and order demonstrates a shifting power relationship between employers and employees. Since the early 1980s, employers, supported by the state, have been engaged in a process of countermobilization against trade unions and collectivism in the institutional structure of the state.[29] Over the short term, this appeared functional; however, to mobilize against trade unions it was necessary to deploy a countercyclical economic policy that not only stalled the economy but substantially weakened the UK's manufacturing sector. Equally, the policies had only a marginal effect on improving the UK's comparative economic weakness.[30]

Over the whole period since 1945, apart from the 1970s, state policy on the industrial relations system has eschewed deviation from an embedded pattern of delegated interests. This pattern retains a particularized structure in which the reform of collective *laissez faire* has reinforced (short term) employer interests at the expense of their longer-term collective interests.[31] This demonstrates that the relative autonomy of the state may reinforce and not overcome contradictions in the functionalism of a particular state.[32]

Reform in the UK's industrial relations system has focused on the institution of collective bargaining because as a process and structure it is of central importance to understanding industrial relations in the UK.[33] For as long as public policy supported collective bargaining, reform in the system structured a coherent but separate conservatism among employers, employees and the state. Crouch[34] describes the process as institutional congruence, yet the utility of this conceptual category is limited because congruence does not create a united pattern of common ideas and aims. For example, in the contemporary period, employer groups such as the CBI, the Institute of Directors (IOD) and the Institute of Personnel and Development (IPD) each express vocal opposition to the introduction of further auxiliary legislation that aims to secure improved individual employee rights in the employment relationship. In addition, all three groups remain opposed on principle to the statutory procedure for trade union recognition in collective bargaining, arguing that voluntary arrangements are always preferable.[35] Differing from congruence, the institutional structure of collective bargaining provides each party with a defensive position, hence it is functional yet contradictory in roughly equal order; similar to other aspects of state policy in the post-war period, collectivism helped to cushion economic decline.[36] In contrast to this, during the 1980s, the state in government was primarily concerned with dismantling the institutions, both economic and democratic, that had cushioned decline since 1945. The industrial relations system, more particularly its deregulation, became an instrument of new right economic policy. As a result of the dismantling process, collective bargaining no longer captured the key issues in job regulation, hence employer opposition to legislative measures designed to legitimize its representative utility. In addition to this opposition, increased managerial control has further reinforced the embedded nature of short-termism in employer interests, measured in profitability as distinct from productivity and participation.[37] The remainder of this section briefly summarizes the process of reform in the industrial relations system since 1945.

The post-war years until 1970

The 1950s reflect 'the high tide of consensus' in the UK's industrial relations system, however the splendour of the system was short lived.[38] Instability became evident from 1958, when sterling convertibility exposed the comparative weakness of the UK's post-war pathway to economic recovery, demonstrating fierce competition beyond the confines of Imperial markets protected by the sterling area.[39] Equally, consensus, although real, is often overstated; as early as 1957, the operation of the system, particularly in a context of full employment, was subject to academic, judicial and political scrutiny.[40] Moreover, the issue of legal regulation in the industrial relations system, particularly over trade unions, became a subject of debate. In 1956, *Political Quarterly* published a special edition under the general heading of 'Trade unions in a changing world'; two years later the *Scottish Journal of Political Economy* published a similar edition titled 'Wage policy and inflation'. Both journals featured industrial relations specialists and labour economists who debated four issues: wage determination (free or fixed), the consequences for incomes policies and productivity, the appropriate level of employment, and finally the role of trade unions in the first three issues.[41]

Industrial relations specialists favoured a voluntary system of regulation, whereas economists pointed to the inflationary consequences of voluntarism in full employment. Flanders advocated incomes policies to structure voluntary regulation in the workplace and further facilitate the deployment of plant level productivity bargaining. Flanders later developed this position in *The Fawley Productivity Agreements* and in his evidence to the Donovan Commission.[42] Judicial scrutiny focused on a 1958 Conservative Inns of Court publication that presented collective bargaining in the workplace as a mechanism which sustained overmanning and the deployment of excessive restrictive practices.[43]

This pattern of scrutiny marked a stall in the UK's post-war recovery and the search for a palliative to cushion comparative economic decline while leaving patterns of regulation in the state and employer interests undisturbed.[44] This process culminated in the Donovan Report and the recommendation for a structural reform of collective bargaining at workplace level.

After 1947 and throughout the 1950s, economic conditions, in particular employment levels, were very favourable to employers and employees.[45] However, this led to opportunism by both groups. Employers recognized that, in relation to workplace industrial relations and interests, the TUC was weak. For example, in the AACP TUC engagement with and interest in more formal workplace industrial relations, procedures through productivity bargaining were effectively rejected by employer action, supported by some union representation from the workplace.[46] In summary, employers in the private sector had little interest in coming to terms with trade unions as an institutionalized bargaining partner in the workplace. Industry-wide collective bargaining remained the normative mechanism for job regulation, although by the late 1950s more direct informal bargaining between shop stewards and plant managers challenged this process especially in engineering and motor manufacturing.

The Donovan Commission identified the apparent breakdown of national collective bargaining in the private sector and the emergence of informal collective bargaining at the workplace as a central problem in the industrial relations system. However, in their subsequent Donovan Report, the commissioners argued that collective bargaining was the best and most democratic mechanism for job regulation in the industrial relations system.[47] Moreover, the report argued that the role of law should be kept to a minimum.[48]

The process of industrial relations reform clearly demonstrates the formative influence on the UK state – libertarianism. Direct legal intervention in the industrial relations system would have been *ultra vires* to collective *laissez faire* almost undemocratic in terms of the UK's particularized pattern of libertarianism. Traditionally – formatively – the state did not intervene in private arrangements as long as they were lawful and reasonable. Voluntary agreements between employers and trade unions were private arrangements more appropriately regulated by formal agreements managed in the workplace. Trade union recognition and formal procedures for personnel management together with the advisory – voluntary – body The Commission for Industrial Relations encompassed the limited state intervention in a private area of delegated responsibility created by enabling legislation between 1871 and 1906.

In addition to procedural matters, the process of formalization in the workplace encompassed more substantial issues, such as work organization, payment systems and job evaluation. The term 'productivity bargaining' is often used to describe this as an integrative process in which higher wages and/or shorter working hours are exchanged for improved work organization. As the following chapter demonstrates, the component elements in the process of substantive formalization in the workplace are similar if not identical to the ideas rejected by UK employers between 1948 and 1952.

The 1970s – the Industrial Relations Act and the social contract

Until the election of the Heath administration in 1970, all post-war governments supported voluntary industrial relations structured by the framework of collective *laissez faire* and the institutional mechanism of collective bargaining. The 1971 Industrial Relations Act appeared to step beyond the collective *laissez faire* framework and to centralize the institutional regulation of collective bargaining in the workplace.

Before the election of Heath, the previous Labour government under Wilson had flirted with the idea of legal regulation in the industrial relations system.

Voluntary proposals appeared democratic but problematic in securing an improved economic performance, particularly in the context of the 14 per cent devaluation of sterling in 1967. However, in the wake of devaluation a combination of fiscal restriction, import controls and incomes policies appeared, in the context of high employment, to make legal intervention unlikely to succeed.[49] The Heath government was undeterred by this and introduced the Industrial Relations Act in 1971. This legislation attempted to enact a centralized legal framework for the industrial relations system by creating a codified framework for workplace order and conflict resolution.

The Act contained several major provisions. First, a trade union registrar empowered to investigate internal union affairs. Second, an assumption that collective bargaining agreements negotiated on a voluntary basis were legally binding unless otherwise stated. Third, the pre-entry closed shop was outlawed. Fourth, a statutory procedure for trade union recognition was created. Last, the legislation created a labour court with the status of the High Court, the National Industrial Relations Court (NIRC).

The 1971 Act resulted in significant union protest and strike activity. Furthermore, it reversed the Donovan policy of procedural reform that legitimized collective bargaining on a voluntary basis. Many managers ignored legal rights given to them by the legislation and stated that collective agreements were voluntary. The Act was a failure both operationally and intellectually.[50]

The NIRC was the central innovation in the Act. It gave life to other elements by creating a new catch-all legal category 'the unfair industrial practice'. The NIRC held the power to codify centrally in an apparently constitutional form a new category – an unfair industrial practice. This reversed the historically embedded practice of enabling legislation in the UK system. By extension, the NIRC reversed the framework of collective *laissez faire* from a process of voluntary negotiation in collective bargaining supplemented by the use of social sanctions and reference to auxiliary legislation where appropriate. The NIRC went beyond collective *laissez faire* by defining what an unfair industrial practice was in absolute terms.

This came to a head in Heaton's case.[51] In their opposition to the Industrial Relations Act, the vast majority of trade unions refused to register with the registrar of trade unions created under the legislation. As a consequence of this action, unions and union members lost immunity for civil liability under the 1906 Act. It was the automatic loss of immunity that created the catch-all category unfair industrial practice. In 1972, Heaton's Transport complained to the NIRC that members of the Transport and General Workers' Union (TGWU), acting under instructions from shop stewards, had refused to handle their containers. The NIRC ordered the TGWU to handle Heaton's containers. However, union officials were unable to secure compliance, resulting in fines and a contempt decision against the union. On appeal, the Court of Appeal held that the TGWU, as an institution, was responsible for the actions of its lay members. Before an appeal to the Law Lords convened, the Official Solicitor had the Appeal Court decision set aside. The Official Solicitor argued that there was insufficient evidence to hold that the particular shop stewards were responsible for organizing unofficial industrial action. The situation appeared solved but it was complicated by a new submission to the NIRC from a second firm complaining of an unfair industrial practice (UIP) relating to unofficial picketing (partly organized by two of the stewards involved in the previous case). An injunction was ignored and the dockers, subsequently referred to as the 'Pentonville Five', were imprisoned. This action resulted in a national dock strike and other sympathy strikes.

The Law Lords still delivered a judgment on the facts in Heaton's case, even though the case had been effectively settled through the intervention of the Official Solicitor. The Law Lords held that a union was liable for the actions of lay activists resulting in the release from prison of the 'Pentonville Five'.

By reinterpreting the NIRC's terms of reference and incorporating them within collective *laissez faire*, the Law Lords rendered the NIRC's catch-all methodology impotent. Intellectually, the constituent elements within both of the above cases represented normal patterns of dispute resolution that the catch-all category unfair industrial practice made unlawful. The vast majority of employers ignored the utility of this category and the Act died on the statute book. By stepping beyond the delegated framework of collective *laissez faire*, the 1971 Act attempted to impose a centralized process of reform and order. However, by creating a separate labour law court which related to the category unfair industrial practice, the legislation attempted to create positive rights for employers and individual union members by suspending collective (negative) immunity for trade unions and their members. This was unsustainable and effectively unconstitutional as it pushed the state beyond its particularized mode of operation in voluntary delegation. The 1979 Conservative government did not repeat this mistake.

The incoming Labour government repealed the majority of the provisions in the 1971 Act to return collective *laissez faire* to its 1906 basis. The efforts of the Labour government to balance economic performance and industrial democracy were more successful in the short term than those of its predecessor, but remained ultimately unsuccessful in economic and political terms. In 1975, the Labour government struck a deal with the TUC referred to as the 'social contract'. Under the provisions of this deal, the government agreed to extend and improve auxiliary legislation on employee rights to protection against unfair dismissal and redundancy in return for moderate wage demands by trade unions. By 1978, many trade unions were unwilling to endure another year of wage restraint and campaigned for a return to free collective bargaining. Equally, in the workplace, many employers negotiated significant pay increases rather than endure sustained industrial action in support of pay claims above agreed norms.

The Labour government, like its Conservative predecessor, sought to manoeuvre its industrial relations policy beyond collective *laissez faire*. As an attempt at corporatism, the social contract was a failure. Corporatism positioned employer associations and the TUC (beyond their traditional enabling role in collective *laissez faire*) as centralized agents responsible for controlling their respective memberships. However, the central power of employer associations and that of the TUC was only weakly articulated in the UK, hence it was unlikely that either party could carry its membership with them for long.[52] Equally, since Donovan, private sector industrial relations management had become increasingly decentralized, a process that substantially weakened the regulatory force of industry-wide agreements negotiated by employer associations as well as the central influence of the TUC. In addition to this, the social contract began (what has become) the sustained focus on public sector industrial relations as the government deflated the economy by a combination of expenditure cuts and cash-limited pay increases in the public sector.[53] The attempt to centralize the delegated framework of collective *laissez faire* with a centralized pattern of corporatism supported by auxiliary legislation failed. The institutional base of the state was unable to operate beyond the particular mechanics of its formative pattern of regulation. Corporatism necessitated centralized institutional control in the hierarchy of the state, whereas the embedded delegated pattern reflected historically formed self-regulated institutional interests.

The contemporary period

The Conservative Party returned to power in 1979 and judiciously avoided the mistakes of 1971. A strategy of disintegrated but cumulative legal intervention running from 1980 to 1993 did not attack collective *laissez faire* as a social process but aimed to rebalance it in favour of employers by tightening the parameters of dispute resolution. This was particularly the case between 1980 and 1984.

The 1980 Employment Act restricted the use of secondary industrial action and made secondary picketing unlawful. The 1982 Employment Act crystallized the significance of both measures in two ways. First, the legislation substantially narrowed the definition of a trade dispute from that contained in the 1906 legislation. This measure restricted trade disputes to those between workers and their employers rather than those between employers and workmen. Second, the 1982 Act introduced institutional liability for unlawful action conducted by the membership of a trade union. The creation of a legal personality for trade unions as institutions marked the cumulative nature of the legislation. Unlawful secondary industrial action or picketing continued until and beyond the provisions of the 1980 Act. However, the 1982 legislation gave employers a legal remedy if they wished to use it because neither secondary picketing nor secondary action were within the new definition of a trade dispute for which immunity from civil liability remained.

The 1984 Trade Union Act introduced a requirement for a correctly worded ballot before the use of industrial action in a trade dispute. This measure had the effect of making a trade union legally liable for unofficial industrial action organized by lay activists without reference to full-time officials or their sanction. Employers were able to deploy injunctions against trade unions that required the institution to control its membership, compelling them to desist from unlawful industrial action. If trade unions failed to do this, they faced substantial fines followed by the sequestration of assets.

Further legislation supplemented these acts to give individuals the right to dissociate from collectively arrived at union decisions, restricted union management membership agreements, allowed employers to dismiss selectively strikers and introduced tighter rules for membership ballots, including advance notice provisions for the employer. The Trade Union Labour Relations Act of 1992 consolidated all measures enacted since 1980.

The institutional and representative role of trade unions in workplace collective bargaining became the central target for Conservative reform. The measures weakened membership at the workplace to undermine collective and representative power. Membership of unions fell, but their influence on work organization within collective bargaining agreements remains significant.[54] More significantly, the interests of UK employers remain short term, as the emergence of integrative and longer-term *strategic human resource management* remains limited at workplace level. The development of direct employee participation in decision-making appears in only a minority of cases. Recent evidence suggests that only 15 per cent of firms have an employee share option scheme, with only 14 per cent guaranteeing job security through a no compulsory redundancy scheme. Only 27 per cent of supervisors are trained in employee relations, whereas only 28 per cent of workplaces have a joint consultative committee.[55]

In contrast to the 1970 Conservative government, the Thatcher and Major administrations used collective *laissez faire* to regulate trade unions. By amending its legal basis as defined in the 1906 legislation, the government maintained immunity provisions but substantially tightened access to them. Moreover, by maintaining but regulating a rebalanced collective *laissez faire*, Conservative governments were able to pronounce the end of incomes policies and a return to unrestricted free collective bargaining in the private sector. The Conservative government promoted a libertarian pattern of employee relations managed through the managerial prerogative. However, the medium-term effects of this failed to improve economic efficiency and reduced industrial democracy for many in the workplace. The election of a Labour government in 1997 marked the beginning of a further phase of order and reform in industrial relations.

This Labour government introduced a minimum wage, signed up to European social charter provisions on European works councils and introduced a statutory procedure for trade union recognition. In addition, the 1999 Employment Relations Act contains numerous auxiliary provisions designed to improve individual rights in the workplace over unfair dismissal, 'whistleblowing' and the use of waiver clauses in fixed-term contracts.[56] While these measures mark a return to regulation – however weak – the vast majority of the previous government's collective legislation remains in force. In addition, it remains to be seen whether the recognition procedure and the minimum wage supplemented by the various auxiliary measures will improve industrial democracy in the workplace and improve the UK's comparative economic performance.[57]

In the period since 1945, the process of reform in the industrial relations system has focused on establishing order in bargaining systems that are decentralized to the workplace, where formally negotiated agreements between management and trade unions are conducted. The Donovan Report argued that employer-led voluntary reform would improve economic performance whereas collective bargaining represented the most democratic form of participation in workplace decisions. Kahn-Freund suggested that legal intervention designed to advance this process was unlikely to be successful.[58] Thirty years later, the evidence suggests that Kahn-Freund was correct. The UK has the most restrictive trade union laws in the EU, one of the poorest records on vocational education and training and one of the lowest levels of collective representation; all in the context of the most deregulated economy in Europe.[59] This pattern has produced a differentiated order in which economic performance, remuneration and democratic participation in the workplace are heavily segmented, reflecting a wider segmentation of the working population, what Hutton refers to as the 40:30:30 society.[60] The evidence suggests that collectively bargained order is efficient, democratic and profitable. Equally, non-unionism and extreme employee flexibility are profitable but less democratic and less efficient in terms of employee absenteeism, productivity and labour turnover.[61]

Legal intervention has, however, stimulated a partial pattern of deregulation that has weakened the integrity of the industrial relations system. The partial erosion of collective bargaining and the hollowing out of auxiliary legislation in the 1980s focused an explicit return to formative influences on the UK state. The historical record laid out in previous chapters suggests that the Donovan proposals supplemented by the measures enacted since 1980 represent a partial route to failure in reform. Both Donovan and deregulation are open to the criticism that they represent 'acts of faith' which failed to connect with and position the industrial relations system as one marginal factor in economic performance.

Economic performance and the industrial relations system

As a mechanism to understand the relationship between the state and the law in the industrial relations system, collective *laissez faire* retains significant explanatory utility.

The restrictive nature of its contemporary structure mirrors the decentralized pattern of industrial relations reforms in which the movement to formal regulation in the workplace has curtailed traditional post-war patterns of dispute resolution, such as solidarity industrial action and localized industrial action sanctioned by lay activists. However, this process has not impaired employer adherence to a pattern of historically embedded short-term interests that focus freedom from the central state – self- or deregulation – the formative influence in the UK state. The particularized relationship between order and reform in the industrial relations system and the performance of the economy remains the subject of generalized, proximate and ahistorical argument. This section positions the industrial relations system in the context of post-war recovery and positions post-war recovery in relation to comparative economic decline. Last, the industrial relations system is examined as an instrument of economic policy.

The industrial relations system and post-war recovery

Since 1980, it has become orthodox to position trade union interests in collective bargaining as the pivotal explanation for the UK's post-war economic decline.[62] Subsequently, it has been argued that the tendency to multi-unionism within the UK industrial relations system impaired productivity, improvement in work organization and a movement to Fordist systems of production.[63] Moreover, retrospectively, these analyses argue that by the early 1950s obsolete working practices emerged as a central impediment to high productivity, low unit labour costs and the installation of Fordist work systems. However, emergence is not the same thing as recognition and rectification.[64]

In the post-war period and (in effect) beyond, the industrial relations system was dominated by the urgency of post-war recovery within the wider context of the UK's historical legacy. The latter meant that the UK played a central role in the emergent Cold War, wherein Marshall Aid funds proved a powerful palliative that cushioned fears of overseas competition particularly from emergent Western European producers. In summary, the UK's post-war markets and production methods retained significant continuities with pre-war interests to emphasize standard but customized products tailored to the needs of established but highly differentiated empire and sterling area markets. In this context, a major restructuring of the industrial relations system was not a priority of the state or employers.[65]

Post-war recovery tightened labour markets and concentrated employers' minds on producing goods for what was until the late 1950s a sellers' market in established export markets and the relatively closed domestic market for manufactured goods. The success of post-war recovery played a major role in generating some significant operational factors that later became problematic, e.g. informal workplace or plant bargaining. As Chapter 6 demonstrates in more detail, the Donovan Report failed to engage with the role and position of the industrial relations system within wider economic performance, particularly labour productivity. Contemporary observers noted this absence but their observations failed to convince.[66] After the failure to engage the issue, economists and economic historians appropriated the relationship between industrial relations and economic performance. By the 1980s, many such had positioned deteriorating post-war economic performance as solely attributable to the UK worker and the looseness of the UK industrial relations system.[67] Singular emphasis on the industrial relations system that highlighted declining economic performance since the late 1950s became so extensive that comparative analyses taking into account factors beyond industrial relations were excluded from consideration.[68]

Reactions to comparative economic performance

It is common to position the attachment of trade unions to free collective bargaining as a central factor in the UK's post-war comparative economic decline. Craft and multi-unionism prevented the deployment of Fordist work systems that led directly to deteriorating economic performance.[69] However, it is far less the case that the central role of employers and management is highlighted in this process.[70] Alternatively, employers and management appear as victims of trade union intransigence – proposing significant changes to improve work organization but unable to achieve this because of trade union obstruction. However, historically this argument is not proven.[71]

As Chapter 3 demonstrates, more common still is the assertion that the UK's comparative economic decline began after trade unions in collective bargaining reached the peak of their power in the 1970s. However, the post-war years until 1973, referred to as the golden age, consolidated comparative economic decline; during this period the UK's growth and productivity performance compared with the recent past was very favourable, although relatively less so. This suggests that factors far beyond the industrial relations system were significant elements in comparative economic performance, whereas from the early 1960s until the late 1970s domestic economic policy cushioned comparative and relative economic decline.

Cushioning economic decline?

Kaldor argues and demonstrates that in an emergent context of relative and comparative economic decline stop–go policies were the most viable, if second-best, option available to government in the post-war period.[72] Kaldor recognized that economic problems such as accelerating unit labour costs, the control of inflation and declining market share in world export markets have sociological and political explanations beyond the confines of economic theory. However, this limitation illustrates the point in Clegg's quotation at the beginning of this chapter. Use of the industrial relations system as a harbinger of reform to decelerate economic decline and cushion or reverse poor economic performance magnifies the problem.

The 1964–70 Labour governments had ambitious plans, summarized under the headings 'the white heat of technology' and 'the Ministry for Economic Affairs', to reposition the UK economy within European if not Atlanticist economies. In addition, the reform of industrial relations detailed by the Donovan Report appeared as a further component in the strategy for improved labour productivity and better management of work organization at plant level. However, economic performance independent of industrial relations challenged the viability of the Donovan proposals. Stop–go policies remained the main instrument of policy and became more severe in the wake of the 1967 devaluation of sterling but continued to cushion decline. However, more crucially, stop–go policies limited the growth trajectory of the economy to the potential of the domestic manufacturing sector not the market potential in export economies. Devaluation improved the price competitiveness of manufactured exports, but to deliver on this the government required a sustained improvement in labour productivity at current costs. However, incomes controls and devaluation combined to reduce disposable incomes, making wage restraint difficult.

Throughout the 1970s, international competition for export markets in the European community and the UK's traditional markets stiffened. More significantly, European and Japanese exporters entered the UK domestic market in many areas of manufacturing. By the early 1980s, economic and political reaction concentrated on efforts to reduce UK labour costs through managerial strategies that deskilled labour or through patterns of organizational change and technological upgrading.[73] Gallie *et al*. suggest that employers utilize both types of policy, with reskilling confined to those who were already skilled and in relatively secure jobs. Moreover, they suggest that cost or quality strategies had limited effects during the 1980s in large measure because of the short-termist nature of UK management.[74]

Between 1979 and 1982, the management of economic policy became more damaging to economic performance than industrial relations when world-wide recession had serious effects on the UK economy. However, the arrival of revenue streams from North Sea oil had the potential to release the UK from the traditionally binding constraint of the balance of payments. However, strict adherence to the doctrines of classical monetarism had further deflationary effects on the economy.[75] Efforts to suppress the rate of expansion in the supply of money forced up interest rates to around 14 per cent. In addition, the abolition of the 1947 Exchange Control Regulation Act saw a surge of investment abroad by UK manufacturing firms and the closure of some domestic plants. The sterling exchange rate accelerated to well over $2, pricing UK manufacturing exporters such as luxury car makers out of the US market in particular.

In the context of a wider world recession, UK economic policy moved beyond cushioning economic decline to a position where it became procyclical. Policy not only cushioned decline but reinforced and accelerated decline beyond the confines of the economic cycle.

The Lawson boom of 1987 repeated this, as did the efforts of John Major to keep the UK in the European Exchange Rate mechanism in 1992. In both cases, domestic recession stimulated interest rates of around 15 per cent, even though the government had moved away from classical monetarism to an interest rate policy.

Throughout the 1980s, the relationship between economic performance and the industrial relations system remained contentious. However, the evidence suggests that movements in the real economy may have improved management ability to control the performance of labour in employment rather than reform of the industrial relations system by legal intervention.[76] The Labour government attempted to side-step the problem of interest rate policy by handing control of interest rates to the Bank of England. The Monetary Policy Committee has an inflation target of 2.5 per cent and if the rate falls below this figure the committee's terms of reference require it to reflate the economy by cutting rates.

The relationship between UK economic decline and the industrial relations system has produced a variety of proximate generalizations, summarized as the 'worker problem', that prevent improved work organization and a delayed deployment of investment. The 1980s heralded legal regulation as the solution to these problems, an intervention that led to a 'transformation of the UK economy and a reversal of economic decline'.[77] The undermining of these arguments exposes one of the problems that Thatcherite economic policies sought to expel – short-termism. Economic performance in the late 1980s had to be better than that in the early 1980s because of economic stagnation at that time. A longer-term – historically informed – assessment appears to indicate two themes, which are followed up by subsequent chapters. First, this period consolidated historically embedded management and employer aims and interests to reinforce short-termism and efforts to reduce costs. Chapter 4 demonstrated that the withdrawal of the state and deregulation can only further reinforce such a tendency. Second, the post-war period was one of cushioned economic decline: the 1980s through to the early 1990s represented a concentrated version of this without the cushion of cyclical macroeconomic policy. The process of reform in the industrial relations system since the 1960s has had only a marginal effect on the economic performance of the UK economy. This is the case because reform here did not solve the main problems in the UK economy.

Short-termism in the state represents a structural framework that inhibits employer deployment of quality-based competitive strategies and productivity, raising value added strategies. In contrast to this, the majority of UK employers deploy management control strategies based on the use of low-cost deskilled labour forces.[78] Low-cost low-skill strategies have a further structural impact on consumer demand – low incomes that result from such strategies also reinforce their deployment. This further embeds short-termism in employer and management strategies, yet the 'worker problem' appears to remain.

The worker problem?

This section briefly reviews the 'worker problem' and repositions it as a derivative of embedded managerial and employer interests. The contemporary ideological and generalized proximate castigation of UK workers as a primary cause of economic decline has a long heritage.[79] In the 1980s, the state specifically identified the worker problem as the key issue in the UK's post-war economic performance.

Trade unions opposed changes in working practices and fed the inflationary expectations of their members.[80]

What is remarkable is the extent to which the role and structure of trade unions, collective bargaining and the industrial relations system are each positioned as operating in manners that are distinct and separate from the interests of employers and the state. Broadberry and Crafts, for example, associate the worker problem with multi-unionism and restrictive practices, to conclude that in the immediate post-war years, this pattern of regulation prevented a movement to US-style Fordist systems of production and remuneration.[81] Barnett goes further than this to argue that the power and restrictive presence of trade unions in the workplace so worried post-war governments that they wasted UK Marshall Aid on creating a 'new Jerusalem' in housing programmes and the welfare state.

The rhetoric of Barnett's argument is more powerful than the evidence provided to support his claims.[82] However, material published in 1951, supported by contemporary historically informed material, throws doubt on Barnett's argument.[83] Zweig demonstrates that in many sectors of the economy management concern with restrictive practices was limited. Such practices were an integral component of the production system. Moreover, these practices were in some sectors a part of delegated systems of work organization and production management. Further, as Clark demonstrates, employer representatives in the AACP were totally against the introduction of US systems of production and management for a variety of reasons.[84] First, they would necessitate the renegotiation of workplace agreements and possibly increase the power of trade unions. Second, the associated scrapping and renewal of plant would damage the UK's post-war recovery and result in the loss of established markets to US competition. Third, the capital costs of such a move were prohibitive. Equally, the move would necessitate costly training programmes which would increase labour costs on the shop floor for supervisors and managers.

Kilpatrick and Lawson argue that the relatively early presence of craft trade unions in the workplace consolidated working-class resistance to the introduction of mass production methods and associated patterns of work organization and remuneration. More peculiarly, they suggest that the presence of decentralized collective bargaining from the 1890s persuaded management to avoid confrontation with trade unions and concentrate on traditional empire and (what become) sterling area markets. In summary, collective bargaining in the workplace has adversely affected productivity rates and technological innovation over the whole of the period since the 1890s.[85] The arguments developed in Chapters 2 and 3 throw some doubt on this conclusion. Empire markets were primary because they sustained existing plant and production methods, where UK manufacturers held a competitive advantage.

In the early 1980s, Conservative governments attempted to destroy the industrial relations system in an effort to repel a major component of the worker problem – their ability to push earnings above increases in labour productivity. Previously, the Donovan Report identified this phenomenon as 'wage drift', a key element in informal workplace industrial relations. The evidence suggests that although governments since 1979 have experienced some success in reforming if not destroying the industrial relations system they have been unable to prevent the UK's comparatively high increases in annual earnings. Between 1980 and 1996, average annual increases in earnings stood at 10 per cent, a figure higher than the UK's industrial competitors and much higher than annual increases in labour productivity in either manufacturing or the economy as a whole over the same period. If earnings rise faster than labour productivity, unit labour costs increase at a rate faster than productivity increases.[86]

The industrial relations system has been restructured to facilitate greater managerial control over work organization, but it has failed to solve a key aspect of the worker problem – excessive increases in earnings. However, collective bargaining, the institution through which 'trade unions resist change and feed the inflationary expectations of their members', has a reduced and reformed coverage than in the 1970s.[87] The worker problem remains because it is structured by the interests of employers and the state.

Gallie *et al*. demonstrate that reform and restructuring in the industrial relations system has stimulated an optimistic and pessimistic scenario about work, its organization, regulation and remuneration.[88] The minority experience the optimistic scenario, those whom Hutton refers to as the 40 per cent in the UK's 40:30:30 society, in secure internal labour markets in which career and promotion prospects are good. In contrast, the majority endure a pessimistic scenario in which technology and computers deskill workers in a manner that is more routine than the alleged situation under mass production Fordism.

In the contemporary period, employer and management interests appear more short term than previously. The reform and restructuring of an already delegated system of industrial relations appears to have further embedded a structure of low pay – low productivity work systems for comparatively and relatively cheap labour. The effects of labour market polarization are that the formally qualified minority receive more training, whereas the poorly qualified or unqualified receive little or nothing.[89] The worker problem remains because the state and employer problem remain. More significantly, the effects of reform in industrial relations on comparative economic performance, particularly rising unit labour costs, appear marginal. As Clegg argues, economics alone cannot provide a theory to diagnose problems in industrial relations or the reform of industrial relations.[90] Equally, its exclusion from institutional analysis has been problematic.

Conclusions

The historically driven, institutionally informed yet empirically underpinned arguments developed in this chapter lead to four broad conclusions.

First, the particularized development or formative influences in the UK state are the central institutional antecedent of the industrial relations system. The partial incorporation of the employed class in the UK state posed no challenge to the political interests of the ruling class or the economic interests of the industrial class. Alternatively, collective *laissez faire* fractionalized the economic and political interests of the employed class to reproduce a contradictory short-termism and self-regulation similar to that secured and retained into the contemporary period by the state and employers. Collective *laissez faire* has outlived policies designed to destroy it and retains intellectual and democratic significance with a reduced if still credible empirical presence in collective bargaining.

Second, since 1945, efforts to secure order and reform in the industrial relations system have sought to improve bargaining systems based on formally negotiated agreements at plant or firm level. The premise of contemporary reform within and beyond such agreements promotes the managerial prerogative to undermine the legitimacy of collectivism in job regulation in the employment relationship. The partial erosion of collective bargaining and the hollowing out of auxiliary legislation in the 1980s focused an explicit return to formative influences in the UK state based not on partial incorporation but on institutional exclusion. Contemporary legal intervention combined with the poor take-up of imported managerial strategies such as HRM have failed to transform the industrial relations system. This demonstrates that the shared economic and democratic benefits of individualism, HRM and non-unionism are beyond empirical articulation or observation for the majority. In the 1980s, order and reform of industrial relations was premised on destroying the post-war system, a determination that pushed economic policy beyond cushioning economic decline to a position that accelerated decline.

Third, the relationships among economic performance, economic decline and the industrial relations system have produced a variety of proximate generalizations, summarized as the 'worker problem'. Over the post-war period, these problems prevented movements towards higher productivity Fordist work organization and the release of investment funds for industry. In contrast, the 1980s was heralded as a transformation in the economic fortunes of UK industry. However, comparative economic analysis over a longer period than the immediate past demonstrates that far from expelling embedded short-termism in UK industry the Thatcher and Major governments reinforced its presence. The 1980s represent a microversion of the whole of the period since 1945. A spurt of recovery from a depressed level of economic activity followed by decline; cushioned in the former but accelerated in the latter – this marks the main difference between the two periods. The evidence suggests that collective *laissez faire* in the industrial relations system had some marginal effects on economic performance, but it was not significant in the scale of its independent effects.

Fourth, the economic effects of reform in the industrial relations system have failed to remove elements of the worker problem previously attributed to trade unions and collective bargaining. Low productivity, high unit labour costs but comparatively low wages remain as central features in the system. Hence, isolation of the worker problem from the employer problem and the problem of the state has only a marginal historical significance. The forcible reform of the former cannot overcome embedded structural constraints particularized in the last groups.

The remaining chapters examine these four issues in more detail. The historical evaluation of the industrial relations system and the failure of UK employers to introduce new structures to regulate pay and conditions in the workplace reveal much about the particularized development of the UK state and its institutional reproduction in the industrial relations system. Positioning industrial relations and the industrial relations system in the wider aims and objectives of the UK state will provide historically informed insights into contemporary issues and problems that confront the system.

6 The industrial relations system and post-war recovery

The failure of the Anglo-American Council for Productivity?

Introduction

A historical evaluation of institutional stability in the industrial relations system and the failure of UK employers to introduce new structures to regulate pay, conditions and the organization of work reveal much about the particularized development and subsequent aims and objectives of the UK state. Equally, this evaluation can provide historically informed insights into contemporary issues that confront the industrial relations system.

The endurance of institutional stability in the industrial relations system and management practice during the initial post-war years rested on two factors. First, securing the international viability of the UK economy and, second and relatedly, the respite that victory in the Second World War afforded to embedded patterns of management practice and associated patterns of industrial relations. This chapter addresses these factors through the vehicle of the Anglo-American Council for Productivity (AACP), in particular its UK section. The AACP researched the issues of management practice and productivity in UK manufacturing with the aim of transforming management practice in order to raise productivity levels to those of the average US firm.[1] US management practice informed the research undertaken by the AACP and its subsequent recommendations. However, the aims and objectives of the UK section successfully diluted US-inspired proposals. This process afforded representatives of UK employers and management an opportunity to secure and sustain embedded patterns in management practice and industrial relations.

The first section briefly recapitulates how the post-war output drive secured the viability of the UK economy. The second section then draws out the implications of the output drive for the industrial relations system. The next section contrasts the aims and interests of representatives of UK employers and management with recent treatments of the period that emphasize the negative effect of the industrial relations system on sustaining the post-war output drive into the 1960s and 1970s. This section demonstrates the isolation of industrial relations as a central explanation of post-war economic decline.

Moreover, the documentary and primary source material illustrates the apparent necessity and embedded nature of short-termism on the part of the state and employers.*

The viability of the UK economy

The UK government used the Marshall Plan as a financial mechanism to secure the viability of the UK economy as a sovereign national economic pathway. In contrast to this, US Marshall planners, particularly those in the ACCP, sought a long-term restructuring, if not transformation, of European capitalism on an integrationist model.[2] The Economic Co-operation Agency (ECA), the centralist body created to administer the Marshall Plan, defined European recovery in terms of 1952 consumption standards. However, these standards were ill-defined and loosely measured against output levels that would enable European economies to finance the necessary level of imports beyond 1952.[3] Hence, the objective was to release European economies from the potentially deflationary effects of national balance of payments constraints. The ECA held that such a level of production would necessitate an intra-European Customs Union – a single European market – and the free movement of goods, services and labour. The US strategy and associated measures aimed to make European currencies 'hard' by raising the scale of European production and reducing costs of production. The recovery programme was strategized as a windfall intervention, yet represented a firm economic and political relationship conceptualized to restructure national economies within a pan-European capitalism.[4] However, as Chapter 2 demonstrates, US strategy was heavily diluted by the intransigence of European states.

In contrast to the US view, European states and the UK in particular viewed the Marshall Plan as a mechanism that would underpin a continuity in national policy.[5] By necessity, within national aims and objectives the outlook was short term. In this respect, the UK's post war recovery of output did not raise the scale of economic efficiency but did have a considerable impact on labour productivity. The output drive was in economic terms marginal, sustaining low capital costs and comparatively low levels of investment in new plant. Here, the volume of output at the existing scale of capital was the main consideration, hence the focus on labour productivity within prescriptive mechanisms such as the AACP.

Marshall Aid had an insignificant effect on the scale of UK manufacturing for three reasons. First, before the arrival of Marshall Aid, the economy was experiencing full employment, hence it was not necessary to undertake considerable investment to create employment. Second, and related, the vast majority of UK Marshall Aid secured funding for imports of food and raw

---

* The documentary research for this chapter was undertaken at the Modern Records Centre at the University of Warwick (MRC), The Public Record Office at Kew (PRO) and the Stack Collection in the University of Leicester Library (LUSC).

materials. In the context of a fully employed manufacturing economy, this was the most sensible course of action. The UK had to export manufactured products for imports of food and raw materials. The finance of imports is the basis of the third factor. The UK's lack of dollars to pay for the necessary imports threatened an export-led recovery. Using Marshall Aid to purchase food and raw materials sustained the recovery of output by funding the dollar gap to secure imports.

There is general agreement that the economic effects of the Marshall Plan on the UK's economy were marginal. The UK allocation – amounting to up to 7.5 per cent of GNP in 1949 – was sufficient to finance two and a half years' national growth.[6] However, although the economic impact of Marshall Aid was marginal, it was critical in maintaining the UK's output and export drives. Economic theory is not necessarily useless in this regard; however, its utility is not, as economists suggest, positive. Alternatively, the deployment of Marshall Aid funds demonstrates how marginal economic theory may be within wider – historically embedded – aims, constraints on and objectives in state policy. In financial terms, maintaining the UK's overseas defence commitments and the sterling area were significant cost constraints on the domestic economy. A cost minimization strategy that excluded the potential of future revenue streams would have suggested an early devaluation of the pound, curtailment of the sterling area and a run down of UK defence commitments. Such a course of action could not prevail, for the UK's whole approach to foreign policy and the Marshall Plan was not governed by economics but by perceived political and strategic necessity.[7]

To sustain the UK's national pathway, it was necessary to maintain the level of exports; this in turn legitimized the marginal output drive, which over the short term precluded the need for large-scale industrial renewal. A volume-based effort delivered by existing plant sustained post-war recovery well into the late 1950s. The UK's wider political economy on the Marshall Plan mediated post-war recovery, hence considerations beyond cost minimization governed strategy and policy. The potential of future revenue streams, the security of the domestic market and disparate export markets, many in the sterling area, were key considerations. Closure of the sterling area may have reduced the costs of recovery but would have simultaneously reduced potential revenue streams. For example, in 1938 empire and sterling area markets made up 45 per cent of UK exports and rose to a level of 50 per cent after the war, where they remained until 1958.[8] In the short to medium term, replacement of these markets was impossible, hence by acting instrumentally in the short term the state secured an efficient deployment of Marshall Aid funds. First, the UK was a manufacturing economy that needed food and raw material imports, which it paid for with exports of manufactured goods. Second, there is no evidence to suggest that the longer-term economic benefits of restructuring and scaling up of UK industry would have been greater than the cost of losing established markets. In summary, a functional if contradictory policy secured the economic viability of the UK state. The policy secured recovery, but its relatively libertarian nature later proved contradictory in terms of comparative systems of work organization, labour productivity and in terms of structural problems in the industrial relations system. This policy was complemented by an industrial efficiency programme that sought to 'Americanize' management practice, industrial relations and work organization in order to reduce unit labour costs and boost labour productivity.[9]

The industrial efficiency programme and the industrial relations system

In large measure, the existing scale of plant and machinery secured the UK's post-war recovery of output.[10] Recovery of the national pathway prevailed in spite of, not because of, the aims and aspiration of US Marshall planners in the AACP's industrial efficiency programme. The AACP's UK section embraced the output drive to legitimize historically embedded employer and management interests. These interests centred around an institutional framework that supported and displayed a strong preference for state abstention to legitimize autonomous and short-termist approaches to management practice and collective bargaining. The issues are examined under four headings. First, the aims of the AACP; second, the position of its UK section; third, the limitations of the AACP's programme of visits to the USA; and last, the AACP and stability in management practice and industrial relations.

The aims of the AACP

The AACP aimed to provide UK manufacturers with prescriptive lessons from US best practice in terms of production management, management accounting and standardization in production. A transatlantic education programme involved sixty-six team visits to the USA, where team members who came from industry and trade unions studied US production management, work organization and management accounting. Some specialist groups examined issues such as factory layout, palletization and materials handling. Each team produced an 'American' best practice report.[11]

The overall conclusion of the best practice reports suggested that improved labour productivity required higher levels of investment in mechanized production sustained over the long term.[12] This would lead to more efficient production management in materials handling and improved systems of cost and management accounting. In combination, such measures would yield management a more accurate measure of unit costs and facilitate lower costs of production and higher labour productivity over longer production runs. The evidence contained in the AACP reports focuses on the deficiencies of UK management in the highlighted areas.[13]

Although AACP research and reports emphasized the deficiencies of UK management, the AACP's UK section diluted many proposals and successfully rejected others. Stafford Cripps, the Chancellor of the Exchequer and co-founder of the AACP, delegated the UK section of the AACP to the Federation of

British Industry (FBI), the British Employers' Confederation (BEC) and the TUC. This process enabled representatives of management and employers to position their established agenda in the UK section.[14]

In 1943, the FBI indicated that UK recovery from war as a sovereign economic power would require immediate output and export drives to take priority over longer-term efforts towards industrial modernization and restructuring. In addition to this, the FBI argued that to recover as a national pathway the UK economy would need protection from US competition through maintenance of the sterling area in empire and middle eastern markets.[15] By 1948, the UK government and industry were not in a position to entertain industrial reconstruction on the scale envisaged by Marshall planners in the industrial efficiency and productivity programme. The disaster of sterling convertibility in the summer of 1947 compounded existing materials and capital shortages and drained UK dollar reserves. Further, the lack of hard currency precluded large-scale imports of capital equipment and materials from the USA.[16]

In 1943, the BOT began to examine issues such as industrial efficiency in the light of an eventual victory in the war.[17] BOT preference, although it was critical of 'bad management', assumed that the UK's manufacturing base would continue to serve a less than standardized domestic market and varied export markets, particularly in the sterling area. Equally, the BOT assumed that domestic modernization in industry, including industrial relations, would be managed on a plural and tripartite basis.[18] The hard currency that was subsequently, if unexpectedly, provided by Marshall Aid served as the basis on which this recovery by continuity was pursued.

The pattern of institutional delegation clearly demonstrates the process of libertarian particularization in the UK state and the prescriptive failure of the AACP illustrates the functional if contradictory effects of the pattern and process. The AACP's prescriptive failure together with the process of delegation appeared functional as the views of the UK section mirrored the overall aims and objectives of the state on UK recovery. However, although functional, this process later demonstrated the limitations of short-termism and its potential for contradiction. First, it was what employers wanted, to the perhaps necessary exclusion of other interests and perspectives. Second, the involvement of employer interest associations in economic policy is rarely progressive in decision-making because such groups lack corporatist central authority.[19] However, the monopoly role of the FBI and BEC in the AACP's UK section enabled them to establish their conservative position on markets and industrial modernization. Hence, the embedded process of institutional delegation in collective *laissez faire* is not an executive process. In the case of post-war industrial relations and economic recovery, delegation was functional for the central state – it allowed them to do very little. It was equally functional for employer and management representatives – it allowed them to position their case that reinforced the position of the state. The potential for contradiction in this position became evident later in the post-war period. The FBI and BEC positioned a strategy for work organization, management practice and associated patterns of industrial relations that subsequently structured the short-term interests of workers and trade unions in increasing labour productivity at the expense of improving and raising the scale of productivity in capital. The records of the FBI and the UK section of the AACP clearly reflect this structure.

The AACP's UK section

Norman Kipping, Director General of the FBI and a joint secretary of the AACP's UK section, made it clear to UK trade associations that there would be no US interference with the UK section. Kipping conceived and managed the UK section as a solely UK initiative that excluded the government and the ECA, representing the interests of the employers but incorporating the institutional representation of organized labour.[20] In addition, he made it clear that in terms of productivity improvement the main criterion for UK industry should be the lowest cost over productivity per man–hour.[21] The notion of lowest cost over productivity per man–hour makes economic sense when 'lowest cost' refers to the scale of operations. If the volume of output is the main consideration, it is possible to improve labour productivity at a low capital cost. This is the case even though increased output encounters the law of diminishing returns to sustain a growing level of allocative inefficiency. For the government and the UK section, this was necessary because in the short term securing the international viability of the UK state precluded raising the scale of UK capital by significant new investment in plant. In contrast to this, the post-war output drive aimed to increase output at the existing scale of plant by focusing on labour productivity. A move to restructure, scrap and scale up manufacturing industry would have shut UK manufacturers out of export markets, weakened the balance of payments and stalled post-war recovery. This combination of effects would have virtually bankrupted the UK economy, the situation that previously prevailed in the summer of 1947.

AACP documents from 1948 support this position. In the view of the UK section, measures to increase productivity per man–hour through greater capital investment would, in the short to medium term, have increased unit costs.[22] This was the case because of the loss in output and the set-up costs created by the deployment of new production systems. Equally, new systems would also require new (US style) systems of management practice and more institutionalized collective bargaining. It was imperative to avoid this because it might strengthen the position of trade unions in the workplace.[23] As an alternative to this, the UK section made it clear that for UK manufacturers output must prevail over productivity, with quantity rather than the quality or scale of production representing the main imperative. Further, this alternative was necessary because of only marginal standardization in UK markets (domestically and overseas) compared with that found in the domestic US market.[24] There was a considerable rationalization of output in the war years, but in the post-war year period a diversity in end-user requirements nullified this process. The UK section cited examples in steel manufacture, metal window frames, gear cutting equipment and the production of cooker hobs.[25] These arguments were short term but necessary to defend the relatively small scale of UK manufacturing plants that served disparate markets.[26] ACCP records demonstrate that at the time the vast majority of UK manufacturing plants employed fewer than 500 workers, with only sixty employing over 5,000 employees.[27]

The themes of marginal improvement in productivity at existing scale are also evident in FBI/ACCP documents on regional productivity conferences and exhibitions. Here, the documents detail an FBI determination always to retain overall control of the conferences. This was the case because the main conference constituency was 'top management', who needed practical information on applications in the current climate not heavily technical explanations.[28] This view prevailed because the introduction of new systems for work organization would require a renegotiation of collective bargaining agreements, existing demarcation agreements and involve considerable expenditure on training. In the planning stages for conferences in Leicester and Nottingham, the FBI's technical director suggested that displays on material handling, storage and factory layout should focus on best practice in the UK. The objective was to indicate how UK best practice could incorporate aspects of US techniques but not be transformed by it.[29] It would appear that practical applications in the context of existing best practice reflected the primary consideration of increasing output while minimizing capital expenditure.

The report of the AACP's fifth session in 1952 consolidated further the cost minimization approach. To improve output and productivity in the short term, the maximum utilization of existing resources was necessary, a direct implication of this was considerable overtime working. The available evidence demonstrates the early institutionalization of overtime working. From 1948 until 1979, employees in the manufacturing sector worked an average of three hours overtime per week. If the total overtime figures are disaggregated, to separate men, women and apprentices, who were not paid on adult rates, the actual number of workers on overtime appears to be between 25 per cent and 35 per cent of the manufacturing workforce. This increases the figure for overtime working to over ten hours per week during the 1950s and eight hours per week throughout the 1960s until 1979.[30]

In addition to a high use of overtime working, the AACP's final report establishes that during the previous four years employers had not experienced significant labour inflexibility because of trade union opposition. However, the report added that over the longer term improvement in output and labour productivity could not be sustained by this route. Alternatively, significantly higher levels of mechanization in production, more power tools for intermediate stages in production and better factory layout and production organization were necessary. Further, the report reiterates that over the past four years an increase in capital expenditure by industry would have reduced output and export levels.[31] This employer-dominated view complements other influential views.

Middlemas suggested that employer support for the cost minimization approach reflected the prevalence of an embedded cartel mentality within employer associations and trade associations based on secure markets and comparatively low wage costs.[32] By placing the FBI and BEC centre stage in the management of the UK's industrial efficiency programme, the state ensured these embedded interests received maximum exposure. This exposure further embedded the FBI's long-standing preference for recovery without significant reconstruction. This recovery was evident in a continuity of management practice, however the AACP's final report portrayed this as a victory of US managerialism.[33]

The aims of the UK section corresponded with those of the government. In addition to this, its aims secured the narrow material interests of employers. However, the victory of US managerialism was considerable in that it incorporated organized labour and the TUC into the productivity programme.[34] Beyond this, however, the operational mechanics of US management failed to dislodge the UK's embedded politics of workplace productivity that the work of the UK section actually sustained.

Within the AACP, the TUC was, in the main, supportive. The General Council actively promoted the productivity drive and saw the AACP as a mechanism that would further strengthen and promote union membership and collective bargaining.[35] However, the TUC indicated that without greater capital investment there would be no material gain on the USA, this was the case even though productivity increases between 1946 and 1949 were significant.[36] In addition to this argument, the General Council made reference to material published in *The Times* newspaper. This evidence suggested that without significant capital renewal the productivity initiative could only deliver a 2–3 per cent increase in productivity per annum.[37] Equally, the TUC was unhappy with the manner in which the UK section appeared to divert AACP findings and direct them specifically to top management without full reference to report findings. This was particularly the case in terms of improved mechanization and training for shop floor operatives.[38] Last, the TUC expressed concern over the manner in which the UK section moulded work study techniques to suit the particular interests of the FBI and the BEC. As a response, the TUC organized its own trips to the USA to examine the issue.[39]

The sustainability of the output drive in the absence of capital renewal and the consequences for shop floor workers was the TUC's main concern. In its submissions to the AACP, the TUC argued that the UK could not compete with nor should be compared with the USA in any meaningful way.[40] This was the case because the US manufacturing sector operated on different measures of productivity and productivity improvement.[41] The TUC production department found that US firms measured productivity in terms of man–hours per unit of output, a method not used in the UK. Equally, in correspondence with the US Bureau of Statistics, British Sugar argued it could not understand the figures, in particular 'trends in man–hour per unit of output'.[42] In addition to these difficulties, after visits to the USA, the TUC appeared unconvinced that under the auspices of the UK section manufacturing industry would be able or inclined to make the necessary improvements on a voluntary basis.[43]

The US programme of visits

The programme of UK visits to the USA sought to demonstrate the benefits of and encourage the take-up of two aspects in US management practice that provided a structure for high productivity. First, a 'scientific approach' to management that presented the manager as a technically informed economic and social engineer. Second, institutionalized pluralism in industrial relations centred on collective bargaining managed in the workplace, constitutional trade union recognition and a commitment to job security.[44]

Hoffman, co-chair of the AACP and Director of the ECA, saw the programme of visits as being of technical importance, but equally visits would expose the UK, particularly UK labour, to the benefits of the 'American way'.[45] Hoffman based his enthusiasm for the visits programme on a belief that 'scarcity' caused all 'distributional' conflicts between management and labour over productivity and wages.[46] Moreover, Hoffman saw increasing productivity and efficiency through measures such as 'scientific management', business planning and constitutional pluralism in the workplace as the only way to reduce scarcity and improve distribution. The material in Chapter 2 demonstrates that apolitical approaches to productivity improvement purport to contain the interests of organized labour by incorporating them into Fordism. Although an intense debate remains over the extent to which UK management, production systems and industrial relations were Fordist, the limitations of Hoffman's success in stimulating convergence suggest only a limited exposure to Fordist systems at this time.[47]

Hoffman's apolitical views on productivity improvement informed his faith in prescriptive mechanisms such as the AACP. However, these views became ideologically charged in the 1950s, when the anti-Communism of US foreign policy further exposed divisions between the US and UK sections of the AACP. US Marshall planners, Hoffman and the US State department advocated the aims of pan-European reconstruction on a centralized basis. In contrast, the UK government advocated recovery of the national pathway on a sovereign basis. Hoffman championed the apolitical benefits of improved productivity for both management and labour, yet he was operating within a series of institutions (AACP and ECA) that were increasingly caught up in the wider aims of US foreign policy. Ultimately, the divergence of views between the US and UK sections disappeared as Hoffman accepted the national distinctiveness of embedded interests in the FBI's responses to the AACP. The maintenance of national distinctiveness rendered the programme of visits and the promotion of constitutional industrial relations managed in the workplace insignificant in post-war UK recovery. Hoffman accepted that the UK section and the UK government wanted the AACP to legitimize and maintain the UK's national pathway not transform it.

The fact that UK management and the TUC came to accept the prescriptive presence of US best practice, if not its adoption in the workplace, cushioned Hoffman's acceptance of UK conservatism. This was the case because the presentation of managers trained in quantitative production control and labour relations positioned a 'scientific' approach to management as an impartial mechanism capable of securing improved productivity for the benefit of firms and workers alike. Marshall planners in the US section argued that these practices had enabled US management to operate in a 'Taylorised' manner since the 'new deal' era. In essence, the new deal, supplemented by the US rearmament programme, saw scientific approaches to production management and constitutional pluralism instituted in many large US workplaces.[48] More significantly, this process moved management control systems and production techniques beyond craft production regulated by simple managerial controls. In contrast to these, technical control strategies regulated by the discipline of the assembly line and collective bargaining managed the process of mass – standardized – production.[49] Numerous AACP reports bear out this point and suggest that US management appeared able to mechanize, standardize, monitor and restructure production with little opposition from the workforce.[50]

The oppositional role of UK trade unions to mechanization, the erosion of craft practices and productivity bargaining appear as a central flaws in the UK's *flawed* Fordism and the prescriptive failure of the AACP.[51] However, US manufacturing firms were more likely than their UK counterparts to invest in mechanized production systems that deskilled labour because of their high wage costs compared with those in the UK. In addition, at the functional level, the sheer size of the US domestic market and its scope for standardization made these innovations economically sensible, whereas in the UK they may have been more marginal. Third, documentary evidence demonstrates that employer and management dominance in the UK section of the AACP eliminated enthusiasm for these innovations. Last, contrary to the generalization of US 'best practice', corporate pluralism, mechanization and high wages were not in evidence throughout the US economy.[52] In submissions to the UK section, the TUC made this point very clear. Equally, trade unions argued this point in their evaluation of individual AACP reports.[53] Moreover, the vast majority of AACP trips concentrated on eastern seaboard states, where institutional pluralism was in evidence, e.g. the AACP building and construction team confined its fieldwork to Washington, DC. This caused the National Federation of Building Operatives to comment that the report tells us very little other than that beyond areas of regulation there is overt discrimination and low wages. Where there is regulation, wages are high and conditions are good. Overall, the Federation concluded that UK wages in this sector were very low compared with the average US wage.[54]

The UK government and the US government favoured a pluralist model of industrial relations, but within the AACP national patterns of regulation held prominence over constitutional patterns of productivity bargaining in the workplace. Although the AACP's UK section, with tacit support from the government, legitimized existing patterns of management practice as efficient, AACP reports on UK industry document incompetent management practice in all sectors of manufacturing.[55] Management practice was unscientific and demonstrated poor production preplanning and ineffective work study.[56] However, the UK section successfully positioned these characteristics as contingent elements within the output drive; in turn, this led strategists within the AACP, in particular Hoffman, to accept the legitimacy of these aims. By 1952, it would appear that a plural, if adversarial, pattern of industrial relations was necessary to sustain 'unscientific management' that the UK section fought so hard to maintain.[57] Congressional propaganda on the use of Marshall Aid supported the intransigence of the UK section. Between 1948 and 1951, the UK industrial output increased by 25 per cent and was 45 per cent above the 1938 level.[58] This recovery prevailed despite the failure of the UK section to accept US labour and production practices and without a transformation of management practice.

Stability in management practice and industrial relations

One implication of stability in management practice for industrial relations was a consolidation of the existing framework for job regulation. In rejecting US proposals for management practice, the UK section did not even consider US proposals for industrial relations. The UK section wrote industrial relations issues out of their agenda in September 1948.[59] However, they conceded that industrial relations issues would crop up and they recommended that existing collective bargaining machinery should deal with these issues.[60]

The FBI and the TUC presented separate and mutually exclusive defences of free collective bargaining within the UK section. Many employers visualized this as a mechanism to re-establish autocratic power in the workplace.[61] In this context, private sector employers sought to avoid institutionalized job regulation negotiated and managed at workplace level. The FBI and individual managers demonstrated considerable concern to prevent the more positive aspects of AACP reports on visits to US firms getting through to workers at productivity exhibitions in the UK.[62] Moreover, many employers saw national agreements as a mechanism to undermine workplace lay activism. This position came to represent one of the major post-war miscalculations by UK management. The miscalculation was particularly evident in sectors that were heavily reliant on overtime working – a central feature of the post-war output drive. This was the case because overtime agreements were, despite managerial preference for national agreements, negotiated at workplace level.[63] In addition to this, employer resistance to the decentralization of collective bargaining structured the emergence of shop floor resistance to piecemeal reforms in job regulation. The accommodation of this problem became the focus of negotiations in an emergent system of informal industrial relations. However, voluntary collective bargaining, multi-unionism and workplace restriction became widely accepted as essential aspects in the productivity programme and its supportive role in the output drive.[64] A further unexpected development did emerge, however.

The consolidation of existing patterns in management practice and industrial relations occurred within a fully employed economy. This further weakened employer concern with productivity and labour costs because the domestic market was secure as was the sterling area for exports. The imperative of output accelerated the shifting focus in collective bargaining away from national agreements to the workplace.[65] As this shift progressed further during the late 1950s, shop stewards emerged as central actors in workplace collective bargaining, favouring a localized if primitive pattern of negotiation that lacked formalized procedure.[66]

Evidence also suggests that employers whose primary concern was with output, such as those in the car industry, routinely accepted potentially problematic local pay deals that supplemented nationally agreed norms as a matter of course. The negotiation of this order did not necessarily secure any quantifiable improvements in productivity, precisely because employer concern focused almost exclusively on output.[67] Employers showed little concern over this because they were able pass increased costs on to purchasers.[68]

The movement in industrial relations activity to the workplace flowed directly from post-war recovery, a process within which industrial relations and management practice remained unreconstructed. The industrial relations system retained stability based on autonomous patterns of collective bargaining, with informal developments consolidating this at workplace level. This pattern of regulation appeared functional, yet it was contradictory. Full employment secured the voluntary nature of the industrial relations system, leaving employer interests relatively intact, but gradually the imperative of output undermined private sector industry level collective agreements. To secure greater control over labour and work organization in the late 1950s and early 1960s, employers attempted to introduce components of productivity bargaining such as measured day work and formalized time and motion studies. However, in the absence of formalized structures in the workplace, these attempts accelerated conflict. It was the Donovan Commission that proposed putting in place structures for plant-wide pay agreements based on formally constituted plant-level collective bargaining, echoing many recommendations made by the AACP fourteen years earlier.

The economy, industrial relations and the industrial efficiency programme, the last under the direction of the UK section of the AACP, were all necessarily tuned to the short term. The manufacturing sector and the industrial relations framework delivered employee participation and involvement but also secured what successive governments needed – output. One outcome of strong institutions within the industrial relations system, particularly at the workplace, is clearly evident here, even if it was unrecognized at the time. The strength, stability and viability of the industrial relations system were more enduring than the capacity of the UK economy to accommodate each category in the post-war period before the 1970s. The quality, strength, stability and viability stimulated an examination of disorder in the industrial relations system as an independent internal factor rather than an internal development structured and sustained, at least in part, by external factors such as economic and foreign policy in the immediate post-war years.

The post-war output drive and revisionist analysis: the issue of industrial relations

This section examines these issues under three headings. Under the first heading, the significance of contemporary revisionist contributions to the literature that highlight the central role of industrial relations in post-war economic decline are critically detailed. Briefly, under the second heading, industrial relations are positioned against the viability of the UK economy after 1958, whereas under the third heading the isolation of industrial relations with respect to post-war economic decline is examined. Selectivity in the use of empirical material on industrial relations that is designed to support the conclusions contained in wider arguments renders each approach revisionist.

Revisionism and the industrial relations system

The contemporary period has witnessed a major revisionism in the treatment of the initial post-war period and the longer-term decline – and comparative failure – of the UK economy. Prominent in this revision are the approaches taken by Broadberry and Crafts, by Barnett and by Broadberry, who each highlight the central role of industrial relations in the UK's post-war economic decline.[69]

Broadberry and Crafts suggest that economic policy in the immediate post-war period was successful in arresting the UK's balance of payments problems. However, the short-term approach to the recovery of output that achieved this prevented the introduction of structural reforms in the supply side of the economy, particularly in the industrial relations system. In turn, this impaired the UK's medium- to longer-term comparative productivity performance until the industrial relations reforms of the 1980s.[70] The presentation of comparative econometric material appears to support this argument, but it merely confirms that UK productivity was weak. Central actors in the UK section established this position as early as 1948.[71]

More centrally, this revisionist position presents the UK's industrial relations system, in particular multi-unionism within voluntary collective bargaining and associated restrictive practices, as a factor that made long-term adjustment in the economy 'marginal to enviable'.[72] However, there is no consideration of management interests in this conclusion and its revisionism is evident in two ways. First, it fails to position industrial relations and the industrial relations system within the wider structure of post-war recovery. The previous section demonstrates that neither the government nor the employers gave serious consideration to institutional reform of work organization, management practice or industrial relations. The failure to consider these issues in this account positions the chosen course of post-war recovery in terms of its unforeseen consequences and not its short-term necessity defined by the UK's wider objectives within the Marshall Plan. Rightly or wrongly, the focus of post-war recovery was output without significant reconstruction of industry, wherein UK manufacturers continued to serve disparate domestic and overseas markets established before 1938.

In 1948, the majority of UK manufacturing plants were small, with 70 per cent of them employing fewer than 500 workers.[73] The small scale of UK manufacturing plants clearly weakened the potential for productivity growth compared with the USA.[74] Regression analyses designed to capture the scale economies of US and UK plants only demonstrate that the size of UK plants limited their potential for labour productivity growth. Of greater historical significance, the small size of UK plants remained into the 1970s.

Clegg demonstrated that in 1972 45 per cent of total employment in manufacturing was in companies with more than 5,000 employees; however, the size of employing units remained small.[75] Prais confirmed this and suggested that, although the largest 100 firms operated an average of seventy-two plants, each manufacturing plant employed a similar number of employees as in 1948. Manufacturing plants averaged 470 employees per plant in the late 1950s and 440 employees per plant in the early 1970s.[76]

Thus, the size of UK firms increased, but average plant size remained small well into the 1970s.[77] As a scale factor, the likely effect of workplace industrial relations in the manufacturing sector on the UK's comparative productivity performance during the post-war period was insignificant. In comparison, the potential of greater plant size, internal structure, levels of investment and diffusion of new technology – factors that were absent in UK firms but secured by European and US firms – were significant.[78] Hence, the effects of workplace industrial relations appear as one of several marginal factors of explanation in post-war economic decline – a proximate explanation of decline.

Second, the arguments on multi-unionism and associated restrictive practices do not sit well with the documentary evidence or academic analysis conducted in the immediate post-war period. TUC and AACP records indicate that employers and trade unions made considerable progress on the issue of restrictive practices as part of the productivity programme.[79] Responses to the TUC's 'Productivity: The Next Step' initiative indicate that although there was some employer disquiet on restrictive practices relating to overtime there was not a general concern.[80] Equally, trade unions and the TUC were not necessarily insistent on the reintroduction of restrictive practices diluted as a result of wartime conditions.[81] A major study of restrictive practices conducted in the immediate post-war period confirms these findings.

Zweig presents a detailed study of job regulation and trade unions in collective bargaining through the vehicle of restrictive practices.[82] The study examined the situation in building and civil engineering, cotton, iron and steel, printing and engineering. The findings are very revealing and pertinent to the issues under consideration. First, there was little agreement on the management side in and between sectors on what constituted a restrictive practice. Second, employers did not view practices such as demarcation rules within multi-unionism as restrictive because they followed naturally from apprenticeship regulations. Alternatively, employers and managers accepted and supported these practices as an integral part of management practice in job regulation. Third, it was only in the printing industry where workplace practices appeared to restrict output, but even here many managers had no view on the necessary corrective action. Some managers indicated that the removal or reform of workplace practices would entail significant upheaval in management practice.

Across the five sectors examined, Zweig demonstrated that many managers viewed restrictive practices as part of a 'negotiated' order (rather than unilateral craft control), which helped to sustain output. A later study of engineering in the late 1960s echoes this view. Almost 50 per cent of management in the sample saw economic and industrial relations advantages of closed shops.[83] By the late 1970s, a survey of manufacturing industry found that 35 per cent of management saw the closed shop as beneficial, whereas only 14 per cent saw it as problematic.[84] As Cannadine suggests, the labour process became fully capitalist in the UK during the nineteenth century and was as much about co-operation and compromise as coercion and conflict. Pluralism in management practice and industrial relations remained a dominant philosophy that helped secure profits and wages well into the post-war period. The acceptability of restrictive practices remains as one manifestation of this process.[85] Zweig's *contemporary* empirical evidence suggests that maintaining output was the primary management concern, whereas workplace industrial relations was of lesser significance. Related to this point, Broadberry and Crafts assert that the effect of restrictive practices on output and productivity were more disruptive than the evidence suggests.

The UK section of the AACP and the manufacturing sector successfully prosecuted their aim of maintaining output. Hence, the effects of restrictive practices on output appear less significant than often suggested. Broadberry and Crafts have subsequently conceded that the AACP and its successor the UK productivity council were part of a low effort equilibrium 'underwritten by the absence of adequate competition'.[86] However, to support the claim that restrictive practices were widespread and corrosive in terms of productivity, Broadberry and Crafts cite Clegg's authoritative view on the extent of restrictive practices.[87] The extent of restrictive practices in UK manufacturing may have been scandalous, yet as Clegg and his colleagues on the Donovan Commission later elaborated this was a management failure.[88]

Post-war recovery secured by a rapid recovery of output was directed to the UK's established pre-war markets. As the previous section demonstrates, this was a sensible course of action – the UK needed to export manufactured goods to secure food and raw materials. However, one of its central consequences was to restrict competition by gearing the UK's export trade beyond the European market. This in turn sustained restrictive cartel arrangements between UK producers.[89] Established markets secured established management and employer interests; these interests in turn secured established patterns of work organization and associated patterns of industrial relations, including workplace restrictive practices. On this evidence, it is difficult to sustain the argument that via restrictive practices trade unions structured the post-war aims and interests of the state and employers. However, this argument is deployed within a second series of influential arguments on the decline of the UK state during the post-war period.

Barnett argues that the post-war Labour government, followed by subsequent governments, missed a clear opportunity to modernize and transform UK industry along the lines of the US model. The 'new Jerusalem' thesis suggests that the welfare state, the public sector and widespread nationalization diverted attention from concern with the real economy. The 'victory' thesis complements the 'new Jerusalem' thesis to argue that post-war governments wanted the best of both worlds, i.e. a domestic 'new Jerusalem' positioned within the status of a great power.[90] These dual strategies prioritized maintaining the value of sterling and its status as a reserve currency, but by association governments felt unable to challenge the organized working class. Barnett suggested that any challenge to the interests of the organized working class would undermine their representation in the new Jerusalem. Opposition to this would take the form of industrial action – threatening post-war recovery – hence government failed to reform industrial relations. In combination, these domestic and external constraints encouraged the government to squander Marshall Aid on food, domestic housing and public debt retirement. This was particularly the case with Marshall Aid counterpart funds.

Counterpart funds represented the domestic currency equivalent of dollars made available to European states under the programme. These funds enabled European purchasers of dollar goods to pay a home government in domestic currency for dollar goods. As a result of this, a government could build up large balances equivalent to the balance of dollars received. The ECA recommended that counterpart funds be used for renewal of manufacturing, in particular scaling up and scrapping.

Barnett argued that the government should have terminated the sterling area and injected Marshall Aid counterpart funds into the domestic economy to restructure the manufacturing sector on the US model. This policy was politically impossible within the wider aims of the UK state under the Marshall Plan. Theoretically, the government's alternative use of 99 per cent of Marshall Aid counterpart funds for debt retirement did preclude using them for industrial renewal.[91] However, the absence of counterpart funds did not impair investment levels.

The recovery of output generated high profit levels and the evidence suggests that private sector firms did not need external sources of finance for investment projects. For example, in 1948 nearly 50 per cent of gross investment came from undistributed profits, the use of reserves and bank advances.[92] Equally, representatives of employers and management in the UK section of the AACP deemed organizational, structural and scale advances in UK manufacturing unnecessary. In this context, it is unlikely that industry would have been able to deploy effectively counterpart funds precisely because the AACP's UK section did not support large-scale reconstruction.

Barnett's assertion that the government felt unable to challenge this preference ignores the wider political economy of the situation. The motivation to use counterpart funds for debt retirement was part of a wider strategy to secure the viability of the economy, the manufacturing sector in particular. In contrast to this established position, Barnett assumes the mantle left by Kilpatrick and Lawson to argue that post-war governments felt unable to challenge trade unions in the manufacturing sector.[93] This was the case even though as a restrictive presence they impaired productivity and by weakening government resolve they denied investment funds to employers.

The main problem with Barnett's approach is the assumption that lies behind the heavy generalization. The generalization of decline positions a version of revisionism that appears to suggest the post-war government deliberately(?) deployed incompetently strategized policies to undermine economic performance. On the contrary, within the wider constraints of the state, the government made the correct decisions. However, decisions on market preferences, sterling and defence spending had future consequences, some of them unforeseen. Equally, economic performance over the whole of the post-war period was acceptable if, as Kaldor argues, marginal – a second-best option. Hence, UK economic performance was not inadequate but less effective than that experienced by European competitors who traded in (what became) a more dynamic market. In addition, Barnett's arguments on industrial relations and restrictive practices are *generalized* from shipbuilding, the only sector examined in any detail.[94] Equally, on the specific issue of industrial relations, cause and effect are reversed, i.e. trade unions prevent management from introducing AACP recommendations. The evidence appears to point to the conclusion that within the UK section of the AACP it was primarily the TUC who was pushing for a more engaged consideration of US proposals on capital investment and work organization. Moreover, the evidence suggests that the attitude and behaviour of organized labour in the workplace did not constitute (at the time) a serious concern for management. The FBI's overall approach legitimized the output drive without significant investment in mechanical production aids, improved management of work organization and management practice or industrial relations to subsume the TUC's guarded criticisms. However, the consequences of this soon became evident.

In 1953, the UK productivity council considered the main factors responsible for high levels of productivity in US manufacturing industry, as reported by twenty AACP teams.[95] Across the twenty sectors that reported technical factors such as the availability of mechanical aids and management technique on costing, production planning and control were the most frequently cited factors. A subsequent study that examined Anglo-American productivity differentials in motor manufacturing established the significance of management incompetence and failures in these areas. In addition, the scale differences in plant size and the potential for standardized production runs were central factors of explanation. Moreover, the study fails to cite trade union restrictionism on either overtime or shift working or the effects of restrictive practices as significant factors.[96] However, a third influential source on the post-war economic performance of the UK economy fails to consider these points.

In a wide-ranging statistical and quantitative analysis, Broadberry examined the performance of the UK manufacturing sector in comparison with its German and US counterparts between 1850 and 1990 and drew three broad conclusions.[97] First, the performance of the UK's manufacturing sector compared with the USA and Germany has over the whole period remained stationary. US levels of productivity are twice those in the UK whereas German and UK levels are on a par, although in the post-war period productivity in the German manufacturing sector pulled ahead of that of the UK. Second, in the post-war period, the failure to adopt US mass production methods in manufacturing opened up a productivity gap between the UK and its European competitors. Third, UK manufacturers geared output to local demand conditions in the domestic market and empire markets. After 1958, the reintegration of the world economy and the convertibility of sterling marked the beginning of an inevitable decline as the UK adjusted to highly competitive markets beyond the Imperial and sterling area.

Although these conclusions are broadly correct, the explanations that Broadberry offers are not always supported by the data and appear to be insignificant causal factors of explanation. This is particularly the case in respect of the treatment of industrial relations. First, Broadberry positions a post-war decline in the level of apprenticeships as evidence of UK manufacturers' enthusiasm for US production methods. However, a failure to take up US methods characterizes the post-war period. Second, union opposition to new technology and work systems with the potential to undermine craft skills appears as a significant factor in the failure to deploy US mass production techniques. For Broadberry, the significance of trade union resistance in the failure to adopt US systems contrasts markedly with management hesitancy – a marginal factor.[98] However, the evidence demonstrates that positioning trade union intransigence over management hesitancy is improbable. Employer representatives in the UK section of the AACP had no interest in adopting US production systems and methods of work organization, positioning this as hesitancy is unconvincing. Clearly, trade union opposition did occur; however, employer and management aims and objectives in established markets structured this as a medium-term response that emerged as a significant if marginal factor after 1958. Moreover, only after secure export markets were threatened and the domestic market for manufactured goods penetrated did employers and managers begin to emphasize the problematic nature of collective bargaining and workplace restrictive practices. It is equally likely that the choices of export markets and of flexible production systems in the domestic economy were themselves a substantive reason for declining comparative productivity. The productivity of UK, German and US manufacturing sectors maintained the trend established after 1850. Thus, it is at least arguable that the negative impact of UK trade unions failed to push the UK's comparative economic performance off trend.[99]

The documentary evidence presented in the previous section combined with Zweig's material throw some doubt on these explanations, if not the conclusions which appear reasonable and agreeable. It seems implausible to conclude that craft trade unions were responsible for a decline in workplace apprenticeships. The maintenance of apprentice methods of training is a function of craft unions and a major source of power in the workplace. The dilution of apprenticeship prevailed in many sectors, particularly where wartime labour shortages remained operative after the war. In other sectors, post-war negotiations introduced dilution agreements.[100]

The international viability of the UK economy?

The international viability of the UK economy substantially weakened between 1958 and 1964 in three ways. First, 1958 saw the reintroduction of full multilateral convertible international trade and really marked the end of the Marshall Plan era. Convertibility and multilateralism exposed emergent consequences embedded within the pattern of post-war recovery. The UK's immediate recovery of output did not lead to dynamic industrial competitiveness and modernization such as the West German economy experienced. Concentration on export trade dominated by the sterling area had two benefits – privileged access to large markets and the availability of sterling area states' dollar surpluses to finance UK dollar trade deficits. The 1958 measures brought both benefits to an end.[101] Second, the dominance of the sterling area positioned UK export trade in a market that was less dynamic than the emerging European market. The relatively secure domestic market and privileged access to export markets sustained and legitimized comparatively low levels of labour productivity yet comparatively high unit labour costs. The significance of this weakness is evident through the third demonstration of weakened international viability. The period saw the UK's share of world trade seriously decline. Numerous studies indicate that the share fell from around 24 per cent in the early 1950s to between 14 per cent and 17 per cent by the early 1960s.[102]

In contrast to emergent economic decline, workplace industrial relations appeared strong and well organized. However, wage drift began to emerge as a source of inflation. The industrial relations system appeared more viable and enduring than the economy that surrounded it. This period marked the beginning of the isolation of industrial relations as a factor central to the problem of UK economic performance.

The isolation of the industrial relations system

Economists and economic historians are, as this chapter previously illustrates, adept at rationalizing and isolating processes such as collective bargaining and institutions such as trade unions as suboptimal interventions in the market that reduce economic efficiency. As post-war recovery stalled in comparison with the higher efficiency and competitiveness of other states, the state and labour economists specializing in industrial relations demonstrated this tendency.

The first case in point is the report of the Donovan Commission, in which a central element within the commissioners' brief was to examine the acceleration of national economic advance.[103] The Commission produced a highly detailed and articulate explanation of the malfunctioning of institutions in the industrial relations system. However, the institutional approach examined the emergence of phenomena such as wage drift, sectional collective bargaining and the frequent use of localized unofficial industrial action to the relative exclusion of harder economic issues. The commissioners argued that the voluntary framework embedded in the UK system of industrial relations could relatively easily formalize the emergent informal system of industrial relations centred on the workplace. In turn, greater formalization would provide a structure to facilitate productivity bargaining, industrial modernization and the deployment of incomes policies.

The commissioners presented a solution to the development and consolidation of workplace industrial relations without positioning the industrial relations system within the wider economy. The Donovan Commission Report emphasized the role of local bargaining often in a multi-union context; however, in the report neither variable was correlated or tested for significance. In addition, the report did not provide significant information on the effect of the industrial relations system in comparatively slow productivity growth over the post-war period to that date. These omissions have enabled subsequent researchers to position the structure of industrial relations, in particular multi-unionism, as the central determinant of staffing levels and productivity but exclude discussion of management inefficiencies as revisionist and 'archive led'.[104]

The acceptance of this position flows in part from the failure of industrial relations academics to position the industrial relations system within post-war economic recovery. Revisionists deploy these factors to legitimize comparisons between the post-war period and the contemporary period that position falling levels of multi-unionism and collective bargaining in the contemporary period as a major source of improved UK economic performance.[105] A second consequence of isolation is evident in much of the empirical work on industrial relations and economic performance in the 1970s and 1980s. Three such heavily cited pieces demonstrate this point.

Pratten presented an international comparison of productivity at company level based on a case study of firms located in the UK who also operated in West Germany and the USA.[106] The focus of the study was productivity differentials among the three countries. The results are presented as 'economic' causes and 'behavioural' causes for US and West German differentials over UK firms.

Economic causes include length of production runs, scale and competitiveness of plant and machinery, quality of materials and capacity utilization. In total, these factors gave West German firms a 12 per cent differential over their UK counterparts, whereas US firms recorded a 32 per cent differential. In contrast, behavioural factors such as strikes, restrictive practices and the efficiency of manning levels gave differentials of 12 per cent and 11 per cent respectively. Compared with West Germany, the two factors are of equal significance, whereas compared with the USA economic factors far outweigh behavioural factors in explaining greater productivity levels. Thus, prima facie, there is no isolation of industrial relations issues. The problem lies not necessarily with the study but with the manner of its employment that concentrates on the large part played by behavioural factors in the supply-side failure of the UK economy during the post-war period.[107] However, such interpretations contain no discussion of management failures or more detailed analyses of proximate explanations, such as the industrial relations system.

A second apparently definitive study on UK economic performance appeared in 1980.[108] The study examined the impact of the industrial relations system on output and labour costs and then highlighted these factors in the UK's poor economic performance.[109] However, the study is more wide ranging than a critique of the UK industrial relations system, e.g. the study suggests that the causes of industrial relations problems are often management failure if not weak incompetent management. The Brookings study does not necessarily separate industrial relations from the organization and performance of management, yet the citation of particular chapters and sections often creates the impression that the isolation of industrial relations is both legitimate and useful. This exaggerates the significance of industrial relations while marginalizing the issue of management practice. Moreover, the study often falls back on 'workplace attitudes' to explain poor industrial relations and low productivity. However, employer and management attitudes were, in large measure, ignored.[110] Hence, the study positions a series of proximate explanations as substantive demonstrations of poor economic performance.

A third heavily cited study of economic performance presented by Metcalf has assumed considerable significance in its isolation of industrial relations.[111] The take-up of Donovan reforms by manufacturing industry failed because they did not deliver the improvements in productivity and economic performance that advocates of voluntarism suggested would follow from the introduction of such reforms. This may be the case, but not for the reasons proffered. Moreover, although the study criticizes Donovan reforms, it repeats some of the limitations of the Donovan approach. In criticizing Donovan, Metcalf specifically inverts the direction of causation to present the failure of productivity improvement in an apparently healthy economy. In contrast to this, the international competitiveness of the UK economy appeared marginal in the early 1970s. Moreover, industry could not sustain significant comparative productivity improvement because for much of the post-war period UK manufacturing industry concentrated on output rather than comparative or relative efficiency. The marginal costs of substantially improving labour productivity required investment to raise the comparative efficiency and scale of UK plants. However, UK manufacturers tend to compete in low-productivity and low-income markets, both at home and abroad. Such markets can sustain comparative scale and marginal inefficiencies because of comparatively low wage levels that compensate for lower productivity.[112]

The argument in each study and the application of each study has sustained and furthered the separation of industrial relations from the wider structure of the state, employer and management interests. In separating economic and behavioural factors, Pratten legitimized an artificial distinction, giving license to subsequent use of his findings that emphasize behavioural factors as significant in themselves. The Brookings study found that problems with the industrial relations system often related to management failure and incompetence but failed to follow up on the latter point, therefore exaggerating the significance of industrial relations alone. Last, although Metcalf points out some failures in the Donovan reform proposals, he exaggerates them out of all proportion. The prescriptive limitation of the Donovan proposals lay in the suggestion that improving the operation of the industrial relations system could slow or reverse UK economic decline. As this chapter and previous chapters demonstrate, reform here could have played a part, but only as one of several marginal factors.

Conclusions

The UK state forged its economic and political aims in the immediate post-war years. Over the whole of the post-war period, the aim of economic policy was trimmed from aiming to secure the UK's national pathway to economic prosperity to cushioning comparative economic decline. In the early 1950s, the aim legitimized and sustained an unreconstructed recovery of industrial output. Equally, until the late 1960s, the international viability of the UK state rested on sustaining sterling as a reserve currency and maintaining the priority of the sterling area for UK export trade. These prerequisites for recovery made wholesale reconstruction of the manufacturing sector impractical and unlikely.

By examining the AACP's UK section, the empirical material and argument of this chapter demonstrates how the objectives of the state afforded representatives of UK employers and management the opportunity to secure and sustain embedded patterns of management practice and industrial relations. Moreover, the chapter draws on empirical material to show embedded patterns of interest in management practice structured, what later became termed informality, in the industrial relations system. Further, this material demonstrates how other analyses of the post-war period underplay the significance of management and employer intransigence to isolate and promote the industrial relations system as a key factor of explanation in post-war economic decline.

The FBI and the BEC were central institutional actors in the UK section of the AACP. Together, they supported if not advocated the conservative approach to post-war recovery taken by the government. The AACP's wider aims were a failure because a prescription for the Americanization of management technique and industrial relations, however forcefully deployed, could not dislodge embedded patterns of interest in employer and management objectives. These interests in turn structured trade union behaviour in collective bargaining. These patterns remained beyond the lifetime of the AACP, in large measure because they developed many years before its introduction.

Continuity in embedded patterns of management practice and industrial relations remained for much of the post-war period as an effect of securing a recovery of output in the immediate period after the Second World War. The embedded patterns of management practice and industrial relations helped to sustain the UK's international economic and political viability. However, both patterns, particularly the industrial relations system, generated unforeseen consequences.

Economic performance throughout the post-war period until the early 1970s was good relative to the recent past, but the prosecution of comparative economic performance appeared less successful. Many revisionist arguments take this position to highlight the significance of absence then failure in industrial relations reform. Archive and institutional evidence demonstrates that trade union behaviour in collective bargaining did not operate as an intransigent independent process. In contrast, it operated within structures that reflected embedded patterns of regulation that neither management nor unions wanted to change. For trade unions, this marked a weakness not a strength.

The long international economic boom, often referred to as Fordism, did not necessarily support the post-war settlement between capital and labour in the state. Alternatively, a costly role in Nato and the Cold War and an economic and political commitment to old empire structured a conservative pattern of domestic reform to constrain economic policy and institutional reform in areas such as industrial relations. In policymaking on industrial relations and management practice, trade unions only became significant actors because of their power on the shop floor. Within institutions such as the AACP, to serve particular short-term interests management and employer representatives succeeded in talking out prescriptive proposals designed to institutionalize shop floor industrial relations. However, the Report of the Donovan Commission reprised these proposals twenty years later. The process of particularization in the UK state that gave trade unions only a partial access to the hierarchy of the state appeared functional, but later developed contradictory tendencies.

The dominant ideology of formative influences in the UK state structure an embedded preference for institutional delegation. In the post-war period, the conservative nature of this delegation generated a series of institutions such as the AACP and its successor the UK productivity council that insulated the *status quo* in management practice and industrial relations from operational criticism. By positioning existing arrangements in management practice and industrial relations as natural and inevitable in the context of the aims and objectives of the post-war state, this was largely successful.

The lack of state intervention in post-war recovery, particularly management practice, secured the economic and political independence of the UK state as a

European great power. However, the short-termism of this approach eventually weakened the comparative economic performance of UK manufacturing industry. This weakness and the wider objectives of the state may have been necessary, but both factors reinforced the defensive power of trade unions on the shop floor as a subsequent contradictory consequence. The Donovan reform proposals helped to re-establish order in the industrial relations system but were unable to slow or reverse comparative economic decline. In large measure, this was the case because the industrial relations system was not of central significance in this regard.

The further isolation of the industrial relations system in the last years of the post-war period followed by legal reform in the 1980s presented employers and management with an opportunity to expel the obstructionism of workplace industrial relations. The next chapter examines the success with which this reform afforded the prosecution of longer-term management interests during the 1980s and early 1990s.

7 Reform of the industrial relations system and economic restructuring since 1980

Introduction

The previous chapter presents an argument supported by empirical material that demonstrates the structural significance of management and employer interests as a key factor in explaining economic decline during the post-war period. Moreover, the chapter demonstrates how these interests structured institutional actors and processes such as trade unions and collective bargaining within the industrial relations system. Further, the chapter demonstrates the marginal significance of job regulation in explaining the process of comparative economic decline during the post-war period.

In the post-war period, voluntary reform in the industrial relations system came to assume a central academic significance in the future transformation of economic performance. In contrast to this, the contemporary period has witnessed the rapid isolation of the system as the key factor in explaining economic decline. This chapter examines the significance of contemporary reform in the industrial relations system on organizational change and development and economic performance which voluntary reform failed to stimulate. The first section examines the central ideological role of workplace obstructionism in the industrial relations system on the state as a contemporary manifestation of formative libertarian values in the state. The next section examines the scope and potential of organizational change and development that reform of the industrial relations system appeared to release during the 1980s and early 1990s. The last section examines the effects of industrial relations reform and the scope of organizational change and development on the UK's economic performance.

The combination of embedded national pathways and the emergence of technological and productivity gaps between leading and following states critically influences the dynamics of economic performance. In the post-war years, the UK assumed a central role in Nato and the Cold War and retained its empire and imperial links. Similarly, the post-war period witnessed a major economic recovery, as distinct from a period of sustained reconstruction. The sociological and political issues that structured these decisions confined the growth potential of the economy, in particular the manufacturing sector; hence, the UK economy could not have grown faster than it did. However, economists, politicians and political scientists and modern historians suggested that reform of the industrial relations system alone could facilitate an improvement in economic performance.

A significant historically embedded feature of UK economic performance is the low rate of growth over the long period since the 1850–70s. This feature assumes greater significance in terms of comparative economic performance, measured through growth of national income per head or measures of capital and labour productivity. In contrast to this, economic performance relative to the recent past has appeared very good, e.g. the immediate post-war period compared with the inter-war period and the 1980s compared with the 1970s. The political and sociological inclusiveness of policy that surrounded economic management during the post-war period constrained the growth potential of the economy. Maintaining traditional markets and associated patterns of management practice and employer interests within the surround of full employment helped to cushion the process of comparative economic decline. Within this inclusiveness, the presence of pluralism in a voluntarist system of industrial relations had only a marginal effect on long run economic performance. The experience of economic performance since the early 1980s demonstrates the last point. Political and sociological exclusion promoted institutions and processes such as collective bargaining and trade unions as monopsonistic obstacles to efficiency. Moreover, both restricted management ability to match real wages with productive capacity and the implementation of broader labour market policies associated with the control of inflation. In the 1980s, the introduction of legislative and managerial policies greatly aided reform of workplace industrial relations and cheapened labour while promoting a plethora of new managerial strategies. However, similar to the rubric of economic policy, they were procyclical, reinforcing not cushioning comparative economic decline.

The argument of this chapter aims not to rubbish industrial relations reform and organizational change and development during the period since 1980 as straw men. Rather, the argument demonstrates how reform of a marginal, if high profile, aspect of state policy cannot bring about scale changes in the course of economic performance. Institutional, political and sociological exclusion from the state contrasts with partial access that was prevalent before 1979. In the contemporary period, institutional and legal processes associated with exclusion from the state provided employers with much needed opportunities to reorganize work systems, contain unit and labour costs, create employment and improve competitiveness. The previous chapter demonstrates how the immediate post-war period afforded employers a similar opportunity. The first section examines the removal of workplace obstructionism in the contemporary period.

Reform of industrial relations: the removal of workplace obstructionism

It is necessary to position the reform of industrial relations and the removal of workplace obstructionism previously ignored by previous states in government as part of a much bigger contextual influence on the contemporary state. The 1979 Conservative government sought an accumulation strategy – a group of separate yet mutually reinforcing policies pitched to make the economy profitable, strong and successful. This process, later termed 'Thatcherism', measured strength and success not by the economic success of its individual components but by the successful mobilization and maintenance of political and popular support.[1] For example, privatization, deregulation of bus services and pensions provision, an artificially high exchange rate, property booms and the libertarianism of the community charge were all longer-term failures. However, over the short term, each was popular and appeared to be a success, receiving considerable political support and populist antistatist support mobilized and maintained over some time.

The procyclical nature of the anti-inflation accumulation strategy reduced industrial output by 14 per cent between 1979 and 1982. At this time, plant closure appeared acceptable on the basis of the emergence of a leaner and fitter manufacturing sector; however, manufacturing output remained below the 1980 level until 1986. More significantly than this, manufacturing output remained weak well beyond 1986, increasing at an average annual rate of only 1.5 per cent between 1980 and 1996.[2] Thatcherism followed by Majorism aimed to cheapen wages both comparatively and relatively. However, the hysteresis effects of plant closure on the capacity of the manufacturing sector and the associated increase in average costs had virtually no effect on comparative economic performance.

The legislative reform of the industrial relations system combined with the ideological rejection of voluntarism by the government led to institutional exclusion from the state for trade unions. Cannadine demonstrates how the 1980s witnessed a renewal of anti-trade union propaganda and rhetoric similar to that generated during the inter-war period, particularly in 1926.[3] The phrase 'the enemy within' was coined during the 1984 coal strike, symbolizing the demonization of the organized working class at its most graphic. More generally, following Hayek, the state in government attacked trade unions and collective bargaining, particularly within the public sector, as anti-working-class institutions. The former because they were militant and unrepresentative, the latter because it often raised sectional and unrealistic expectations for union members.

Thatcherism as a wider phenomenon was relatively successful because it reconciled sectionalism in the industrial relations system with its supporting accumulation strategy. For example, supporting the managerial prerogative to promote organizational change and flexibility through free collective bargaining in the private sector received considerable popular support from union members as it banished incomes policies. Quite remarkably, the crisis in production appeared of marginal significance as distributional reform within and between the public and private sectors intensified labour and restructured production, by extensive means, often by plant downsizing or closure. However, within this process, wage drift, where earnings run ahead of productivity increases, continued throughout the period 1980–96.[4] Although substantial windfall gains in labour productivity appeared, they failed to improve the UK's comparative position. The cheapening and intensification of labour appear similar to that of the initial post-war period, whereas the contemporary period saw the emergence of a more flexible workforce replacing intensification by extensive overtime working. Over the short term, again similar to the post-war period, this process enabled many employers to extend the life of comparatively less competitive capital.

The institutional and political defeat of organized labour is often overstated; however, over the short term 'defeat' further reinforced the formative influence of libertarian *laissez faire* in the state and capital. In attacking trade unions and collective bargaining, the Thatcherite project followed by that of John Major sought to undermine and exclude labour as a collective institution. There is no evidence that either industrial relations or the economic performance of non-union firms is superior to those that maintain collective bargaining arrangements. However, although this may be the case, it does not prevent the spread of non-unionism that the trade union recognition procedure contained in the 1999 Employment Relations Bill may or may not temper.[5]

Of greater significance is the negligible difference to long-term economic performance that followed the process of retrenchment and reform in the industrial relations system. To substantiate this argument, the next section examines the not inconsiderable organizational change and development that took place during the 1980s and 1990s.

Organizational change and development

The processes of organizational change and development result from innovations in the economic and social dynamics of employment and production, hence it is necessary to examine these factors at several levels of analysis. First, for many, the major change in the Western economic system over the contemporary period is the emergence of 'post-Fordism', which replaced ailing Fordist systems of production in the late 1970s. A second associated level of analysis centres on a more detailed evaluation of the state of training and development in the UK. A third level focuses on the emergence and deployment of new managerial strategies, such as HRM, that appear to exemplify notions of organizational commitment and training and development. Finally, the emergence of 'flexibility' in the labour market and employment regulation provides a good empirical measure of the parameters of organizational change and development. The category 'post-Fordism' may or may not describe a wider accumulation strategy for Thatcherism. However, one of its central components – reform of the industrial relations system – afforded the expectation of improved management and work systems and greater levels of training and development, secured by management, for a more committed and flexible workforce. By grounding 'post-Fordism' against the concept of historically embedded national pathways, it provides a framework within which to examine contemporary organizational developments such as greater training and development, HRM and flexibility.

The emergence of post-Fordism

Chapter 2 demonstrates the conceptual significance of 'Fordism' in debates on the UK's post-war recovery and economic and industrial decline during the post-war period. However, the chapter further demonstrated that the concepts of Fordism and regulation appear analytically and empirically flawed when examined against historically embedded patterns of regulation in nation states as national pathways. Chapter 6 consolidates this argument by a documentary and empirical examination of the UK's post-war economic recovery.

The labels Fordism and post-Fordism generalize and divide the period since 1945 into two broad headings, yet as a frame of reference the regulation literature only captures the dynamics of the UK economy in the post-war period as a 'flawed Fordism'.[6] Hence, it is at least probable that post-Fordism in the UK will be equally flawed. Moreover, as Table 2.1 illustrates, the elasticity of prefixes to Fordism demonstrates the compelling nature of embedded national pathways over generalized if accommodative categories.

The mass production of standardized commodities, institutionalized collective bargaining and full employment welfare state capitalism constitute the central features of Fordism.[7] In contrast, the contemporary period associates the demise of mass standardized markets with the emergence of dynamic niche markets dominated by branding and the erosion or hollowing out of the social democracy in the state.[8] In the UK's case, a particular feature of the latter was the rejection of collective bargaining, trade union recognition and proceduralized personnel management in the workplace as 'good' industrial relations.

Post-Fordism has several identifiable features. First, a renaissance of craft workers operative within small to medium-sized enterprises. Second, the deployment of decentralized production systems that employ extensive worker autonomy and discretion. Third, post-Fordism features considerable production specialization.

Thatcherism promoted these features as central in the movement to a libertarian and populist enterprise approach to economic restructuring that emphasized the stifling bureaucracy of social democracy as a contextual influence on the state. The phrase 'the enterprise culture' captured this promotion. However, an authoritative study of economic restructuring that focuses on upskilling and training and development draws rather different conclusions.[9] Some aspects of each feature within the post-Fordist paradigm prevailed in the UK during the 1980s and early 1990s, yet they fell short of a movement towards post-Fordism. For example, already skilled labour was the primary beneficiary of training, development and upskilling designed to promote specialized production based on task autonomy and worker discretion. In contrast to the experience of further skill development and multiskilling for skilled workers, less skilled manual and white collar workers often experienced deskilling and task intensification or unemployment. Post-Fordist systems did not necessarily supersede Fordist conceptions of work organization. Alternatively, the collapse of manufacturing industry curtailed much training and development, in services and manufacturing, because of the procyclical nature of macroeconomic management.

The accumulation strategy behind Thatcherism and Majorism failed as a transmission mechanism to post-Fordism. The prescriptive mechanism of post-Fordism and Fordism are included as a presumed role for the state. However, Chapter 6 demonstrates that the UK state supported by employers and management interests was unable to provide this in the immediate post-war period. A new structure for production such as Fordism could not dislodge the presence of historically embedded interests and structures. Equally, in the contemporary period before 1997, historically embedded structural interests – formative influences in the state – were no longer mediated by contextual influences over the state, such as the welfare state and full employment. Rejection of the post-war settlement by the Thatcherite state in government, in particular the procyclical control inflation between 1979 and 1982, led to a permanent loss of capacity in the manufacturing sector, large and small. More particularly, withdrawal and loss of capacity failed to provide the conditions for post-Fordist restructuring. The state withdrew from industry and enterprise to promote and privatize the managerial prerogative. Legislative deregulation of employment protection and legislative intervention in otherwise legitimate patterns of dispute resolution represented contemporary, if individualist, manifestations of libertarianism in the state. Crouch described the process of promoting and privatizing the managerial prerogative as 'there is no such thing as good industrial relations other than what employers say it is'.[10]

Rejection of the post-war settlement and a renewed emphasis on skills training and development is for some the result of advances in information and production technology that flawed Fordism actually prevented the diffusion of before 1979.[11] Moreover, Broadberry argues that the UK competes in labour-intensive yet highly skilled sectors such as chemicals, pharmaceuticals, aerospace, motor vehicles and electronics. Here, flexible skilled shop floor labour operates within flexible work systems that emphasize customized production.[12] However, while Broadberry's argument contains considerable empirical material, not all of it supports its twin claims. First, that Fordism was a failure in UK because of excessive shop floor control of industrial relations. Second, that Thatcherism transmitted a movement to a flexible post-Fordist production paradigm which resulted in a more skilled workforce across the board. For example, Broadberry's material illustrates that the number of apprentices in UK manufacturing and engineering fell dramatically between 1980 and 1989, whereas in Germany the number of apprentices in both sectors fell far less dramatically. Moreover, German apprentice qualified labour, as a share of employment in each sector, increased between 1980 and 1989.[13]

More than this, Steadman demonstrates that in 1987 the UK's figure for mechanical, electrical and electronic engineering qualifications awarded at craft and technician level was 78 per cent short of the German figure and 69 per cent short of the equivalent French total.[14] More generally, for the UK and German manufacturing workforces, O'Mahoney and Wagner found that in 1989 only 26 per cent of the German workforce held no qualifications whereas the UK figure was 57 per cent.[15]

The Thatcher governments followed by those of John Major succeeded in reforming, if not destroying, the UK system of industrial relations. However, the latter and the associated improvement in the managerial prerogative did not release the potential of new technology and a related upskilling of the workforce across the labour force within an emergent post-Fordism. A more voluntarist approach to the regulation of employment appears to have made employer attitudes to the introduction of new technology and training and development more short term. To substantiate this aspect of the discussion, the argument now moves to an examination of organizational change and development in terms of training, development and reskilling.

Skills, training and development

Before 1980, the industrial relations system was commonly cited as a major factor that restricted employers adopting improvements in the organization of work. Reform of the industrial relations system would lead to the adoption of improved systems of work organization, often allied to new or more advanced technology. Improvement in the managerial prerogative at the workplace could decentralize responsibility for work allocation to employees as individuals or work groups with either no or far less sectional intervention from trade unions. In turn, improved work systems and higher technology justify increased expenditure on training and development in order to capture the greater productivity potential of new work systems. Moreover, improvement in the managerial prerogative would rationalize and make more realistic worker expectations in unionized and non-union workplaces, therefore expelling some of the corrosive effects of trade unions. Greater levels of employee commitment and performance would go hand in hand with improved job security and new consultative and participative structures for workplace job regulation.

However, as Gallie *et al.* demonstrate, it is necessary to measure this optimistic scenario against a more polarized and pessimistic reality.[16] The familiar shortage of skilled workers remains, so too does the demand for skills training in which many employers have effectively rejected supply-side policies on vocational training. This is the case even though employers manage much of the current training provision through their control of local TECs.[17] The withdrawal of the state from direct control and sponsorship of training provision demonstrates the contradictory effects of libertarianism. Deregulation and local flexibility – the absence of nationally administered and regulated control mechanisms – pushes employers further back into short-termism. The provision of training is polarized between skilled workers for whom there is excess demand and the unskilled for whom there is little demand and who have little voluntary demand for the training provision made available to them.

The managerial strategies of command and control associated with the pessimistic reality appear to minimize or deny the need for an improved skill base. Alternatively, the association among autonomy, discretion and upskilling strategies and the optimistic scenario positions training as a prerequisite for improved economic performance. Further, the evidence suggests that employers position the rhetoric of upskilling in work systems that do the reverse.[18]

An EU-wide study of mechanical engineering found that although labour cost is the main element in production value added this sector is susceptible to high wages across the EU.[19] However, this susceptibility reflects the necessity for highly qualified human capital and associated packages of training and development within internal labour markets or via the state. For the UK sector, the study found that whereas labour costs appear comparatively low firms are unable to take advantage of this because the comparative lack of training and development inhibits skill development and innovation. In summary, the costs of tooling and skilling up restrict the capability of UK mechanical engineering as a low-cost sector. More critical than this, the study found that for small to medium-sized enterprises fully or part foreign-owned firms conducted the highest levels of training and development.

The problems encountered in taking advantage of comparatively low wage costs appear confirmed by a 1998 British engineering industry survey that cites recruitment and retention as a major difficulty.[20] However, only 8 per cent of the firms in the survey attempted to remedy the difficulty by improving training or retraining, whereas 40 per cent of the survey constituency opted to increase efforts to recruit staff, preferably already qualified.

In the food and drink sector, UK firms are in the order of 10 per cent less efficient than overseas competitors because of inadequate training.[21] In particular, this study suggests that UK workers have great difficulty dealing with modern work systems and production equipment, leading employers to spend more time and training for a comparatively poorer outcome. The study found that UK employees have lower levels of formal (GCSE) qualifications and lower levels of vocational qualifications than European equivalents.

The aggregate effect of training and skill development since the early 1980s appears contradictory. Both national governments and EU policymakers argue that improved access to workplace training and development in association with higher technology and more flexible work systems have raised skill levels. However, the distributional effects appear polarized, with higher-skilled employees in more secure jobs experiencing the greatest increase in skill content.[22] In contrast to this finding, lower-skilled employees appear extremely flexible, yet this is not necessarily within production or work systems. Alternatively, the manner by which employers recruit, terminate and deploy labour in relation to demand appears to be the main feature of flexibility. Here, the cost savings derived from the use of non-standard employment contracts appear dominant, reinforcing the suggestion that on balance cost reduction and command and control strategies prevail over autonomy and upskilling across the whole labour force. Cully *et al.* found that 90 per cent of workplaces contract out at least one service, including training (38 per cent), whereas 63 per cent of workplaces reported that the use of fixed-term contracts had either increased or remained at the same level over the past five years.[23] Cully *et al.* conclude that there are clear negative effects of the use of non-standard 'flexible' labour – it restricts functional task flexibility to less than 50 per cent of workplaces; by implication, similarly restricting training and the deployment of new managerial strategies such as HRM.

The emergence of human resource management

The extent to which reform of the industrial relations system since the early 1980s has contributed to more systematic and strategic management of industrial relations can be evaluated against the findings in successive workplace industrial relations surveys. These surveys are particularly revealing in relation to the adoption of improved – strategically integrated – systems of production and work organization.

Millward *et al.* found some evidence that employers had improved mechanisms for internal communication during the late 1980s. However, implementation of the component elements in this process appeared disintegrated and non-strategic. Similarly, there was no evidence of any relationship to new systems of production organization.[24] Millward found fragmentary evidence for the use of an HRM approach to management. However, this did not constitute a new form of employee representation and participation in the workplace. The evidence did not support the claim that employers bundle – integrate – the measures.[25] In contrast to this, the preliminary findings from the latest survey suggest that clusters of new management practices may represent a new form of employee participation. However, these management practices represent an extremely limited movement to individualism measured against the prescription of HRM.[26]

Case study and survey evidence indicates that strategic HRM, such as high-commitment or high-performance work systems, containing appropriately bundled initiatives are more likely to prevail in high-technology high-value added sectors. However, even in cases where bundles are present, little of the strategy is discernible on the shop floor.[27] In the absence of strategic HRM, high-commitment and high-performance bundles appear to represent a loosening of conceptual and theoretical testing that may sustain the rhetoric that skill training, development and workplace flexibility are central components of management practice in the deployment of new managerial policies.

Flexibility

Under the previous two headings, the confinement of positive scenario organizational and technical innovation in production and work organization systems over the past twenty years are demonstrated. Thus, on balance, it appears safe to conclude that legislative intervention in the industrial relations system combined with procyclical economic management of the real economy to sweep away trade union 'rigidity' in the workplace. However, both measures failed to reform the structurally embedded short-termism in UK management and employer interests. The pessimistic reality appears to prevail over the optimistic, even though employers have far greater levels of flexibility than during the 1970s. However, the presence of flexibility has failed to shake off structural constraints that surround the managerial prerogative.

The term 'flexibility' has a variety of possible meanings. First, it can relate to labour market flexibility. This appears confined to a movement away from permanent employment and associated patterns of democratic participation and remuneration. For example, pension fund access, holiday and sick pay, protection against unfair dismissal or redundancy, all had much reduced coverage for part-time and non-standard employees during the 1980s. This remains so in the current contemporary period for some non-standard employees, but to a lesser extent. For example, part-time employees now have the same redundancy and unfair dismissal protection as full-time workers. Second, flexibility can refer to the concept of the flexible firm. Here, employers segment internal labour markets to emphasize upskilling and task flexibility for some and deskilling subject to simple supervisory or technical controls for others. Pollert argues that 'flexibility and the flexible firm' became fetishized during the 1980s as a management tool, whereas its empirical presence was not necessarily proven and its impact on gender inequality ignored.[28] A third way to understand the omnipresence of flexibility over past twenty years is as an ideology in the state. UK governments and employers are consistent in their view that maximum relative employment and labour market flexibility represent the best route to competitiveness and employment creation. The prefix 'relative' relates to the juxtaposition of formative and contextual influences on the state. For example, in the post-war period, the introduction and subsequent extension of individual employment rights aimed to limit problematic and overtly discriminatory aspects of voluntarism such as redundancy, unequal pay and racial and sexual discrimination in employment. However, although particular governments sought to restrict voluntarism, in general governments were supportive, if sometimes reluctantly so.[29] In contrast to the post-war years, the 1980s and early 1990s saw formative influences also become contextual influences. The post-war period and particular policies such as social democracy, the welfare state and state intervention became demonized. As a consequence of this, removing, marginalizing and minimizing interventions and rigidities in the labour market became a preoccupation of government policy to promote flexibility in recruitment, termination and hours of work. This preference remains in the current contemporary period and although UK employers via the CBI have agreed a trade union recognition procedure many remain opposed to it on principle, preferring voluntary arrangements. For example, the Newspaper Society, the regional press employer association, recently circulated a confidential briefing document that outlines how to avoid trade union recognition under the provisions of the 1999 Bill.[30] Equally, employers pressed for and succeeding in getting restrictions on the coverage of and opt-outs from European working time regulations.[31]

The evidence suggests that labour market flexibility is significant, whereas innovation in production and work organization and related upskilling associated with flexibility in the flexible firm are less in evidence. For example, in 1993, 38 per cent of the employed labour force was employed flexibly, i.e. working long hours or shift patterns.[32] By 1998, the extent of flexible working was clearly evident, 1.3 million men and 5.4 million women worked on a part-time basis, whereas 10 per cent used flexitime arrangements, with 14 per cent of employees undertaking shiftwork.[33] However, the use of flexible work practices within new systems of work and production organization is not in evidence. Equally, the figures for shift working and variable 'bank' hours within flexible work practices remain comparatively low. One reason for this might be that flexible work practices as distinct from labour market flexibility mainly affects workers in higher productivity manufacturing economies that produce industrial machinery. Together, Germany, Japan and the USA produced 67 per cent of world machinery, much of it manufactured in modern production systems that are less in evidence in the UK.[34] Moreover, the International Labour Organization (ILO) report concluded that this type of flexibility would be most likely to maintain and create employment in richer nations where industrial restructuring raises growth and labour productivity. In 1999, a CBI report found that UK workers continue to become more flexible, with 46 per cent of employers sampled deploying shiftwork. However, this flexibility appears unrelated to the deployment of flexible work systems that remain less in evidence.[35] Last, Cully *et al.* found that 26 per cent of all workplaces used mostly part-time labour, particularly those in hotels and catering and health and education, where at least 50 per cent of workplaces in each sector used part-timers. However, the study found that 16 per cent of all workplaces used no part-timers yet only 5 per cent of workplaces reported the presence of autonomous trained teamworkers within designated production systems who had to work together.[36] However, although practitioner bodies such as the CBI and the successive governments position the UK labour market as highly flexible, recent comparative data throw some doubt on this claim.[37]

Robinson cites OECD data to demonstrate that in 1995 the UK had an above average level of part-time employment, similar to the level found in Australia and Sweden at approximately 24 per cent of the labour force. More significantly than this, the UK level of part-time employment in 1979 was greater than the EU average. Labour market deregulation since 1979, designed to promote flexibility, appears to have failed to generate a significantly faster growth of part-time employment than that found in other EU nations. In addition to this comparative limitation, the data suggest that the UK level of temporary employment – 6.9 per cent of employees – appears lower than in Germany (10.5 per cent), France (12.4 per cent) and Scandinavia (13.9 per cent), with only the USA experiencing a lower level in 1995 (2.2 per cent). Thus, states with greater labour market regulation such as Germany and France do not appear to have significantly lower levels of flexibility than the less regulated UK labour market. Equally, the US labour market, which is less regulated than the UK labour market, appears to have a greater level of full-time employment and a lower level of temporary employment.

In the contemporary and current period, the ideology of flexibility remains embedded in the state. The current government recently recognized a productivity gap of 30–40 per cent between the UK and its main competitors in Europe. This admission illustrates some recognition that the crude pursuit of flexibility during the 1980s had little positive impact on comparative economic performance.[38] Labour market deregulation in the 1980s resulted in the worst aspects of social exclusion and poverty prevalent in the US economy, but with few if any of its benefits.[39] This argument led some observers to conclude that during the 1980s and early 1990s flexibility became the aim in state policy rather than expressing a means to an end. However, the contradiction of this strategy was its never-ending course, in which more flexibility promoted the need for more of the same. It appeared that Conservative governments attempted to compete with states whose labour costs and social conditions in civil society the UK could never compete with, unless those conditions were reproduced in the UK.[40]

The key point made by critical observers of flexibility relates to its apparently catch-all coverage. Anything that the state, employers or managers want to introduce can express flexibility. As the next section demonstrates, during the contemporary period this is often irrespective of democratic consequences or wider long-term impact on comparative economic efficiency and performance.

Economic performance in the contemporary period

This section examines the effects of industrial relations reform and the scope of organizational change and development detailed in the previous sections on the UK's economic performance since 1980. The relationship between economic performance and the industrial relations system is both controversial and complex, hence it is necessary to discuss the issue under several headings. First, it is essential to examine the merits and limitations of relative and comparative measures of economic performance since 1980, not only in themselves but in the course of the whole period since 1945. Second, the effects of reform in the industrial relations system and the effects of organizational change and flexibility are important considerations in the evaluation of labour costs in the UK. Third, consideration of investment in the economy may consolidate arguments developed on relative and comparative economic performance and labour costs. Fourth, both economically and politically, Conservative governments have dominated the period since 1980. As a result, it will be useful to examine the effects, however marginal, that follow from changes in public policy associated with the election of the current Labour government. Last, this section demonstrates how consideration of measured economic performance in the 1980s and early 1990s both illustrates and consolidates the effects of short-termism on the state, capital and labour.

Comparative and relative economic performance in the contemporary period

Previous chapters demonstrate that during the height of the golden age UK economic performance, although relatively good compared with the inter-war period, was comparatively poor. Between 1955 and 1973, the annual trend growth rate for manufacturing output was just over 3 per cent, whereas the figure for the USA was only 4.7 per cent and the trend figure for France and (west) Germany was double that of the UK.[41]

Kaldor has convincingly demonstrated that historically embedded political and sociological factors play a significant role in the relative and comparative economic performance of a state.[42] The presence of small often family-controlled firms that serve local markets, a low level of investment in labour-saving equipment, associated slow innovation and research and development (R & D) expenditure represent one series of factors. Equally, a pattern of post-war recovery dominated by Cold War interests express the above factors while the continued dominance of empire and sterling area markets represent a second series of significant factors. At the workplace, an absence of Fordist management structures and techniques and a continued reliance on craft production represent a third series.

Thus, an explicit focus on the industrial relations system may reveal factors that do inhibit economic performance. However, in isolation processes such as collective bargaining reform and the legislative control of trade union activity in dispute resolution cannot inhibit or improve performance other than on the margin. Moreover, although comparative economic performance deteriorated less than previously during the period 1979–88, poor performance and decline remained significant features of the UK economy. Further, although this period coincided with the impact of interventionist reforms in the industrial relations system, the significance of reform was confined to a significant short-term impact on management and trade union prerogatives. Over longer periods of analysis, such reforms make no impact on comparative economic performance. For example, annual average increases in manufacturing sector productivity were 3.6 per cent compared with 2.4 per cent for the whole economy.[43] Attempts to relate rapid productivity improvement in the manufacturing sector to reform of the industrial relations system suggest that over the long term productivity in manufacturing increases faster than in services and the economy as a whole. Further, in the post-war period, the presence of multi-unionism and trade union obstruction in the workplace prevented management from achieving necessary downward adjustments in the size of the manufacturing labour force. Moreover, in the contemporary period, the closure of manufacturing plants, redundancy and unemployment – downsizing – represented more efficient industrial production.[44] However, whereas most industrialized states experienced a relative decline in the numbers employed in the manufacturing sector, the UK suffered an absolute decline, reflected in a differential between productivity increases and stalled output. More critically, improved economic performance in the economy between 1979 and 1988 was less favourable relative to that between

1950 and 1973. However, during the earlier period, the institutional significance of trade union actors and the process of collective bargaining was far stronger than during the latter period. Irrespective of these points, obstructionism in the industrial relations system was identified as a prime factor in poor economic performance during the earlier period.

The procyclical deflationary management of the macroeconomy during the recessions of 1979 and 1982 combined with reform in the industrial relations systems between 1980 and 1984 so damaged the manufacturing sector that output failed to recover its 1979 level until 1987. Hence, it follows that by 1988 economic performance measured from 1979 showed considerable short-term improvement in productivity if not output. This demonstrates the limitation of relative improvement in isolation from comparative measures of performance. Economic performance was better than that previously but showed little or no substantive improvement compared with the UK's industrial competitors. This was particularly the case in the manufacturing sector, but the relative nature of the improvement – better than that previously – was not without cost in terms of the sector's overall capacity. More specifically, a failure to match the economic performance of other states represents comparative economic decline, measured in terms of labour productivity or rate of growth of national income per head. The major limitation of relative measures of economic performance is the failure to position recent performance relative to ten or twenty years ago into a comparative context.

Equally, this failure shows the marginal nature of arguments that highlight the scale significance of reform in the industrial relations system.

The substantive reform of a particular political and sociological factor such as the industrial relations system, if isolated from the other groups of factors cited above, may reinforce the continuation on an embedded course. Several such factors appear equally, if not more, significant than the industrial relations system in explaining the UK's current productivity gap. However, although the current state in government recognize the seriousness of the UK productivity gap, New Labour policy blames low national income per head on the productivity gap.[45]

Comparative levels and rates of change of national income per head provide a good measure of real income and changes therein – a measure of individual and collective prosperity. By placing the blame for low income levels on poor comparative productivity, the government provides only a proximate explanation of poor performance and decline. Low productivity can only result in low per capita incomes and increases in incomes. For example, an OECD study found that the UK's relative productivity performance improved significantly between 1987 and 1993 in sectors such as chemicals, oil refining and electrical equipment manufacturing.[46] But what the study termed absolute productivity remained well behind other states such as the USA, Japan, Germany and France. In other words, comparative productivity growth remains a significant problem. The study concluded that, historically, the UK has sustained and competed in low-value added areas, where comparatively low productivity appeared less problematic – perhaps, as previous chapters demonstrate, because of relatively secure markets domestically and abroad in the post-war period. Hence, raising relative productivity cannot raise comparatively low incomes as a matter of course. As UK experience demonstrated during the 'productivity miracle' of the 1980s, higher levels of relative productivity are achievable by cutting output and cheapening labour. More critically than this, cutting wage costs while deploying labour more extensively through measures such as flexibility and empowerment in the workplace may extend the life of comparatively poor capital equipment that is worked harder. In the early post-war period, extensive overtime working performed a similar role to flexibility and empowerment. The OECD found no evidence that comparative income levels increased as relative productivity increased. Attempts to raise income levels through measures such as the minimum wage, improved skill and investment levels within new production systems may do little to encourage employers to compete beyond low-cost extensive methods.

More positively, the present government appears to recognize that factors beyond the industrial relations system are critical to the UK's comparative economic performance.

> Britain suffers long-standing shortcomings, which may hold us back. Too many British Companies fail to match the performance of their overseas counterparts not just in terms of productivity but in innovation and quality. We have invested too little in modern plant and machinery, as well as research and development and other intangible assets. Skill levels, including marketing and design skills, are too low across much of the workforce.[47]

Over the long term, comparatively poor productivity – the productivity gap – results from the UK's comparatively low level of investment in plant and machinery, training, development and research and development. The operation of the industrial relations system is likely to have an impact upon each area, yet each is an independent factor with historically embedded, qualitative and substantive explanations for their respective low levels. Since the reforms of the 1980s, marketing, design, innovation and diffusion of new systems and technologies have retained a comparative lag. Quality is a cumulative, long-term development related to the above issues, which combine to generate a high-value technical composition of capital. In contrast to this, cheapening relative labour cost is likely to improve comparative competitiveness only marginally perhaps over the short term.

In the food and drink sector, poor levels of training, comparatively poor levels of innovation and investment have resulted in the perverse situation in which companies with the oldest plant appeared to be the most competitive.[48] This is the case because the availability of cheap untrained labour stimulates low investment and poor technological diffusion that extends the life of capital stock.[49] However, the replacement of plant and machinery and the absence of a training and a quality culture within management and the workforce reduces the potential for greater efficiency. It appears that firms fail to consider skill and training needs until commission and delivery of new equipment. Some firms cited the problems of appropriate skills training and increased downtime as reasons for delaying or not investing in new systems. The data show that 70 per cent of firms examined with an overall effective efficiency of 85 per cent or more at world-class manufacturing standards achieved this with very old plant. Here, good maintenance systems sustain efficiency and reliable plant operation in which *skilled* labour operate systems very effectively. The comparative cost of labour appears to be the key factor in competitiveness, not technology. This is likely to be the case in other sectors. However, over time, as a reason for not investing, the food and drink study indicates that a reliance on comparatively cheap *skilled* labour will limit competitiveness as equipment and related labour skills become comparatively obsolete.

In the motor manufacturing sector, the Ford Dagenham plant was in the late 1980s 30 per cent less efficient than its sister plant in Cologne, Germany. In contrast to this, by 1997 Dagenham had become Ford's most efficient plant in Europe, with an output of sixty-two vehicles per person per year.[50] However the Dagenham plant only improved its output per employee–year relative to the late 1980s. As a recent Ford announcement concedes, only increases in the capacity of the plant can raise scale efficiency, which doubling Dagenham's capacity to 450,000 vehicles per year will provide. To achieve both the reforms of the late 1980s and the current increase in production capacity, Ford negotiated agreements with the recognized trade unions. An Amalgamated Engineering and Electricians' Union (AEEU)–TGWU partnership agreement with management led to the current 'modern operating agreement' between the management and the workforce. However, evidence suggests that Dagenham retains a comparative productivity gap – measured by output of cars per person– year – compared with other car manfuacturing plants in Europe.[51] More significantly, past underinvestment at the site played a major role, whereas poor labour productivity and labour relations were less significant as independent factors. However, it appears that Dagenham's comparatively low wage levels combined with improved labour productivity in the late 1980s did sustain the absence of capital investment.[52]

As a measure of comparative prosperity, a low level of gross domestic product (GDP) growth per head may result from the UK's productivity gap. However, this does not demonstrate or explain why a current contemporary gap of between 20 per cent and 40 per cent with France, Germany and the USA remains. Like the fall back of the industrial relations system, it is a marginal and proximate explanation. Organizational change and development, including changes in industrial relations management, failed to improve the long-term comparative productive performance of many UK employees but may have reduced labour costs. The latter has assumed a greater level of importance in measures of short-term profitability and shareholder value. In the period up until 1987, when output remained below the 1979 level, reducing labour costs and output improved the profitability of firms but not necessarily or conclusively efficiency or economic performance.

Labour costs in the contemporary period

As a strategy for making capital profitable, Thatcher governments specifically pursued economic policies oriented towards financial and multinational capital. A central element within this approach was the control of inflation and trade union activity. Hence, the Thatcherite accumulation strategy focused on cheapening UK labour costs to promote and finance the export and import of multinational capital. More specifically, reform of the industrial relations system appeared to be a prerequisite for the processes of organizational change and development necessary to promote the UK's international competitiveness within and beyond the EU.

The Thatcherite focus on cheapening labour costs attempted to remove a persistent problem in the UK labour market since 1945 – the manner in which increases in money earnings exceed productivity increases. This problem causes unit labour costs – the labour cost per unit of output – to increase even where productivity is rising. The theory behind attempts to cut labour cost was simple. By cutting labour costs, the government could make the manufacturing sector leaner and fitter – more internationally competitive. Although it is contentious whether economic policies during the 1980s achieved this goal, on a comparative basis there are additional concerns that the process actually limits competitiveness rather than boosting it.

The available evidence suggests that UK labour costs rose significantly between 1980 and 1996, averaging over 9 per cent per annum increase in the manufacturing sector and nearly 12 per cent per annum increase in the economy as a whole.[53] On a comparative basis, Table 7.1 shows a fall in the annual average labour cost increases; however, the process is common across all the cited OECD states. More significantly than this limitation, the increase in UK unit labour costs over both periods exceeds the OECD average by some margin. This suggests that although the acceleration of money wages over productivity may have slowed during the 1980s and 1990s on a comparative basis the UK made only marginal progress. Moreover, as Nolan demonstrates, whereas wage costs in the UK are comparatively low, unit labour costs are comparatively high; as the Ifo study of mechanical engineering in the EU further demonstrates, low wages often sustain high unit costs. This is the cases as employers sustain comparatively inefficient plant and machinery through low wages, that is the latter compensates for the former.[54] A recent Dresdner Bank study found that in a comparison of seven countries – the US, the UK, France, Germany, Italy, Japan and Spain – only France recorded lower unit labour cost increases between 1991 and 1998 than Germany. Moderate wage agreements since 1993 negotiated under nationwide bargaining procedures or increasingly at workplace level are cited as the major reason for increased productivity, flexibility and output.[55]

Table 7.1   Increases in business sector pay and unit labour costs in the OECD, 1980–95 (annual averages %)

Country	Pay per employee		Unit labour costs[a]	
	1980–90	*1991–5*	*1980–90*	*1991–5*
USA	5.0	4.3	4.1	2.8
UK	8.6	5.1	5.9	2.9
Canada	6.4	3.2	4.9	1.8
Germany[b]	3.6	5.0	1.8	2.4
Japan	3.9	1.9	0.9	0.7
France	7.3	2.8	4.7	1.0
Italy	11.5	5.2	9.4	3.0
OECD	6.0	4.0	4.2	2.3

Source: B. Towers, *The Representation Gap* (Oxford University Press, 1997); figures calculated from *Employment Outlook* (Paris, The OECD, 1994), p. 8, Table 1.5.

Notes
a At 1991 purchasing powers parities.
b West Germany up to, and including, 1991; Germany thereafter.

Any improvement in productivity during the 1980s and early 1990s was of an extremely short-term windfall nature. To close the UK productivity gap requires sustained productivity improvement over the longer term. Equally, it requires levels of capital investment, R & D expenditure and investment in training and development to increase and exceed levels achieved by OECD and EU competitors. The absence of these factors severely limits any benefits derived from organizational restructuring other than cheapening labour. While reforms in the industrial relations system may have contributed to this process on a relative basis, comparatively cutting wage costs as opposed to unit labour costs limits the comparative competitiveness of the UK economy.

Developments in the management of industrial relations, for example the decentralization of personnel to line managers, has combined with low wage costs across the economy, reinforcing a comparatively low technical composition of capital in the manufacturing sector. The previous chapter demonstrates how and why this process continued in the immediate post-war years and how it later affected economic performance over the post-war period, particularly in the 1960s. However, that process cushioned comparative economic decline during the post-war period. In contrast, in the contemporary period, measures that promised to reverse comparative decline both reinforced and telescoped its effect over a much shorter period. The cheapness of UK wages appears to have extended the life of comparatively obsolete capital, whereas the scope of labour market flexibility compensated for comparatively high unit labour costs and indifferent levels of labour productivity. Nichols argues that by paying workers peanuts it is possible to compensate for low capital intensity. Unless employers are able or prepared to work the workforce to death through long hours, low wages alone will limit comparative competitiveness. Equally, the

UK economy is like a Morris Minor— it can go on forever but over time its performance becomes less and less competitive.[56]

Evidently, low-cost areas of UK manufacturing such as mechanical engineering are unable to take advantage of internationally favourable labour costs. A contributory factor in this is the dominance of small to medium-sized enterprises in the UK sector that secures low labour costs, but the smaller scale of operations compared with other EU states caps investment in human capital.[57] However, one particular reason for increases in money wages throughout the manufacturing sector drift ahead of inflation and productivity is difficulty in retaining staff with sought-after skills. For example, in 1998, 23 per cent of employers in a study of 1,300 wage settlements cited inflation plus wage increases as necessary to recruit and retain labour.[58] Hence, in combination, low wage costs, low output relative to the 1980 level and a flexible labour force do not necessarily translate into a comparatively low level of unit labour costs.

The comparatively low level of UK labour costs may also be a factor that inhibits innovation. Innovation is essential if higher labour cost economies are to retain competitiveness, e.g. in engineering, technological competitiveness – a measure of innovation – is the base for wider infrastructure development in which diversified quality production in manufacturing justifies and maintains the need for high labour costs. A particular problem experienced by the UK engineering sector is a high dependence on investment activity by domestic purchasing companies in the textile and clothing sectors. However, movements in the value of the exchange rate have led to significant numbers of plant closures or the retention of current plant. The evidence suggests that in the UK the recessions of 1986 and 1991 reduced the UK share of EU capacity in mechanical engineering to 12.5 per cent of the European total in 1992 from a level of 17.3 per cent in 1985. The historically low level of investment in the UK reduced the domestic and export market share of UK textiles and clothing as they both became less technologically competitive.[59]

Michael Porter argues that the UK ranks thirteenth out of seventeen industrial nations for innovation in terms of its ability to derive commercial benefits from science and technology. Efforts to increase productivity by cutting labour costs appear inappropriate because excessive cost cutting encourages entrepreneurs and large firms to play safe – not risk innovation. Porter's argument concentrates on the need for incentives, particularly in the fiscal system where capital gains tax claws back wealth generated by investments for the Treasury. However, his analysis suggests that a contradictory effect of low labour costs is the reinforcement of low productivity, where the emergence of assembly plants can undermine the R & D and innovation capacity in domestically owned industry. This appears to consolidate further the argument that over the longer term key areas of UK industry are unable to take advantage of low costs because of (un)foreseen consequences that were ignored in the short term. Hence, cheapening labour in terms of low wages appears to have succeeded. However, this does not necessarily appear to translate into a significant comparative reduction in UK unit labour costs. To consolidate this argument further, UK investment levels in the contemporary period require brief examination.

Investment levels in the contemporary period

The discussion of labour costs in the contemporary period suggests that for many firms product market strategies emphasize low-price/low-cost competition, premised on relatively and comparatively low wages in a flexible labour market. However, in addition, the discussion demonstrated that although both are often the subject of favourable political rhetoric the reality, in particular at the comparative level, is open to dispute. Moreover, following on from the discussion of training and development, product market strategies clearly dictate the scope and scale of investment in human capital. Investment in plant and machinery underpin productivity, added value and company growth. However, whereas firms are instrumental in following the profit motive, they follow the guide of public policy in the state. Within this framework, companies themselves determine the appropriate level of capital assets and investment necessary to motivate and retain the labour force. The challenge for the current Labour government is to persuade firms to move beyond short-term time horizons and consider the longer term. As the discussion demonstrates, this is a particular challenge because during the 1980s public policy appeared overtly to support short-termism.

A specific, if negative, effect of the above shows up in official estimates of investment by UK companies. The DTI's capital expenditure (capex) scoreboard published in 1998 demonstrates that the level of underinvestment by UK firms limits their international competitiveness.[60] The report benchmarks the UK's largest 500 spenders on capital investment in the workplace and compares them with an international list of 300 global investors. To measure competitiveness, the report calculates the level of accumulated capital stock in UK companies in terms of gross tangible fixed assets (GTFA) per employee. For general manufacturing, the figure was £61,000, whereas the international average was more than twice this level. In contrast, for consumer goods, manufacturers and service sector UK firms had figures of £44,000 and £63,000 respectively, sustaining gaps against the international average of £73,000 and £ 113,000 respectively.[61]

The international scoreboard calculates current and accumulated capital expenditure in several ways. The most significant measures are GTFA per employee, capex per employee and capex as a percentage of GTFA. Across all three measures, the scoreboard reveals a level of underinvestment that appears to constrain international competitiveness in UK industry.

GTFA per employee measures how much fixed capital is invested to support each employee. As Table 7.2 illustrates, in mineral extraction which is very capital intensive and a sector where the UK is dominant UK firms have a £61,000 investment per employee lead over international competitors. However,

Table 7.2 Capex and GFTA data – UK sector groups and international counterparts

(a) GTFA per employee

	GTFA per employee (£000)	
Sector groups	UK group level	International–UK lag
Mineral extraction	589	-61
General manufacturers	61	67
Consumer goods	44	29
Services	63	50
Utilities	659	296
National	96[a]	53

(b) Capex per employee

	Capex per employee (£000)	
Sector groups	UK group level	International–UK lag
Mineral extraction	52.1	-9.5
General manufacturers	6	4.5
Consumer goods	4.4	2.3
Services	7.7	5.9
Utilities	36.4	22.5
National	9[a]	4.7

(c) Capex as % of GFTA

	Capex % of GTFA	
Sector groups	UK group level	International–UK lag
Mineral extraction	8.8	−0.5
General manufacturers	10.2	−1.6
Consumer goods	10.0	−0.6
Services	12.2	−0.8
Utilities	5.5	1.1
National	9.6[b]	−0.5

Source: *Capex Scoreboard 1998* (London, DTI).

Notes
a This figure was calculated at the national rather than sectoral/group aggregate level.
b This figure was calculated at the national rather than sectoral/group aggregate level Figures for 1997.

in other sectors the UK deficiency is significant particularly in general manufacturing.

Capex per employee measures capital expenditure spent in the previous year to add power to the labour power of each employee. In the UK, capex measures approximate to 65 per cent of international counterparts except in mineral extraction, where high investment in the oil sector buoys the group figure. This measure of capex suggests that accumulated capital assets in the UK are deficient compared with the international average. In addition to this, except for minerals, current levels of capex per employee are also deficient, suggesting that the UK is not converging or closing its productivity gap.

The ratio of capex to GFTA provides a measure of the rate at which companies replace assets. The study assumes that most equipment has a ten-year life, to suggest that an annual capex level of 10 per cent represents the norm. Compared with international competitors, UK groups appear to replace assets at a faster rate. However, as UK firms have a lower GTFA base, a capex/GTFA figure indicates a marginal level of investment on a smaller scale base, suggesting little if any catching up of investment levels.

Although the information contained in the capex scoreboard index is very revealing, it has some limitations. The value of sterling in December 1997 was relatively high, biasing sterling values downwards. Equally, the impact of inflation may affect GTFA levels in the current year in terms of current equivalent prices of assets purchased in previous years.[62] The report concludes that investment per worker in the UK is £9,000 – one-third of the international average. These general data become more daunting when combined with evidence on mechanical engineering in the UK.[63]

The innovative and marketing capacities of domestically owned firms are insufficient to enable them to take advantage of comparative low wages. It appears that the lack of qualified labour is a major factor in the drag effect. This is especially so in the technological field which sustains relatively high unit labour costs – limiting the UK as an emerging low-cost engineering sector. Evidence from a recent US study appears to confirm this.

Foreign direct investment by US firms tends to flow into states that have well-established collective bargaining systems, sophisticated systems for employee rights, a skilled work force and higher rather than lower labour costs. The study found that the erosion of collective bargaining and the emergence of non-unionism in deregulated systems of industrial relations appear less significant to foreign investment decisions made by US firms than the stereotype of US firms suggests.[64] Equally, the study concluded that low-skill/low-wage countries suffer serious comparative competitive disadvantages over more regulated systems. Excessively deregulated industrial relations systems that are too flexible corrode the ability and incentive of employers to find mechanisms to promote competitiveness beyond such constraints. The highest levels of US foreign direct investment in the EU are in France and Germany, which are high labour cost/high-productivity economies with low unit labour costs.

The accumulation strategy pursued by the Thatcher governments followed by those of John Major orientated towards financial and multinational capital. For example, the abolition in 1979 of the Exchange Control Regulation Act of 1947 encouraged UK-based multinational firms to extend and internationalize further operations by direct foreign investment. This, combined with deregulation in the City, created significant short-term benefits. As UK firms further internationalized investment, foreign earnings from interest, profits and dividends appeared to compensate for erosion of the domestic manufacturing base.[65] In the early 1980s, banks and finance houses focused overseas, where profits had risen. For the domestic economy, the rate of return on investment, on which the City provides investment funds already geared to the short term, became higher and more short term.[66] Banks and financial institutions dictate the terms for investment funds and therefore profitability. A low-investment strategy appears legitimate when other aspects of the wider accumulation strategy such as cheapening labour costs enable firms to increase profitability by extending the life of capital equipment. Evidence from the food and drink sector tends to support this argument.[67]

The extent to which UK employers adopt a strategic approach to their employees is the subject of sustained debate. The evidence on skills development and training and investment suggests that in the contemporary period the policy of many employers was strategic if not developmental. In particular, training and skill development become more polarized as the core 'standard' labour force declined; in contrast, the expansion of non-standard employees further limits training and skills development opportunities.[68] This reflects comparatively low investment levels, which in turn suggest that there is little need to train flexible employees further because existing competence levels are appropriate for the scope and level of equipment and technology. In 1995, the Department for Education and Employment (DfEE) suggested that by 2000 40 per cent of the UK labour force would be flexible or non-standard.[69] Equally, the CBI recognizes that relying on non-standard employees to accelerate flexibility will further limit the need for investment and investment in training and skill development for flexible employees.[70] At current levels of capital investment and investment in skills development and training, 'Britain has no future as a low skill, low wage, low quality, low value economy'.[71] The present government appear to recognize the seriousness of the no future scenario, hence it is necessary to examine briefly what effect the change in public policy is likely to have.

A Blairite vision for the state?

The political rhetoric of Tony Blair's foreword in the 'Fairness at Work' White Paper details the 'no future' pessimistic scenario as the legacy of Conservative rule during the 1980s. Moreover, there appears the promise of a longer-term approach to governance, regulation and industrial relations.[72] However, although subsequent government statements identify the need for a new model in public policy, the government has explicitly stated that there will be no return to the interventionist policies of the 1960s and 1970s.[73] Moreover, Blair's foreword to the document together with the identification of measures to tackle the UK productivity gap appear to highlight the central significance of formative influences in the UK state. The historically embedded influence of libertarian *laissez faire* appears to have precedence over contextual influences such as stakeholding and social partnership. Indeed, the former are reinvented in phrases such as 'the encouragement of entrepreneurialism and venture capitalism' and 'the promotion of a corporate culture where fairness underpins competitiveness'.[74] For example, the government expresses both measures as matters for employers and employees beyond the auspices of the state and the framework of employee relations. It appears that the New Labour government concedes that many contextual, if European-inspired, influences over the economy and state are unavoidable, but equally they must not impinge on the UK's traditional pattern of voluntary arrangements. The rejection of interventionism by the government indicates that formative influences over the UK state honed during the 1980s remain significant in the current framework for economic policy.

New Labour appears to adopt the rhetoric of social reform in phrases such as social inclusion while reinforcing the narrowly Thatcherite reinvention of historically embedded economic and political influences over the state. More critically than this, measures such as the national minimum wage, the dilution of *fairness* measures in the 1999 Employment Relations Bill and the governments perfunctory implementation of EU working time regulations continue to embed fragmentation and polarization in the employment relationship. For example, the minimum wage, although of symbolic significance, is at a level that does not threaten the competitiveness of most employers. A survey by Reed Personnel Services found that, of 846 employers questioned, 87 per cent agreed in principle with the implementation of the minimum wage.[75] Equally, a CBI survey found that 75 per cent of employers believe measures such as the minimum wage, the Working Time Directive and the statutory union recognition procedure will have an insignificant effect on their competitiveness.[76]

The fallacy of short-term windfall measures to improve relative statistical competitiveness, such as greater labour market flexibility and labour cost reduction as distinct from measures to reduce unit labour costs via greater investment, are clear. Divisions between and movement in the boundary between what Gallie *et al.* term the optimistic and pessimistic scenario for employment seriously inhibits longer-term approaches to improving international competitiveness.[77] Currently, the efforts of *New Labour* to break the chains of short-termism appear distinctly marginal.

The permanence of short-termism?

Short-termism represents a failure to adopt, to decline and to recognize the need for corresponding change in civil society through economic and institutional reconstruction. In the contemporary period, the UK state followed an accumulation strategy that judged successful economic advance by the lowest standards – deregulation, flexibility and associated measures to cheapen labour. Ferner and Hyman demonstrate that in the late 1990s competitiveness measured in terms of cost and quality are no longer polar alternatives.[78] The particular problem for the UK state in the wider EU context is the 'stickiness' of low wage competition whereby embedded patterns of regulation in national pathways threaten the possibility of economic transformation. For example, the productivity miracle of the 1980s now appears as a productivity gap in which any short-term benefits of the former are unsustainable in the longer term. Supply-side economics and supply-side measures to increase the availability of skilled labour floundered on the contradiction in lack of demand. The closure of partial institutional access to the state via trade unions and collective bargaining during the 1980s deepened this problem. In the contemporary period, deliberate measures enacted by the state – designed to erode pluralism in industrial relations – clearly demonstrate that the industrial relations system was not a significant problem. As Kaldor argued and demonstrated, for the post-war period, the removal of non-quantifiable institutional measures does not necessarily lead to an improvement of economic performance. Whereas in the post-war era pluralism in the industrial relations system helped cushion economic decline, a further retreat into shorter-termism in the contemporary period has accelerated this process. In the post-war period, the perhaps necessary but unrealistic view of the UK's international interests and role did not damage relative economic performance, although comparative economic performance exhibited a decline to trend. In the contemporary period, relative improvement in economic performance appears as a windfall. In contrast, comparative economic decline accelerated further.

Conclusions

The arguments and evidence presented in this chapter demonstrate that institutional and legal reform in the industrial relations system did provide employers with opportunities to reorganize and restructure work systems. The latter resulted in considerable organizational change, if not development; however, it appears that neither reform in industrial relations nor organizational change has contributed to improvement in comparative competitiveness.

The evidence suggests that the procyclical nature of economic policy combined with employer reticence on workplace innovation and investment resulted in the pessimistic reality prevailing over the optimistic scenario. A peculiar – if historically embedded – process, previously blamed on archaic privileges that structured the industrial relations system. In contrast to this, the withdrawal of institutional and legal support for trade unions and collective bargaining represented one component in the wider process of deregulation. The latter led to a renaissance of formative influences over the economy and state which the erosion of partial institutional access to the state, previously acquired by trade unions, reinforced and made more crude.

In terms of organizational change and development, the pessimistic reality outweighs the optimistic. This is the case because although reform of the industrial relations system may have facilitated the process of change management, on balance for the majority of workers, employers have failed to upskill or improve training. Several factors might explain this reluctance. First, misguided managerial efforts to reduce labour costs and improve managerial command, commitment and control may improve workplace performance in terms of shareholder value and profitability but fail to improve organizational commitment. The last requires integrated or strategic managerial policies that promote organizational rather than worker flexibility. Such an approach necessitates better mechanisms for training and development – the illusive high-commitment managerial strategy centred within a high-performance work system.

As the Ifo study of mechanical engineering in the EU concludes, high technology manufacturing industry needs inclusive support from the state not merely an accumulation strategy that promotes cost reduction.[79] The absence of the former demonstrates the fallacy of cost reduction strategies which in isolation limit the international competitiveness of UK engineering. This precludes the emergence of a flexible post-Fordism in engineering, but promotes a pattern of organizational change and development that struggles to be optimistic.

The emphasis throughout the 1980s on improvement in UK economic performance relative to the recent past positioned 'transformation' as a short-term shield for continued comparative economic decline, now manifest as the 'productivity gap'. In the UK, the short-termism of cost reduction is a deeply embedded priority, but misguided in the concentration on cheapening labour. The priority of 'cost reduction' passes to another body, e.g. the state in higher unemployment benefits or suppliers who may find it necessary to further cheapen labour by negotiating or imposing poorer working conditions on their employees. In contrast to this, efforts more prevalent in competitor states appear designed to reduce unit labour costs and therefore improve productivity over the longer term and maintain labour standards. The miracle of transformation appears extremely marginal when examined over the longer term. Its short-termism failed to arrest the declining competitiveness of the manufacturing sector that was evident some time before the 1970s. Moreover, the success of cost reduction in the 1980s reinforced short-termism to embed further the UK's comparatively low-investment culture.

Improvement in economic performance measured relative to the recent past is the central manifestation of short-termism in the state and economy. The success of cost reduction has done little to improve the quality of UK competitiveness in manufacturing and engineering. In the latter, the evidence is profound: within the comparative EU context, the UK sector cannot combine high quality with cost competitiveness. The weakness of trade unions in collective bargaining in the contemporary period makes it possible for employers to legitimize the pessimistic reality as optimistic. The UK's productivity gap now evident in the 1990s demonstrates that *ceteris paribus* short-termism remains. Change and development during the 1980s inspired by reform in the industrial relations system ignored historically embedded weaknesses beyond industrial relations, many of which remain.

The Thatcherite accumulation strategy continued by John Major and in part by Tony Blair made capital more profitable but at a considerable cost in terms of lost output. By stressing the ideology of the market, the customer and the individual, the inclusiveness of post-war economic management was demonized along with trade unions and collective bargaining. Attacks on the post-war state and its institutional components such as collectivism, pluralism and organized labour as a productive force reinvented formative influences in the state. The rhetoric of the market and individualism mobilized support for non-interventionism and the withdrawal of the state from the economy and civil society. Cannadine demonstrates that freedom from the state and libertarianism meant freedom to be unequal.[80] The remarkable quality of this strategy was its successful sale as the source of improved economic performance. As previous chapters demonstrate, the social and political inclusiveness of the post-war period, however contested and marginal, did not make UK economic performance any worse than its potential held.

Reform of industrial relations during the 1980s was a marginal to insignificant factor in the course of comparative economic performance, suggesting that the Thatcherite project was more political than economic. The strategy aimed to eradicate the post-war orthodoxy in the state and this necessitated defeating organized labour politically and institutionally. The political economy of the state since 1979 has reinforced embedded tendencies in the UK's national pathway, not removed them. Short-term profitability appeared to improve without a balanced movement to an optimistic scenario for capital and labour, a process similar to that promoted by the state and capital in the immediate post-war period. The main difference between the two periods is that the former policy cushioned decline, whereas in the latter decline was accelerated.

8 Economic decline

The state, regulation and industrial relations?

Introduction

An attempt to draw together the separate but thematically linked arguments developed in the previous seven chapters is fraught with difficulty. Movement between different levels of analysis blunts analytical precision and on occasion results in the reader being asked to do something more difficult than the author. Any writer who moves between different subjects and literature sets faces these difficulties. However, this is necessary to draw out and to expose the proximate nature of many declinist arguments that highlight, isolate and separate the industrial relations system from other aspects of the state and capitalist regulation.

Each chapter takes general arguments and theories and blends them with particularized detail on the UK state. Contemporary organizational restructuring, the effects of industrial relations on economic decline, the failure of the state to take a more realistic view of the UK's role in the post-war world are complex issues surveyed in and between disputed literature sets. Movement between different subjects and literature provides the material to develop a particularized argument derived from general material but significantly different from it.

In the contemporary period, the reform of the industrial relations system has failed to improve the UK's comparative economic performance or remove organizational problems previously blamed on the industrial relations system throughout the post-war period. This may have been the case because the short-term pattern of the UK's post-war economic recovery sustained and structured embedded patterns of industrial relations and management practice throughout the post-war period. This is characteristic of the UK's highly conservative and particularized state. In turn, conservatism and particularization determined a series of post-war aims – economic, military and political – that precluded, perhaps necessarily, restructuring in the economy and state modelled on what is now termed Fordism. The following headings detail summary and concluding arguments that aim to make connections between the arguments of individual chapters.

Decline: governance and industrial relations since 1945

> No state in the twentieth century has ever been able to recast its economy, political structures and society to the extent that Britain must do, without suffering defeat in war, economic collapse or revolution. Only traumatic events on that scale delegitimise the existing order to such an extent that a country concedes the case for dramatic change.[1]

Governance refers to the control and co-ordination of activities to attain a range of outcomes. In the main, it is the arena of the state, particularly in the external arena. However, in the domestic sphere, the state may delegate the regulation of economic and social institutions to representative groups from capital and labour. Policymakers, academics and politicians find it necessary to search for economic and social interpretations of decline when historically embedded institutions appear to undermine the political aims of governance, in particular economic performance.

Attention to particular institutions such as those in the industrial relations system often appear to provide an interpretation of decline that is less true than the facts. The 'other' facts remain insignificant while a particular interpretation of decline remains plausible. However, a particular interpretation may 'crowd out' other complementary interpretations as a result of familiarity. For example, those that emphasize the aim, pattern and structure of governance rather than the isolated effects of particular institutions.

The industrial relations system reflects the broad contours of the economic, political and social development and decline in the UK. However, the last group structures the former institution. Historically and intellectually, it is impossible to separate the industrial relations system from the broader contours of development and decline; however, theoretically and empirically the avoidance of historical formation makes separation plausible. Equally, the structure and internal operation of the industrial relations system are not an abnormal graft onto otherwise functional institutions of corporate, economic and political management. Chapters 4 and 5 detail an examination of economic, political and social contours that remain deeply embedded in the contemporary period. Both chapters reveal the importance of prior significance, which suggests that historically embedded − formative − influences in a particular state directly structure contemporary economic performance.

The partial incorporation of the employed class into the UK state represents the central institutional antecedent of the industrial relations system. Incorporation posed no challenge to the political interests of the ruling class or the economic interests of the industrial class. Alternatively, collective *laissez faire* fractionalized the economic and political aims and interests of the employed class to reproduce a contradictory short-termism and self-regulation similar to that secured and retained by the industrial and ruling classes into the contemporary period.

The quote from Hutton that opens this section defines the conservative and short-term structure that makes up and surrounds the UK state. For example, institutional reform in the industrial relations system cannot recast economic performance or political structures. However, as Chapters 5 and 7 demonstrate, industrial relations reform from the Report of the Donovan Commission to the Thatcherite project has aimed to do this. Institutional reform without wider reform of governance in the state merely reinforces continuity in the latter although it has only a marginal effect on improving economic performance and political accountability.

A legacy of connections

The contemporary period is pregnant with the presumption of an inexorable movement to convergence. Economic pressures for convergence result from globalization or the emergence of the single European market at the regional level. Such pressures will (allegedly) homogenize particularized patterns of development associated with individual nation states. However, developing a historically embedded argument that establishes the distinctive structures and processes that particularize a state – what makes it individual – challenges the movement and presumption of convergence. This is particularly the case if the substance and rhetoric of convergence are unable to erode the legacy of historically embedded connections within and between the institutional structure of the state and economy.

In the contemporary period of 'economic convergence', the comparative deficiencies in the UK pattern of capital formation reflect and are similar to those of the post-war period. The immediate post-war era saw the legacy of unconstructed or organic industrialization and the subsequent effects of empire renewed. This was necessary to support the wider goals of the state in *realpolitik* and international relations – nuclear power, permanent membership of the UN Security Council, sovereign *European* great power and supporting actor in regional conflicts. Although these objectives remain, the UK's post-war economic performance has struggled to maintain them. However, a legacy of connections remains whereupon the contemporary institutionalization of economic and political values that were formative during the process of industrialization and empire structures political governance and limits economic functionalism.

The UK is a modern state, yet simultaneously conservative to the point of obsession with the past. Since 1945, the political success of policies in economic management appears not in terms of comparative competitiveness but in the degree to which they secure national sovereignty. For example, policies that secured the reserve status of sterling, securing the recovery of national pathways within the Marshall Plan – as a precursor to not joining the EC in 1957. Equally, in the post-war period, the maintenance of established if disparate non-standard markets, associated patterns of management practice and industrial relations were demonstrative of this measure. Further, in the contemporary period, opt-outs from integrative EU strategies such as the social chapter, withdrawal from the European Exchange Rate Mechanism (ERM) and reticence over membership of the Euroland area are indicative of this measure. Each policy has maintained sovereignty, yet each was contradictory – where short-term political necessity, defined formatively in terms of sovereignty, seriously damaged longer-term economic performance.

The transformational premise of economic and political management in the UK state since 1979 has been unable to break this legacy. The evidence presented in Chapter 7 demonstrates that the political economy of the state has reinforced the legacy. An accumulation strategy focused on improving short-term profitability appeared to improve economic performance without a balanced movement to the elusive, but often espoused, optimistic scenario for capital and labour.

Proximate explanations of decline during the post-war period followed by proximate explanations of transformation during the contemporary period result in a contentment for scholars, policymakers and politicians. The argument that decline occurred because of the industrial relations system may hold some truth, but it explains nothing. The key issue is why the system was problematic and what was its connection to other economic, political and ideological factors such as those detailed in Chapters 2–4. Equally, counterfactual explanations that position alternative courses for the post-war period are theoretically conceivable, but fanciful. This is the case because a different course would have required different causes which, as Chapters 2, 3 and 5 demonstrate, could not prevail.

First indications of UK economic decline became evident in the late nineteenth century, suggesting its long-term nature. Yet, only since the early 1960s has the link between decline and the industrial relations system preoccupied scholars and governments. However, the attention of this focus has failed to break the legacy of other connections in the development of UK capitalism. These connections range from the localized development of industrialization in the seventeenth century to its consolidation during the industrial revolution in the nineteenth century. These patterns connected with and trailed the slow diffusion of new technologies and systems of work organization in the twentieth century and the pursuit of sovereignty and its attendant necessities since 1945. The historical legacy of early development buoyed by empire and the subsequent attachment to comparatively slow growth/low-productivity markets remains significant. In contrast to this, the impact of reform in the industrial relations system, when isolated from continuity in other significant areas of UK capitalism, appears marginal.

The aims of the UK state in the period since 1945

The limitations of post-war aims in the UK state remain significant in the contemporary period. They reflect the continuous and conservative development of the state whereby the effects of early industrialization have created a particularized approach to governance in the state. This pattern permeates international relations and domestic, economic and political management. Positioning the industrial relations system and embedded patterns of management interests and associated patterns of job regulation in this wider framework exposes the limitations of proximate explanations of decline that isolate the industrial relations system as a primary causal factor.

The economic and political aims of the state were forged early in the post-war era. Over the post-war period, the aim of economic policy trimmed from securing the UK's national pathway to prosperity to a political aim of cushioning economic decline. Despite the rhetoric of New Labour, the latter remains the central political aim of the state. The aim of sovereignty in national policy remains to demonstrate national reassertion in an internationalized world, formerly dominated by superpower conflict now dominated by the pressures of globalization and apparent economic and political convergence. The dominance of these factors has over the periodic short term made national policies appear viable and necessary, e.g. the maintenance of established markets and defence interests, and established patterns of management and patterns of job regulation. Each played a role in sustaining the comparatively low-investment/low-capital stock of UK industry that has appeared necessary to sustain the wider interests of the UK state in international relations.

The central difference between state policy in the post-war period and the contemporary period is the erosion of institutional inclusion for the employed class. This has separated the interests of the state and capital from wider civil society. Reform of the industrial relations system is a case in point. Carr demonstrates that all history is contemporary history whereby the past informs contemporary evaluation of policy and strategy.[2] Moreover, Carr demonstrates that scholars must evaluate the thought processes behind events and decisions. From the early twentieth century until the end of the post-war period, the state attempted to cushion economic decline by tolerating the partial inclusion of trade unions and the institution of collective bargaining. In contrast to this, in the contemporary period, the state has sought to sustain its political and economic objectives by excluding trade unions and the representative institution of collective bargaining.

The evidence presented in Chapter 7 suggests that the strategy of exclusion has done little to improve comparative economic performance. More critically than this, exclusion appears to have accelerated economic decline, whereas the relative measurement of economic performance appeared to justify exclusion. By contrasting the post-war period and the contemporary period, the recent thought processes within state actors become clear. The political motivation for exclusion informs and interlocks with a series of ideas, ideologies and interests within an embedded framework of delegated institutions. In amalgamation, during the contemporary period these have reinvented formative influences in the governance of the state. However, the contradictory limitations in the aims of the post-war state lay beyond trade unions and the institution of collective bargaining. The former remain in the contemporary period to demonstrate this.

The consequences of national distinctiveness

Nation states organize political power both domestically and externally in order to maintain patterns of governance in a highly particularized manner. For the UK state, the course of particularization remains historically significant in the contemporary period. Particularization and conservatism create a 'national distinctiveness' that reflects sociological and institutional factors and interests that once internalized or enacted appear to preserve sovereign identity. For example, successive post-war governments resisted the course of European integration, whether in the economic, in the military or in the political arena. Subsequent to the arrival of economic and political integration, the UK state has sought to preserve its national distinctiveness by resisting then blunting aspects of political integration, e.g. the promotion of subsiduarity as a foil to 'shared sovereignty' and/or aggressive negotiating positions on the implementation of EU directives that may 'erode' national sovereignty. The negotiation of exclusions and opt-outs from the provisions of the European working time directive are a case in point, whereas the maintenance of passport and border controls are another.

Maintenance of a distinctively UK pathway in the management of economic interests and economic policy is only one aspect of sovereignty. Material in Chapters 2, 3, 6 and 7 demonstrate that although this may appear necessary it does not always result in an economic performance that matches the comparative performance of other states. Equally, Chapters 6 and 7 demonstrate that distinctively particularized aims and objectives in a state are pivotal to the course of economic management, which in turn structures employer interests in the industrial relations system. Nationally distinctive processes of regulation become embedded – voluntarism in the industrial relations system – and subsequently institutionalized. The accumulated views and perceptions of key actors in the state, capital and labour prevail over hegemonic patterns of dominant regulation prescribed in the post-war period and over the contemporary period.

Since 1945, the UK state has operated within but against economic and political frameworks that appear to imply an end to national sovereignty and with it national distinctiveness. Chapters 2, 3 and 5 demonstrate this most clearly in terms of post-war recovery – the Marshall Plan, threats to the embedded interests of capital in established markets, systems of work organization, management practice and associated patterns of job regulation. More critically than this, the chapters demonstrate how the fear of an end to sovereignty creates contradictory tendencies within a defined national pathway. In the post-war period, UK economic decline demonstrates the fallacy of national ambition in a superpower Cold War dominated by integrative pressures within the European states system. The fallacy – the UK's short-term isolation from the emergent *European state* – soon became apparent and by the early 1960s negotiations for membership of the EC commenced.

Although fallacious, policies designed to secure national distinctiveness expose and limit the generalization of proximate explanations for longer-term decline in comparative economic performance. Proximate explanations for economic decline, for example the UK's 'flawed Fordism', a failure to adjust to the emergence of post-Fordism and the subsequent pressures of globalization and convergence, only acquire credibility at a level of abstraction too high for historical observation or empirical evaluation. Chapter 2 develops this argument, whereas Chapters 6 and 7 provide empirical illustration for the post-war and contemporary periods. More particularly, both chapters demonstrate that proximate explanations are themselves explainable not as general movement but in terms of historically embedded – historically significant – influences in particular states such as the UK.

National distinctiveness remains significant in the contemporary period of political integration and economic convergence. UK membership of the EC and EU illustrates the limitations of following an independent economic and political pathway during the early post-war period. However, national distinctiveness remains significant as the UK state seeks to generalize the Anglo-American model of economic management and industrial relations throughout the EU.

A failure to match the performance of other nations is a measure of economic decline, more particularly decline results from a failure to adjust to a more realistic view of national interests. In one respect, the UK state has overcome the latter by membership of the EC, now EU. However, the contradictory results of national distinctiveness remain. The UK state remains, together with France, a *European* great power with extra-European interests. The cost of becoming a great power in the post-war period appears to be economic decline. In the contemporary period, this remains the case. These factors appear of greater significance in explaining economic decline than the associated effects of the industrial relations system.

Capitalist regulation, post-war recovery and contemporary decline

'Regulation' implies order and common purpose, a set of rules that describe orderly behaviour. Regulation theory offers a general catch-all system of ideas that explain the material dynamics of the post-war period and subsequently the contemporary period independently of historical facts. Regulation theory as either Fordism or post-Fordism offers a plausible explanation of the internal and material dynamics in capital during the post-war and contemporary phases of capitalist development. However, the analytical precision and the empirical presence of both categories of regulation remain controversial and questionable. Equally, as Chapter 2 demonstrates, regulation theory contains no historical dimension of any significance.

In the period 1941–7, US foreign policy strategized institutional regulation in the following manner. A multilateral fixed exchange rate system for international trade in Fordist goods between states where Americanized management practice would institutionalize industrial relations, undermine craft control in the workplace and align wages and productivity. The historically informed theoretical category 'Atlanticism' developed in Chapter 2 positions US foreign policy as the architect of Fordism in the UK and the Western European states system more generally. Moreover, Chapter 2 further demonstrates, by moving beyond the regulation literature, that by 1947 the initial aims of US foreign policy were defunct. In the UK, the policies created virtual economic collapse and in France and the Western occupation zones of Germany they stimulated political support for Communism.

In contrast to its initial post-war phase, from 1947 US foreign policy focused on geopolitics in Western Europe. To secure US economic, military and political interests, US foreign policy moved away from an all-encompassing economic theory to an aid programme – the Marshall Plan. The design of the latter aimed to suppress the Communist threat by promoting the material freedom and prosperity of US capitalism. As Chapters 2, 3 and 6 demonstrate, the only way to secure this was to allow individual states to maintain or reinvent national pathways, and markets therein, and associated patterns of interest for capital, management interests and job regulation. The UK is the primary example of the former, whereas West Germany is the primary example of the latter.

The regulatory framework of anti-Communism and the Marshall Plan formed the basis of regulation in the post-war period. The apparent imperative and bluntness of Cold War measures necessarily created a complex of Western European nations in which highly particularized patterns of interest and regulation resurrected historically embedded national pathways: sooner in the case of the UK and later in the case of West Germany. In both cases, the economic performance of each state returned to trend relatively quickly. Chapter 6 demonstrates that for the UK by the early post-war period Fordism in the state and capital, 'flawed' or otherwise, was a historical fiction – a historically insignificant concept.

Jessop, the leading UK commentator on regulation theory, has recently argued that national economies are increasingly unable to regulate national economic space because of the emergence of international economic trends, often termed globalization or internationalization.[3] The historical evidence suggests that this assertion will over the longer term prove partial. The global project launched by the USA in the post-war period was equally as powerful as contemporary globalization, yet accumulation regimes in national pathways contained and legitimized the project. The UK's recent experience in the ERM and the growing reluctance of the state to entertain membership of Euroland illustrate the political limitations of integrationist regulation. Integration requires politically and socially unacceptable levels of deflationary bias or, alternatively, a mechanism to legitimize the economic and political consequences that will result from integration for a declining nation state. The continued centrality of the nation state as the driver for national pathways seems assured.

Particularized patterns of national regulation

The primary objective of the UK state is maximum material freedom in an independent national pathway to capitalist accumulation and structured class conflict. Liberty and freedom from the state represent the ideological base of the state in civil society; the maintenance of free will – control and coercion – before capitalist accumulation, the literal meaning of libertarian *laissez faire*. A national system for industrial relations is central to this process.

A national study that integrates *realpolitik* with a discussion of domestic political economy provides an explanation of the UK's comparative economic decline beyond the proximate limitations of *flawed* Fordism. The history of the UK's movement to capitalism is highly distinctive – particularized to the point of unique. The process was highly organic and localized containing little instrumental management by the state, in contrast to this the process itself structured the state and its relative autonomy from capital. The movement from feudalism to industrial capitalism is distinctive among European states as the UK's sovereign integrity has remained uninterrupted since medieval times. Territorial integrity creates a form of sovereign nationalism in the state that during the twentieth century has replaced economic and political protection previously secured by empire.

In the post-war period, sovereignty fused with influences that were formative during the process of industrialization, the significance of embedded structures in libertarian *laissez faire* and its ideological, if rhetorical, expression as freedom from an emergent *European* state. The embedded structure in the institutional ensemble that constitutes the UK state constrains UK economic performance while securing its national sovereignty. The relationship between the UK state and the emergent *European* state during the post-war period and the contemporary period demonstrates the difficulty faced by new forms of governance, in which deeply embedded economic and political structures remain significant yet contradictory.

A particularized theory of the UK state specifies a hypothesis that illustrates the contradictory course of economic functionalism. A historically informed structural theory appears able to specify the post-war and contemporary pathway of the UK state. The emergence of liberal capitalism created a hierarchical state that became accessible to the working class through the impact of contextual influences from the late nineteenth century. However, although collectivism reached a high point during the post-war period, it fragmented working-class resistance to the capitalist interest into narrowly defined short-term economic and political interests. Equally, the expulsion of these interests from the state in the contemporary period further fragmented the working class while overtly resurrecting the interests of the capitalist class under the label of economic restructuring. The UK state is an increasingly *ancien régime*, dominated by the aim of restoring unbridled libertarian *laissez faire*. This aim has done little to improve economic performance and nor has the restrictive reform of the industrial relations system, indicating its marginal role in decline since 1945.

As this study of the UK demonstrates, nation states cling to national pathways in economic and political management to create barriers to international economic interdependence that appear to threaten national sovereignty. The continued short-termism of this approach in the UK results in the question 'can capital and labour do better in a state where libertarian *laissez faire* is so deeply embedded?'. *Laissez faire* is short-termism, and the experience of the 1980s and 1990s suggests that compared with the post-war period the state can do better. However, the erosion of national inclusiveness so prevalent since 1979 appears designed with little concern for improved economic performance but the concentration of economic and political power. Hence, distribution could be better, but concentration of economic and political power perhaps could not. The treatment of the employed class in the industrial relations system demonstrates this position quite clearly.

Notes

1 Governance, regulation and industrial relations

1   E. H. Carr, *What is History?*, second edition (London, Penguin, 1987).
2   E. H. Carr, op. cit., p. 14.
3   E. H. Carr, op. cit., Chapter 4, pp. 8–9.
4   N. Kaldor, *Causes of the Slow Rate of Economic Growth in the United Kingdom* (Oxford University Press, 1966); N. Kaldor 'Conflicts in national economic objectives', *Economic Journal* (1971) 81: 1–16; N. Kaldor 'Capitalism and industrial development: some lessons from Britain's Experience', *Cambridge Journal of Economics* (1977) 1: 193–204.

2 Regulation and the post-war order

1   H. J. Morganthau, *Politics Among Nations* (New York, McGraw Hill, 1993).
2   For critical summaries of the Atlantic alliance, see A. Deporte, *Europe Between the Superpowers*, second edition (New Haven, Princeton, 1987). Deporte argues that superpower competition in Western Europe created a stable Western Europe within an Atlantic alliance which developed out of the Marshall Plan, the North Atlantic Treaty, Nato and the rearmament of West Germany in 1958. See also, D. Calleo, *Atlantic Fantasy* (Baltimore, Johns Hopkins Press, 1971). Calleo suggests that 'Atlantic alliance' is a euphemism for US domination. A similar approach is applied to 'federalism' in Nato by Osgood. See, R. Osgood, *Nato: The Entangling Alliance* (Chicago, University of Chicago Press, 1962).
3   M. Aglietta, *A Theory of Capitalist Regulation* (London, New Left Books, 1979).
4   Ibid.
5   B. Jessop, 'Post-Fordism and the State', in A. Amin (ed.), *Post-Fordism: a Reader* (Oxford, Blackwell, 1994).
6   S. Marglin, 'Preface', in S. Marglin and J. Schor (eds), *The Golden Age of Capitalism Reinterpreting the Post-war Experience* (Oxford, Clarendon Press, 1991).
7   R. Jessop, 'Regulation Theory', in P. Arestis and M. Sawyer (eds), *The Elgar Companion to Radical Political Economy* (Aldershot, Elgar, 1994).
8   M. Aglietta, op. cit.
9   Ibid.
10   H. Braverman, *Labour and Monopoly Capital – The Degradation of Work in the Twentieth Century* (New York, Monthly Review Press, 1974). For a recent review of Braverman, see M. Noon and P. Blyton, *The Realities of Work* (London, Macmillan, 1997), Chapter 6.
11   M. Aglietta, op. cit.
12   Edwards extended the approach of Braverman through an examination of different types of controls (simple, technical and bureaucratic) which management utilize at different stages of capitalist development and in different size of firm. R. Edwards, *Contested Terrain* (New York, Basic, 1979).

13   A. Tickell and J. A. Peck, 'Social regulation *after* Fordism: regulation theory, neo-liberalism and the global–local nexus', *Economy and Society* (1995) 24 (3): 37–86.

14   A. Lipietz, *Mirages and Miracles and the Crisis of Global Fordism* (London, Verso, 1987).

15   A. Glyn, A. Hughes, A. Lipietz and A. Singh, 'The rise and fall of the golden age'; S. Marglin and A. Bhaduri, 'Profit squeeze and Keynesian theory'; S. Bowles and R. Boyer, 'A wage-led employment regime: income distribution, labour discipline and aggregate demand in welfare capitalism'. All in: S. Marglin and J. Schor (eds), *The Golden Age of Capitalism: Reinterpreting the Post-war Experience* (Oxford, Clarendon Press, 1991).

16   Glyn *et al.*, op. cit.; S. Bowles and R. Boyer, op. cit.; and, especially, Marglin and Bhaduri, op. cit.

17   R. Boyer, 'Capital–labour relations in OECD countries: from Fordist golden age to contrasted national trajectories', in J. Schor (ed.), *Capital, the State and Labour* (Aldershot, Elgar, 1996).

18   B. Jessop, 'The welfare state in the transformation from Fordism to post-Fordism' and 'Thatcherism and flexibility: the white heat of a post Fordist revolution', in B. Jessop, H. Kastendeik, K. Neilsen and O. Petersen (eds), *The Politics of Flexibility: Restructuring State and Industry in Britain, Germany and Scandinavia* (Aldershot, Elgar, 1991); R. Boyer, 'The evolution of wage/labour relations in seven European countries', in R. Boyer (ed.), *The Search for Labour Market Flexibility – The European Economy in Transition* (Oxford, Oxford University Press, 1988); T. Ward, 'From mounting tension to open confrontation: the case of the UK', in R. Boyer (ed.), *The Search for Labour Market Flexibility – The European Economy in Transition* (Oxford, Oxford University Press, 1988).

19   Boyer (1988; 1996), op. cit.; R. Boyer and D. Drache, 'Introduction', in R. Boyer and D. Drache (eds), *States Against Markets: The Limits of Globalization* (London, Routledge, 1996).

20   G. Hodgson, 'Thatcherism: the miracle that never happened', in E. Knell (ed.), *Free Market Conservatism: A Critique of Theory and Practice* (London, Allen and Unwin, 1984).

21   Glyn *et al.*, op. cit.; Ward in Boyer (1988), op. cit.

22   Glyn *et al.*, op. cit.; C. Kindleberger, 'Why did the golden age last so long?', in F. Cairncross and A. Cairncross (eds), *The Legacy of the Golden Age: The 1960s and their Consequences* (London, Routledge, 1992).

23   A. Gamble, *The Free Economy and the Strong State: The Politics of Thatcherism* (London, Macmillan, 1988).

24   R. Hyman, 'Plus ça change. The theory of production and the production of theory', in A. Pollert (ed.), *Farewell to Flexibility* (Oxford, Blackwell, 1991), pp. 27–77.

25   C. Lane, *Industry and Society in Europe Stability and Change in Britain, Germany and France*. (Aldershot, Elgar, 1995), p. 26.

26   Boyer (1996), op. cit.

27   I . Clark, 'Institutional stability in management practice and industrial relations: the influence of the Anglo-American Council for Productivity', *Business History* (1999) 41 (3): 64–92.

28   H. Bull, *The Anarchical Society: A Study of Order in World Politics*, second edition (London, Macmillan, 1995); M. Wight, *Power Politics* (London, Penguin, 1979).

29   Bull, op. cit.

30   Taylor argues that alliance systems combined with the momentum of mobilization caused the First World War. Moreover, Taylor illustrates that alliance systems necessitate the creation of disputes. For example, it has been established that Germany had no real quarrel with France or the UK. Further, Taylor illustrates how the Second World War was caused by the conclusion of the First. The inequality and unworkable points contained in the Versailles Treaty prefigured German attempts at redress. Equally, the UK's alliance with Poland ensured that the UK would enter the war if the balance of power was disturbed. A. J. P. Taylor, *The Origins of the Second World War* (London, Hamish Hamilton, 1961).

31   For the definitive treatment of this argument, see A. Deporte, op. cit.

32   Definitive treatment of revisionism in G. Kolko and J. Kolko, *The Limits of Power: The World and US Foreign Policy 1945–1960* (New York, Harper and Row, 1972).

33 Deporte, op. cit., and M. Hogan, *The Marshall Plan: America, Britain and the Reconstruction of Western Europe 1947–1952* (London, Cambridge University Press, 1987).

34 F. Block, *The Origins of International Economic Disorder: A Study of US International Monetary Policy from WW2 to the Present* (Berkeley, University of California Press, 1977).

35 R. N. Gardner, *Sterling Dollar Diplomacy in Current Perspective* (New York, Columbia University Press, 1980). During the war, foreign exchange earnings of residents of the overseas sterling area were commandeered under sterling area pooling arrangements and deposited in London for common use by the central dollar pool. As Gardner demonstrates, sterling area balances increased from £856 million in 1941 to £2,723 million in June 1945. The main reason for this rapid growth was that the UK's current account with the sterling area was heavily in deficit, largely as a result of the cessation of peacetime exports. Dollar surpluses pooled from the overseas sterling area piled up as the government issued inconvertible sterling credits in return. Egypt and India were particularly hard hit by this practice, as was any other Empire nation where troops were garrisoned. For details, see pp. 16–72.

36 At the 1947 International Trade Organization conference in Geneva on tariff reduction, the Americans were outmanoeuvred by the UK. The agreement concluded that the majority of UK exports to Empire nations retained pre-war levels of tariff preference; see Gardner, op. cit., Chapter 18.

37 The US loan was supplemented by a $1.25 billion loan from Canada.

38 A. Sked and C. Cook, *Post-War Britain* (London, Penguin, 1979), p. 29.

39 Block notes the change in emphasis once Truman replaced Roosevelt, suggesting that Morganthau's ideas on international economics retained a significance in political rhetoric and propaganda while losing importance in terms of power politics. Block, op. cit., pp. 38–42.

40 X, 'The sources of Soviet conduct', *Foreign Affairs* (1947) July. Also, see G. Kennan, *Russia and the West Under Lenin and Stalin* (Boston, Little Brown and Company, 1960).

41 Bull, op. cit., pp. 97–8; D. Calleo, *The Imperious Economy* (Massachusetts, Harvard University Press, 1982).

42 Deporte, op. cit.; see also J. Ikenberry, 'The myth of post-war chaos', *Foreign Affairs* (1996) May/June. Ikenberry argues that containment and the liberal economic order were independent yet mutually reinforcing, with the latter responsible for a large degree of institutional co-binding between the US and Europe.

43 Clark, op. cit.

44 Kolko and Kolko, op. cit., pp. 435–6.

45 P. Armstrong, A. Glyn and J. Harrison, *Capitalism Since 1945* (Oxford, Blackwell, 1991), p. 100.

46 A. Van der Pijl, *The Making of an Atlantic Ruling Class* (London, Verso, 1984), pp. 94 and 162–6.

47 A. Milward, *The Reconstruction of Western Europe 1945–51* (London, Methuen, 1984). This is Milward's thesis, its argument is controversial and contrasts strongly with that of Hogan. Milward provides a powerful counterfactual revisionism which suggests that the Marshall Plan had only a marginal impact on the moves to European integration. Equally, Milward suggests the Marshall Plan was not necessary. Further, Milward argues that the Marshall Plan was merely a technical device to bridge the dollar gap, which had no impact beyond this. However, this last argument is not without significant criticism. See A. Cairncross, *The British Economy Since 1945* (London, ICBH, 1992), p. 55. Cairncross repeated these criticisms of Milward during the UK Academy/Marshall Plan Foundation Conference at the University of Leeds, May 1997. For an orthodox systems international relations perspective on European Integration, see Deporte, op. cit. For a more radical perspective, see Mary Kaldor, *The Disintegrating West* (London, Penguin, 1979). Kaldor predicted that the superpower states system would eventually collapse and usher in new power centres – Europe and Japan – to rival the USA.

48 F. Romero, *The United States and the European Trade Union Movement* (New York, University of North Carolina, 1993); R. Filippelli, *American Labour and Post-War Italy, 1943–1954* (Massachusetts, Stanford University Press, 1989); J. Harper, *America and the Reconstruction of Italy, 1945–1948* (Cambridge, Cambridge University Press, 1986).

49 For evidence of this in the car industry see D. Thoms and T. Donnelly, *The Motor Car Industry in Coventry Since the 1890s* (London, Croom Helm, 1985).

50 Milward, op. cit.

51 M. Hogan, 'American Marshall planners and the search for a European neo-capitalism', *American Historical Review* (1985) 90: 44–73; C. Maier, 'The politics of productivity: the foundations of American international economic policy after WW2', *International Organization* (1977) 31(4): 607–35.

52 Text of Marshall's speech.

53 The central factor in European economic destabilization during the inter-war period was the debilitating effect of German reparations, both the Dawes and the Young Plans were designed to repackage German reparations. The Dawes Plan also contained a grant of 800 million goldmarks in order to assist Germany in a return to the gold standard.

54 Austria, Belgium, Denmark, Norway, Sweden, Iceland, Holland, Luxembourg, Great Britain, Portugal, Italy, Greece, Turkey, France, Eire and the Western occupations zones in Germany.

55 A. Bullock, *The Life and Times of Ernest Bevin*. Vol. 3. *Foreign Secretary* (London, Heinemann, 1983).

56 Milward, op. cit., p. 65.

57 Hogan, op. cit., 1987, pp. 45–53. This approach was not explicit, it rested on an agreement to publicly position integration as the basis of the Marshall Plan. The Soviets were unlikely to accept an invitation to join on this basis, a likelihood even more remote if the plan included the Trizonia area of Germany.

58 Hogan, op. cit., 1987, pp. 76–82.

59 For a summary of this argument, see J. Bulpitt, 'The European question', in D. Marquand and A. Seldon (eds), *Ideas that Shaped the Post-War Britain* (London, Faber, 1996).

60 Kolko and Kolko, op. cit., Chapters 1–8.

61 For the definitive account of Nato's fictional Federal Structure, see Osgood, op. cit.

62 For a useful documentary account of this, see J. Tomlinson and N. Tiratsoo, *Industrial Efficiency and State Intervention in Labour 1939–1951* (London, Routledge, 1993).

63 E. Van Der Beugal, *From Marshall Aid to Atlantic Partnership: European Integration as a Concern of American Foreign Policy* (Amsterdam, Elsevier, 1966), p. 183.

64 P. Hoffman, *Peace Can Be Won* (New York, Joseph, 1951), pp. 108–10.

65 Counterpart funds were a central component of the Marshall Aid programme, they represented the domestic currency equivalent of the dollars made available to European states. The availability of counterpart funds meant that Western European purchasers of dollar goods paid their government in domestic currency, thereby a government could accumulate large balances equivalent to the value of dollars received. Hoffman in his capacity as Head of the ECA recommended that these funds should be used for renewal of domestic industry (scrap, renew and scale up). However, in its terms of reference, the ECA specified that counterpart funds could be used for debt retirement, the use to which the vast majority of UK and Norwegian funds were used. France, West Germany and Italy used the vast majority of their funds for domestic production; see W. Brown and R. Opie, *American Foreign Assistance* (Washington DC, Brookings Institute, 1953), Table on p. 244. For detail of resistance by UK employers, see Clark, op. cit.; Tomlinson and Tiratsoo, op. cit. For primary source on Hoffman's view, see Hoffman, op. cit.

66 Clark, op. cit.; Tomlinson and Tiratsoo, op. cit.

67 Block, op. cit., pp. 38–42.

68 This reflected the ascendancy of the State Department in the formulation of foreign policy.

69 Kolko and Kolko, op. cit.; Milward, op. cit.; Van der Pijl, op. cit.

70 At this time, the UK had $14 billion in sterling balances and about $2 billion in gold and convertible currency.

71 See Block, op. cit., pp.100–2 and 130–1.

72 Hogan, op. cit.

73 Bank of International Settlements, *Annual Report*, Basle, Switzerland (1949), p. 20.

74 Ibid.

75 J. Tomlinson, 'Economic planning: debate and policy in the 1940s', *Twentieth Century History* (1992) 3(2): 154–74.

76 Milward, op. cit.

77 C. Barnett, *The Lost Victory: British Dreams British Realities 1945–1950* (London, Macmillan, 1995), see Chapter 19 'Marshall Aid', pp. 373–79.

78 A. Carew, *Labour under the Marshall Plan* (Manchester, Manchester University Press, 1987).

79 M. Dintenfass, *The Decline of Industrial Britain 1870–1980* (London, Routledge, 1992); S. Broadberry, *The Productivity Race: British Manufacturing in International Perspective 1850–1990* (Cambridge, Cambridge University Press, 1997).

80 A. Maddison, *Economic Growth in the West: Cooperative Experience in Europe and North America* (New York, 20th Century Fund, 1982); H. Van der Wee, *Prosperity and Upheaval: The World Economy, 1945–1980* (California, University of California Press, 1980); Marglin and Schor, op. cit.; Kindleberger, op. cit.; Cairncross and Cairncross, op. cit.; N. Crafts, 'The golden age of economic growth in Western Europe 1950–1973', *Economic History Review* (1994) XLVIII (3): 429–47; Armstrong *et al.*, op. cit., part 2, Chapter 8.

81 A. Cairncross, 'Introduction: the 1960s', in Cairncross and Cairncross, op. cit.

82 Glyn *et al.*, in Marglin and Schor, op. cit.

83 See also J. Ball, *The British Economy at the Crossroads* (London, Financial Times/Pitman Publishing, 1998).

84 Jessop (1994), in Amin, op. cit.

85 Similar arguments are developed in Bull, op. cit., Chapter 11; Lane, op. cit.; A Tickell and J. Peck, 'Social Regulation *after* Fordism: regulation theory, neo-liberalism and the global-local nexus', *Economy and Society* 24 (3): 357–86.

86 J. Holloway and S. Picciotto (eds), *The State and Capital* (Aldershot, Elgar, 1978); S. Clark, 'Overaccumulation, class struggle and the regulation approach', *Capital and Class* (1986) 36: 59–91; S. Clark (ed.), *The State Debate* (London, Macmillan, 1991).

87 W. Hutton, *The State We're In* (London, Jonathan Cape, 1995); 'Rover Makes the Wrong Kind of Headlines', *Financial Times* (London), 22 October 1998.

88 I. Clark, 'The state and new industrial relations', in I. Beardwell (ed.), *Contemporary Industrial Relations A Critical Analysis* (Oxford, Oxford University Press, 1996). The closure of the Siemens semiconductor plant in the summer of 1998 and BMW's threatened closure of the Rover Longbridge plant in November of the same year bear this point out.

89 M. Sawyer, *The Challenge of Radical Political Economy: An Introduction to the Alternatives to Neo-Classical Economics* (London, Harvester Wheatsheaf, 1989), pp. 96–102.

90 D. Calleo, op. cit. Calleo argues that US-inspired Atlanticism was a recognition that its capacity to dominate, i.e. act hegemonically, was limited; however, Calleo demonstrates that the US sought domination.

91 Hogan (1985), op. cit.

92 Bull, op. cit.

93 Bull, op. cit., Chapter 3, summary, p. 51.

3 The UK's competitive decline during the golden age 1945–79

1 N. Kaldor, 'Conflicts in National Economic Objectives', *The Economic Journal* (1971), March.

2 Respectively S. Broadberry, *The Productivity Race* (Cambridge, Cambridge University Press, 1997); F. Hayek, *The Road to Serfdom* (London, Routledge, 1944); S. Broadberry and N. Crafts, 'British economic policy and industrial performance in the early post-war period',

Business History (1996) 28 (4): 65–91; R. Boyer, 'Capital–labour relations in OECD countries: from Fordist golden age to contrasted national trajectories', in J. Schor (ed.), *Capital, the State and Labour* (Elgar, Aldershot, 1996).

3   This issue is the focus of detailed examination in Chapter 7.

4   Broadberry, op. cit., p. 4.

5   See Chapter 2.

6   Kaldor, op. cit., p. 3.

7   Kaldor, op. cit., p. 14.

8   Kaldor, op. cit., p. 15.

9   J. C. R. Dow, *The Management of the British Economy 1945–1960* (Cambridge, Cambridge University Press, 1964).

10   For a general discussion of this period, see B. Tew, *The Evolution of the International Monetary System 1945–1985* (London, Hutchinson, 1985). For a *contemporary*, if hopeful, account of the movement to floating exchange rates, see W. Keegan and R. Pennant-Rea, *Who Runs the Economy?* (London, Hutchinson, 1979).

11   A. Deporte, *Europe between the Superpowers* (Connecticut, Princeton University Press, 1987), p. 206; P. Hall, *Governing the Economy* (Cambridge, Cambridge University Press, 1986).

12   R. Dornbusch, 'Expectations and exchange rate dynamics', *The Journal of Political Economy* (1976) 84: 1160–76.

13   A. Maddison, *Phases of Capitalist Development* (Oxford, Oxford University Press, 1982), p. 93.

14   Maddison, op. cit.; see also C. Kindleberger, 'Why did the golden age last so long?', in A. Cairncross and F. Cairncross (eds), *The Legacy of the Golden Age* (London, Routledge, 1992).

15   R. Matthews, 'Why has Britain had full employment since the war?' *Economic Journal* (1968) 77 (September): 558–69.

16   A. Cairncross, 'Introduction: the 1960s', in Cairncross and Cairncross, op. cit.

17   This view was prosecuted by Paul Hoffman, the US Head of the AACP, however with little success. Hoffman was outmanoeuvred by the UK section of the AACP and by changes in US foreign policy away from integration and internationalism to geopolitics as the Cold War deepened. See I. Clark, 'Institutional stability in industrial relations and management practice: the influence of the AACP 1948–1952', *Business History* (1999) 41 (3): 64–92. On US policy, see C. Maier, 'Hegemony and autonomy with the Western alliance', in M. Leffler and D. Painter (eds), *The Origins of the Cold War: An International History* (London, Routledge, 1994).

18   Note the concern of the 1997 Labour government with the UK European Union productivity gap; equally, BMW's sale of the Rover Longbridge plant is a specific case in point. See, *The 1998 UK Capex Scoreboard* (London, DTI, November 1998). The DTI-commissioned report establishes that the UK's poor level of international competitiveness is in the main the product of low investment in all sectors of the economy. In particular, the report provides comparative analysis on gross tangible assets per employee; in most sectors, the UK is some way behind the international average, e.g. in general manufacturing £61,000 compared with an average of £128,000 and service companies £63,000 compared with an average of £113,000. More disturbingly, a recent report commissioned by the European Commission puts the UK's engineering industry eleventh out of fourteen in the EU in terms of productivity measurements. In 1996, the value added productivity of the UK's mechanical engineering sector was 35,000 ECU (approximately £25,000) per worker, the Union average was 48,000 ECU. The report concedes that UK productivity has improved by 7.1 per cent relative to 1990; however, on a comparative basis Italian productivity increased by 62 per cent. See *Competitiveness in European Union Mechanical Engineering* (Ifo, Munich, December 1998).

19   P. Armstrong, A. Glyn and J. Harrison, *Capitalism Since 1945* (Oxford, Blackwell, 1991), p. 9, Table 2.1.

20   Broadberry, op. cit.

21 S. Davies and R. Caves, *Britain's Productivity Gap* (Cambridge, Cambridge University Press, 1987).

22 R. Matthews, C. Feinstein and J. Olding-Smee, *British Economic Growth 1850–1973* (Oxford, Oxford University Press, 1982), pp. 89–92.

23 E. Hobsbawm, *Empire and Industry* (Penguin, London, 1968).

24 J. Bullpitt, 'The European question', in D. Marquand and A. Seldon (eds), *Ideas that Shaped Post-War Britain* (London, Faber, 1996).

25 Clark, op. cit.

26 Broadberry, op. cit.

27 M. Dintenfass, *The Decline of Industrial Britain 1870–1980* (Routledge, London, 1992).

28 Dintenfass, op. cit., p. 71.

29 W. Lewchuk, *American Technology and the British Vehicle Industry* (New York, Basic, 1987); W. Lewchuk, 'The motor vehicle industry', in B. Elbaum and W. Lazonick (eds), *The Decline of the British Economy* (Oxford University Press, 1986).

30 See S. Tolliday, 'The failure of mass production unionism in the motor industry 1914–1939', in C. Wrigley (ed.), *The History of British Industrial Relations*, Vol. 3 (Brighton, Harvester, 1987).

31 S. Bowden 'Supply and demand constraints: the inter-war UK car industry', *Business History* (1991) 33 (2): 241–67.

32 For summary, see Dintenfass, op. cit., Chapter 2, pp. 13–26.

33 J. Walsh, 'The performance of UK textiles and clothing: recent controversies and evidence', *International Review of Applied Economics* (1991) 5(3): 277–310.

34 Dintenfass, op. cit.

35 Iron and Steel Productivity Team Report, *Anglo American Council on Productivity* (London, AACP, 1952), p. 13; L. Rostas, *Comparative Productivity in British and American Industry* (Cambridge, Cambridge University Press, 1948).

36 Iron and Steel Report, op. cit., p. 123.

37 Ibid.

38 Dintenfass, op. cit.

39 Broadberry, op. cit.

40 Ibid.

41 Kaldor, op. cit.; see also N. Kaldor, *The Causes of the Slow Rate of Economic Growth of the United Kingdom* (Cambridge, Cambridge University Press, 1966); N. Kaldor 'Capitalism and industrial development: some lessons from Britain's experience', *The Cambridge Journal of Economics* (1977) 1: 193–204.

42 *The Royal Commission on Trade Unions and Employers' Associations 1965–1968* (London, HMSO, 1968).

43 C. Lane, *Industry and Society in Europe* (Aldershot, Elgar, 1996).

44 S. Lash and J. Urry, *The End of Organized Capitalism* (London, Sage, 1987), p. 43.

45 P. Mathias, *The First Industrial Nation: An Economic History of Britain 1700–1914* (London, Methuen, 1969); D. Landes, *The Unbound Prometheus: Technological Change and Industrial Development in Western Europe from 1750 to the Present* (Cambridge, Cambridge University Press, 1969); D. Landes, *The Wealth and Poverty of Nations* (London, Little Brown and Company, 1998), Chapters 1–5.

46 H. Perkin, *The Origins of Modern English Society, 1780–1880* (Routledge, London, 1969), pp. 17 and 38–56.

47 A. Fox, *History and Heritage: The Social Origins of the British Industrial Relations System* (London, Allen and Unwin, 1985), Chapter 3.

48 J. Barrington-Moore, *The Social Origins of Dictatorship and Democracy: Lord and Peasant in the Making of the Modern World* (London, Penguin, 1976), part three, Chapter 7.

49 Dow, op. cit.; Kaldor, op. cit. 1966, 1971; Matthews, op. cit.; see also J. Tomlinson, 'Why there was never a "Keynesian Revolution" in economic policy', *Economy and Society* (1981) 10(1): 72–85.

50 See Cairncross and Cairncross (1992), op. cit., p. 7.

51 J. Hughes and A. Thirlwall, 'Trends in cycles of import penetration in the UK', *Bulletin of the Oxford University Institute of Economics and Statistics* (1977) 39: 301–17.

52 G. Reid, 'An economic comment on the Donovan Report', *The British Journal of Industrial Relations* (1968) 6(3): 303–15; H. Turner, 'The Donovan Report' *The Economic Journal* (1969) LXXIX: 1–10.

53 See Armstrong *et al.*, op. cit., Chapter 4; see also A. Glyn, A. Hughes, A. Lipietz, A. Singh, ' The rise and fall of the golden age', in S. Marglin and J. Schor (eds), *The Legacy of the Golden Age* (Oxford, Oxford University Press, 1992).

54 N. Crafts, 'The golden age of economic growth in Western Europe, 1950–1973', *Economic History Review* XLV111(3): 428–47.

55 Broadberry, op. cit., Chapter 1.

56 Broadberry, op. cit., Chapter 1 and concluding Chapter.

57 Ibid.

58 S. Pollard, *The Genesis of Modern Management* (London, Arnold, 1965), Chapters 1–4; P. Hall, *Governing the Economy: The Politics of State Intervention in Britain and France* (Cambridge, Polity, 1986), p. 42.

59 L. Hannah, *The Rise of the Corporate Economy* (London, Methuen, 1976).

60 Lash and Urry, op. cit., pp. 42–53

61 Ibid.

62 S. Aaronovitch and M. Sawyer, *Big Business: Theoretical and Empirical Aspects of Concentration and Mergers in the UK* (London, Macmillan, 1975).

63 This point is further developed and supported by archival and documentary evidence in Chapter 6

64 A. Kilpatrick and T. Lawson, 'The nature of industrial decline' *Cambridge Journal of Economics* (1980) 4: 85–102.

65 Kaldor (1971), op. cit., p. 7.

66 J. Eatwell, *Whatever Happened to Britain?* (London, BBC/Duckworth, 1982).

67 G. Ray, 'Labor costs in OECD countries 1964–1975', *National Institute Economic Review* (1976) Vol. 78.

68 Hall, op. cit., pp. 30–3. Hall's argument and explanation are reminiscent of Dow's destabilization thesis. Dow, op. cit.

69 C. Bean and N. Crafts, 'British economic performance since 1945: relative economic decline and renaissance?', in N. Crafts and G. Toniolo (eds), *Economic Growth in Europe Since 1945* (Cambridge, Cambridge University Press, 1995); N. Crafts, *The Conservative Government's Economic Record: An End of Term Report* (London, Institute of Economic Affairs, 1998).

70 See E Keep and H. Rainbird, 'Training', in P. Edwards (ed.), *Industrial Relations* (Oxford, Blackwell, 1994). The authors conclude that although government has increased the amount of training available during the 1980s it has not necessarily improved on the previous system of employer-focused responsibility for training. The lack of a legislative base or a social partnership approach to training is in marked contrast to other EU states. More significantly, the authors argue and demonstrate that the low-cost/low-productivity trajectory of the UK economy over the post-war and contemporary period has encouraged many employers to peruse low-cost/cost-minimization strategies which eschew the value added in training. Equally, the erosion of the UK's manufacturing sector has further reduced the apparent need for value added end-user training, i.e. resulting in a recognized award.

71 C. Feinstein, 'Economic growth since 1879: Britain's performance in international perspective', *Oxford Review of Economic Policy* (1988) 4: 1–13.

72 Kaldor (1971), op. cit.

73 Broadberry, op. cit.; Feinstein, op. cit.

74 C. Barnett, *The Lost Victory: British Dreams, British Realities 1945–1950* (London, Macmillan, 1995).

75 I have previously described the phenomenon of UK economic decline as that of a Morris Minor economy; one that goes on forever but, comparatively, one which falls further and further behind. I. Clark, 'The state and new industrial relations', in I. Beardwell (ed.), *Contemporary Industrial Relations: A Critical Analysis* (Oxford, Oxford University Press, 1996).

76 Broadberry, op. cit.
77 For example, Crafts (1998), op. cit., is in marked contrast to some of the authors earlier statements. Here, it is acknowledged that the improvement in industrial relations had little effect on macroeconomic performance during the period 1979–97 because overall macropolicy was a failure. Equally, microreform had no impact on training and development or a reduction in wage inequality; contrast this to N. Crafts, 'Reversing economic decline? The 1980s in historical perspective', *Oxford Review of Economic Policy* 7(1991) (3): 81–98, in which the reform of industrial relations is positioned as the corrective to the UK's relative economic decline.

4 A particularized theory of the UK state

1 P. Mathias, *The First Industrial Nation: an Economic History of Britain, 1700–1914* (London, Methuen, 1969).
2 R. Hartwell, *The Causes of the Industrial Revolution in England* (London, Methuen, 1968); E. Hobsbawm, *Labouring Men: Studies in the History of Labour* (London, Weidenfeld, 1964); E Hobsbawm, *Empire and Industry* (London, Pelican, 1968); Hartwell debates.
3 The movement from feudalism to workshop manufacturing and then the factory system has provoked intense debate on the issues of control and efficiency. Steven Marglin and David Landes entered into a major debate on the issues of economic efficiency and management control with Margin asserting that the movement led to no technical improvement in economic efficiency merely greater technical control. Moreover, he accused Landes of technological determinism, a charge Landes refutes vehemently.

   Maxine Berg suggests that the process of industrialization was, in its changes to production, much slower than is often presented in introductory or general summaries. Berg argues that cottage industry and outsourcing continued well into the heyday of factory manufacturing. Pollard summarized the movement to industrialization as creating management systems and structures based on employment and the separation of ownership and control rather than what he terms feudal or workshop entrepreneurialism. S. Marglin, 'What do bosses do?: the origins and functions of hierarchy in capitalist production', *Review of Radical Political Economy* (1974) 6: 33–60; D. Landes, 'What do bosses really do', *Journal of Economic History* (1986) XLVI (3), September; M. Berg, *The Age of Manufacturers* (London, Penguin, 1985).
4 For contrasting accounts of the development of the industrial working class, see Hartwell, op. cit.; Hobsbawm (1964; 1968), op. cit.; E. Thompson, *The Making of the English Working Class* (London, Penguin, 1963).
5 D. Cannadine, *Class in Britain* (London, Yale University Press, 1998); H. Perkin, *The Origins of Modern English Society* (London, Routledge, 1969).
6 J. Barrington Moore, *The Social Origins of Dictatorship and Democracy: Lord and Peasant in the Making of the Modern World* (London, Penguin University Books, 1973); S. Pollard, *The Genesis of Modern Management* (London, Arnold, 1965).
7 Barrington-Moore, op. cit., p. 429.
8 Just as the industrial revolution is seen by many historians as a pivotal change agent or motor of history, the bourgeois revolution is viewed similarly. See Barrington-Moore, op. cit.; H. Perkin, *The Origins of Modern English Society* (London, Routledge, 1969).
9 D. Cannadine, op. cit., p. 5.
10 Barrington Moore, op. cit., p. 418.
11 D. Cannadine, op. cit.
12 A. Fox, *History and Heritage: The Social Origins of the British Industrial Relations System* (London, Allen and Unwin, 1985).
13 K. Morgan, *Labour in Power* (Oxford, Oxford University Press, 1984); I. Gough, *The Political Economy of the Welfare State* (London, Macmillan, 1979), Chapter 4; D. Marquand and A Seldon (eds), *Ideas that Shaped Post-War Britain* (London, Fontana Press, 1996).

14 S. Clark (ed.), *The State Debate* (London, Macmillan, 1991), p. 49.

15 P. Dunleavy and B. O'Leary, *Theories of the State: The Politics of Liberal Democracy* (London, Macmillan, 1987), p. 43.

16 H. Clegg, 'Pluralism in Industrial Relations' *British Journal of Industrial Relations* (1975) 13(3): 309–16.

17 A. Fox, 'Industrial relations: a social critique of pluralist ideology', in J. Child (ed.), *Man and Organization* (London, Allen and Unwin, 1973), pp. 185–234; see also A. Fox, *Manmismanagment* (London, Hutchinson, 1985).

18 P. Nolan, 'Walking on water: performance and industrial relations under Thatcher' *Industrial Relations Journal* (1989) 20(2): pp. 81–92.

19 These views are commonly associated with F. Hayek, *The Road to Serfdom* (London, Routledge, 1944); see also F. Hayek, *The 1980s Unemployment and the Unions* (London, IEA, 1984).

20 A Gamble, *The Free Economy and the Strong State: The Politics of Thatcherism* (London, Macmillan, 1988); see also B. Jessop, K. Bonnett, S. Bromley and T. Ling, *Thatcherism* (London, Polity, 1988).

21 N. Crafts, *The Conservative Government's Economic Record: An End of Term Report* (London, Institute for Economic Affairs, Occasional Paper 104, 1998).

22 I. Gough, *The Political Economy of the Welfare State* (London, Macmillan, 1979); see also B. Jessop, 'The welfare state in the transformation from Fordism to post-Fordism' and 'Thatcherism and flexibility'. Both in: B. Jessop, H. Kastendiek, K. Nielssen and O. Pedersen (eds), *The Politics of Flexibility: Restructuring State and Industry in Britain, Germany and Scandinavia* (Aldershot, Elgar, 1994).

23 For the latter, see Dunleavy and O'Leary, op. cit., Chapter 4.

24 M. Weber, *The Theory of Social and Economic Organization* (New York, The Free Press, 1964); J. Schumpter, *Capitalism, Socialism and Democracy* (London, Allen and Unwin, 1944).

25 Dunleavy and O'Leary, op. cit., p. 141.

26 See R. Hyman and R. Price (eds), *The New Working Class? White Collar Workers and Their Organisations* (London, Macmillan, 1983); C. Smith, D. Knights and H. Willmott (eds), *White Collar Work: The Non-Manual Labour Process* (London, Macmillan, 1991).

27 J. Holloway, 'The state and everyday struggle', in S. Clarke (ed.), *The State Debate* (London, Macmillan, 1991).

28 The key phrase here is 'appear not to' that is they may have a clear-cut class dimension but it has proved too difficult to mobilize interest on this basis.

29 J. Holloway and S. Piccotto (eds), *The State and Capital* (London, Arnold, 1978); S. Clark (ed.), 'The state debate', in S. Clark, *The State Debate* (London, Macmillan, 1991); I. Wallerstein, *Historical Capitalism* (London, Verso, 1981).

30 See T. Parsons, *Sociological Theory and Modern Society* (New York, The Free Press, 1967).

31 R. Miliband, *The State In Capitalist Society* (London, Quartet Books, 1973).

32 For summaries, see B. Jessop, *The Capitalist State* (Oxford, Blackwell, 1982); Clarke, op. cit., pp. 3–5.

33 B. Jessop, *State Theory: Putting Capitalist States in their Place* (Cambridge, Polity Press, 1990).

34 See Chapter 5 for more detail on this issue. Also see M. Cully, A. O'Reilly, N. Millward, J. Forth, S. Woodland, G. Dix and A. Bryson, *The 1998 Workplace Employee Relations Survey – First Findings* (London, DTI/ESRC/ACAS/PSI, 1998); J. Monks, 'Trade unions, enterprise and the future', in P. Sparrow and M. Marchington (eds), *Human Resource Management* (London, Financial Times Business Books, 1998); British Institute of Management (Control Publication – Quick Reaction Survey of Members) 'Trade Union Recognition', (1998) June. For a summary of the survey, see 'Business backs plans for union recognition' *Financial Times*, 23 June 1998.

35 For a detailed discussion of these issues, see Clarke, op. cit.

36 See Cannadine, op. cit.

37 For a more detailed discussion of Labourism, see D. Coates, *The Crisis of Labour: Industrial Relations and the State in Contemporary Britain* (Oxford, Phillip Allen, 1989).

38 For discussion of particularization, see Jessop (1990), op. cit., Chapter 12.

39 See the following articles in the *Financial Times*: 'Morris warns of employer threat to White Paper', 15 September 1998; 'CBI denies wrecking White Paper', 24 October 1998; 'CBI lobbying produces results for employers', 18 December 1998.

40 Cannadine, op. cit., discusses hierarchy as a model for the UK state See also H. Perkin, *The Origins of Modern English Society* (London, Routledge, 1969).

41 See A. Milward, *The European Rescue of the Nation State* (London, Routledge, 1992).

42 Milward, op. cit., p. 410. Society of Motor Manufacturers and Traders material indicates that by 1958 both West German output of cars and the export ratio of completed cars to output exceeded UK levels.

43 D. Thoms and T. Donnelley, *The Motor Car Industry in Coventry since 1890* (London, Croom Helm, 1985).

44 I. Clark, 'Stability in management practice and industrial relations 1948–1952: the influence of the Anglo-American Council for Productivity', *Business History* (1999) 41(3): 64–92; S. Strange, *Sterling and British Policy: A political Study of an International Currency in Decline* (Oxford, Oxford University Press, 1971).

45 Clark (1999), op. cit.

46 For a comprehensive discussion of UK policy, see Milward, op. cit., Chapter 7.

47 Ibid.

48 N. Kaldor, 'Conflicts in national economic objectives', *The Economic Journal* (1971) March.

49 N. Kaldor, *The Causes of the Slow Rate of Economic Growth in the United Kingdom* (Cambridge, Cambridge University Press, 1966); N. Kaldor, 'Capitalism and industrial development: some lessons from Britain's experience', *The Cambridge Journal of Economics* (1977) 1: 193–204.

50 J. C. R. Dow, *The Management of the British Economy 1945–1960* (Cambridge, Cambridge University Press, 1964), pp. 75–7.

51 Kaldor, op. cit.

52 Gamble, op. cit.

53 For a comprehensive treatment of this argument, see H. Overbeek, *Global Capitalism and National Decline: The Thatcher Decade in Perspective* (London, Unwin, Hyman, 1990).

54 B. Jessop, 'Post Fordism and the state', in A. Amin (ed.), *Post-Fordism – A Reader* (Oxford, Blackwell, 1994). Here, Jessop presents a 'regulation' theory of the state that suggests the erosion of contextual influences on the state, in particular those in employment relations are necessary and unavoidable where the post-war state is 'hollowed out' to exclude elements of social democracy.

55 P. Nolan, 'The productivity miracle?', in F. Green (ed.), *The Re-structuring of the British Economy* (Brighton, Harvester Wheatsheaf, 1989).

56 For data and discussion of this issue, see G. Ray, 'Labor costs in manufacturing', *National Institute Economic Review* 120: 71–4; P. Nolan and K. O'Donnell, 'Industrial Relations and Productivity', in P. Edwards (ed.), *Industrial Relations in Britain* (Oxford, Blackwell, 1995); I. Clark, 'The state and new industrial relations', in I. Beardwell (ed.), *Contemporary Industrial Relations* (Oxford, Oxford University Press, 1996).

57 'Our Competitive Future: Building the Knowledge Driven Economy', (London, DTI/The Stationery Office, Cm 4176, December 1998); 'Company Reporting: Capex Scoreboard, 1998', *The Department of Trade and Industry/Company Reporting Limited* (London, DTI, November 1998); H. Kriegbaum, A. Uhlig and H. Gunther Vieweg, *The EU Mechanical Engineering Industry* (Munich, Ifo (Institute fur Wirtschaftorschung), 1997).

58 S. Broadberry, *The Productivity Race* (Cambridge, Cambridge University Press, 1998); Cannadine, op. cit.

59 Kaldor, op. cit.

60 W. Greenleaf, *The British Political Tradition*. Vol. 1. *The Rise of Collectivism* (London, Methuen, 1983).

61 For a definitive account of this argument, see Cannadine, op. cit.

5 The industrial relations system in the UK state

1 H. Clegg, *The Changing System of Industrial Relations in Great Britain* (Oxford, Blackwell, 1979), p. 447.

2 N. Kaldor, *The Causes of the Slow Rate of Economic Growth in the United Kingdom* (Cambridge, Cambridge University Press, 1966); N. Kaldor, 'Capitalism and industrial development; some lessons from Britain's experience', *Cambridge Journal of Economics* (1977) 1: 193–204.

3 Clegg, op. cit.; Kaldor, op. cit.

4 For comprehensive discussion of this framework, see W. McCarthy, 'The rise and fall of collective laissez faire', in W. McCarthy (ed.), *Legal Intervention in Industrial Relations* (Oxford, Blackwell, 1992); C. Crouch, 'Review essay: atavism and innovation: labor law since 1979 in historical perspective', *Historical Studies in Industrial Relations* (1996) 2 (September): 111–24. In reviewing Davies and Freedland, *Labor Legislation and Public Policy: A Contemporary History* (Oxford, 1993), Crouch observes that the erosion of collective *laissez faire* reflects a shift to greater employer power caused by changes in the economic and political priorities of the state. What might be described as Liberal *laissez faire* not individualist *laissez faire*, for as Crouch points out individual and collective employment rights have been eroded since 1979. K. Ewing, ' The state and industrial relations: collective laissez faire revisited', *Historical Studies in Industrial Relations* (1998) 5 (Spring): 1–31. Ewing concludes that the state was instrumental in creating a pattern of collective *laissez faire*. As an active stimulant to building collective bargaining, this and what the previous chapter refers to as active delegation by the state described rhetorically in phrases such as *laissez faire* as freedom from the state.

5 O. Kahn-Freund, 'Intergroup conflict and their settlement', *British Journal of Sociology* (1954) 5: 193–227; O. Kahn-Freund, 'The legal framework', in A. Flanders and H. Clegg (eds), *The System of Industrial Relations in Great Britain* (Oxford, Blackwell, 1954).

6 I. Clark, 'Institutional stability in management practice and industrial relations: the influence of the Anglo-American Council for Productivity', *Business History* (1999) 41(3): 64–99.

7 Kaldor, op. cit.

8 S. Broadberry and N. Crafts, 'British economic policy and industrial performance in the early post-war period', *Business History* (1996) 38: 65–91.

9 C. Crouch, *Industrial Relations and European State Traditions* (Oxford, Oxford University Press, 1993).

10 Ibid.

11 The lock-out may sound like an antiquated device, but it still features as an employer threat or sanction, e.g. the 1993 Timex dispute in Dundee, the Magnet Kitchens dispute in Doncaster, the Liverpool Dock dispute between 1996 and 1998 and the British Airways Heathrow dispute in 1997.

12 D. Cannadine, *Class in Britain* (London, Yale University Press, 1998).

13 The concept of pooling sovereignty is very complicated and controversial. For Milward, pooling sovereignty is the basis by which the European nation state has survived in the post-war period. For others, the notion of pooling sovereignty is illegitimate. Sovereignty is either something states have or do not have. Territorial sovereignty and the legitimate use of force, i.e. the maintenance of national power, represent the basis of sovereignty in this conceptualization, see Bull (below). A. Milward, *The European Rescue of the Nation State* (London, Routledge, 1994); H. Bull, *The Anarchical Society: A Study of Order in World Politics*, second edition (London, Macmillan, 1995).

14 The European Court held in Brown v. Rentokil that dismissal at any time during or after a pregnancy for workplace absence which has been caused by an illness related to confinement is unlawful. This makes contractual terms that allow an employer to dismiss an employee after a defined period of continuous absence (in this case 26 weeks) discriminatory and unlawful. This precludes employers comparing pregnancy-related illness to sustained illness that might be suffered by a man for a similar continuous period of time. The ruling requires further amendment of the 1975 Sex Discrimination Act. European Court Ruling, 30 June 1998, Brown v. Rentokil Ltd, case number C 394-/96.

15 For more detail on this argument, see H. Clegg, *Trade Unionism Under Collective Bargaining* (Oxford, Blackwell, 1976).

16 Crouch, op. cit.

17 *Union Membership Survey, Labor Force Survey*, Trades Union Congress, May 1999. WERS4 initial findings are in M. Cully, A. O'Reilly, N. Millward, J. Forth, S. Woodland, G. Dix and A. Bryson, *The 1998 Workplace Employee Relations Survey – First Findings* (London, DTI/ESRC/ACAS/PSI, 1998), pp. 14–18, Tables 7 and 8 and Figure 18.

18 Crouch, op. cit., see Tables 6.4, 6.11, 7.5 and 7.9.

19 J. Purcell, 'The end of institutional industrial relations', *Political Quarterly* (1993) 64(1): 6–23; K. Sisson and P. Marginson, 'Management: systems , structures and strategies', in P. Edwards (ed.), *Industrial Relations* (Oxford, Blackwell, 1995). For current data that support this view, see M. Cully, A. O'Reilly, N. Millward, J. Forth, S. Woodland, G. Dix and A. Bryson, *The 1998 Workplace Employee Relations Survey – First Findings* (London, DTI/ESRC/ACAS/PSI, 1998).

20 Cully *et al.*, op. cit.; D. Gallie, M. White, Y. Cheng and M. Tomlinson, *Restructuring the Employment Relationship* (Oxford, Oxford University Press, 1998).

21 See J. Kelly, *Re-Thinking Industrial Relations* (London, Routledge, 1998), Chapters 1 and 2, where this argument is developed.

22 K. Middlemas, *Power, Competition and the State*, Vol. 1 (Macmillan, London, 1986); A. Carew, *Labour under the Marshall Plan* (Manchester, Manchester University Press, 1987).

23 Middlemas, op. cit.

24 McCarthy, op. cit.

25 E. Keep and H. Rainbird, 'Training', in Edwards, op. cit.; P. Nolan and K. O'Donnell, 'Industrial Relations and Productivity', in Edwards, op. cit.

26 McCarthy, op. cit.

27 Even in the case of automatically unfair sex or race discrimination, employees have only an automatic right to bring their complaint to an employment tribunal. This is not the same as a positive or constitutional right not to be discriminated against on grounds or race or sex.

28 For more discussion of these issues, see J. Kelly, op. cit., Chapter 1; P. Blyton and P. Turnbull, *New Dynamics of Employee Relations* (London, Macmillan, 1994), Chapter 1.

29 Kelly, op. cit., Chapter 6.

30 See Chapter 3. For an institutional polemic on this, see W. Hutton, *The State We're In* (London, Jonathan Cape, 1995).

31 Hutton, op. cit.

32 This argument is developed in detail in Chapter 4.

33 Clegg, op. cit., p. 444.

34 Crouch, op. cit., p. 21.

35 For the position of the IPD, see *Statutory Trade Union Recognition, Issues in People Management* (London, IPD, 1996). For the position of the IOD, see R. Lee, 'Let firms decide on recognition', *The Times*, 5 May 1998. The CBI eventually agreed a procedure for recognition but remain opposed to statutory recognition on principle.

36 See Chapter 3 on economic policy in the post-war period and the argument developed therein on the utility of the interpretative approach of Kaldor.

37 Edwards, op. cit., p. 9.

38 W. Brown, 'The high tide of consensus: the system of industrial relations in Great Britain revisited', *Historical Studies in Industrial Relations* (1997) 4 (September): 135–50.

39 See material in Chapters 2 and 3 on this point.

40 'The Economic Consequences of Full Employment' (London, HMSO, Cmnd. 1417, 1957).

41 *Political Quarterly* (1956), special edition under the general heading 'Trade unions in a changing world'; *Scottish Journal of Political Economy* (1958) on the wages question, significant contributions in the latter included: A. Cairncross, 'A wages policy and inflation', pp. 81–4; A. Flanders, 'Can Britain have a wage policy', pp. 114–25; H. Johnson, 'Two schools of

thought on inflation', pp. 149–53; H. Phelps-Brown, 'Conditions for the avoidance of the spiral', pp. 145–8; B. Roberts, 'Centralized wages policy', pp. 154–9.

42 Flanders (1958), op. cit.; A. Flanders, *The Fawley Productivity Agreements: A Case Study of Management and Collective Bargaining* (London, Faber, 1964).

43 The Conservative Inns of Court Association, *A Giant's Strength* (London, The Conservative Inns of Court Association, 1958).

44 See Chapter 3 on the economics of decline and Chapter 6 for further demonstration of this argument supported by primary source material.

45 See Chapter 3 for detailed analysis.

46 Clark, op. cit.; see also Chapter 6 for more detail and documentary evidence.

47 'The Royal Commission on Trade Unions and Employers' Associations 1965–1968 Report' (London, HMSO, Cmnd. 3623, June 1968).

48 The Royal Commission on Trade Unions and Employers' Associations 1965–1968 Report, op. cit., Chapter XIV, paragraphs 751–993.

49 See W. Beckerman (ed.), *The Labour Government's Economic Record 1964–1970* (London, Duckworth, 1972); M. Stewart, *The Jekyll and Hyde Years: Politics and Economic Policy Since 1964* (London, Dent, 1977).

50 For comprehensive discussion of the 1971 Act, see B. Weekes, B. Mellish, L. Dickens and J. Lloyd, *Industrial Relations and the Limits of the Law* (Oxford, Blackwell, 1975).

51 Heaton's Transport (St. Helens) Ltd. v. Transport and General Workers Union (1973).

52 Crouch, op. cit., Chapter 7.

53 Stewart, op. cit.; D. Winchester, 'Industrial relations in the public sector', in G. Bain (ed.), *Industrial Relations in Britain* (Oxford, Blackwell, 1983).

54 N. Millward, *The New Industrial Relations?* (London, Policy Studies Institute, 1994), Chapter 2; M. Cully, A. O'Reilly, N. Millward, J. Forth, S. Woodland, G. Dix and A. Bryson, *The 1998 Workplace Employee Relations Survey – First Findings.* (Department of Trade and Industry, 1998), Table 7, p. 15.

55 Cully *et al.*, op. cit., Table 4, p. 10.

56 I. Clark, *Stakeholders in Social Partnership* (Leicester, Leicester Business School Occasional Papers, 1999).

57 Ibid.

58 See McCarthy, op. cit., for the definitive position on Kahn-Freund.

59 Keep and Rainbird, op. cit.

60 W. Hutton, *The State We're In* (London, Jonathan Cape, 1995).

61 See Gallie *et al.*, op. cit.; J. Monks, 'Trade unions, enterprise and the future', in P. Sparrow and M. Marchington (eds), *Human Resource Management* (London, Financial Times Business Books, 1998).

62 F. Hayek, *Unemployment and the Unions* (London, Institute for Economic Affairs, 1980); see also S. Pollard, *The Wasting of the British Economy* (London, Croom Helm, 1982).

63 S. Broadberry and N. Crafts, 'British economic policy and industrial performance in the early post-war period', *Business History* (1991) 38: 65–91; S. Broadberry, *The Productivity Race* (Cambridge University Press, 1998).

64 See Chapters 3 and 7 for detailed analysis.

65 Clark, op. cit.

66 G. Reid, 'An economic comment on the Donovan Report', *British Journal of Industrial Relations* (1968) 6(3): 303–15; H. Turner, 'The Donovan Report', *The Economic Journal* (1969) 79: 1–10.

67 S. Pollard, *The Wasting of the British Economy* (London, Croom Helm, 1982); D. Metcalf, 'Water notes dry up: the impact of the Donovan Reform Proposals and Thatcherism at work on labour productivity in British manufacturing' *British Journal of Industrial Relations* (1989) 27(1); 1–33.

68 K. Joseph, *Solving the Union Problem is the Key to Britain's Recovery* (Conservative Central Office, 1979), very similar to Hayek, op. cit.; M. Olsen, *The Rise and Decline of Nations* (New Haven, Yale University Press, 1982); S. Broadberry, 'The impact of world wars on

the long-run performance of the British economy', *Oxford Review of Economic Policy* (1988) 4: 25–37. Both Olsen and Broadberry produce general theses on decline but appear to position trade unions and industrial relations as central factors.

69 Broadberry and Crafts, op. cit.; Broadberry, op. cit.; The 'flawed Fordism' thesis, see R. Boyer, 'Capital–labor relations in OECD countries: from Fordist golden age to contrasted national trajectories', in J. Schor (ed.), *Capital, The State and Labor* (Aldershot, Elgar, 1996).

70 Clark, op. cit.

71 See M. Dintenfass, *The Decline of Industrial Britain 1870–1980* (London, Routledge, 1992); B. Alford, *British Economic Performance 1945–1975* (London, Macmillan, 1988).

72 Kaldor, op. cit.

73 D. Gallie, M. White, Y. Cheng and M. Tomlinson, *Restructuring the Employment Relationship* (Oxford, Oxford University Press, 1998).

74 Ibid.

75 The Quantity Theory of Money that postulates a theoretical relationship between the quantity of money in the economy and the price level. $MV = PT$, where M is the stock of money, V is the income velocity of circulation, i.e. how many times a unit of money is used, P is the average price level and T represents the total volume of transactions. Under this equation, the total value of expenditure (M.V) must equal the value of goods and services bought and sold (PT). Moreover, if over the short term or in conditions of full employment V and T are constant, a direct relationship between M and P must exist, i.e. an increase in the supply of money must increase the price level and vice versa. For introductory material, see K. Chrystal, *Controversies in British Macro Economics* (London, Phillip Allen, 1979).

76 Metcalf, op. cit.; W. Brown and S. Wadhwani, 'The economic effects of industrial relations legislation since 1979', *National Institute Economic Review* (1990) 131: 57–70; S. Deakin, 'Labour law and industrial relations', in J. Mitchie (ed.), *The Economic Legacy 1979–1992* (London, The Academic Press, 1992), pp. 173–91.

77 N. Crafts, 'Reversing economic decline? The 1980s in historical perspective', *Oxford Review of Economic Policy* (1991) 7(3): 81–98.

78 E. Keep in Edwards, op. cit.

79 T. Nichols, *The British Worker Question* (London, Routledge, 1986), reviews this phenomenon. Recent contributions to the literature that emphasize the worker problem include: Broadberry, op. cit.; Broadberry and Crafts, op. cit.; and C. Barnett, *The Lost Victory – British Dreams British Realities 1945–1950* (London, Macmillan, 1995). For an earlier view, see: M. Shanks, *The Stagnant Society – A Warning.* (London, Penguin, 1961); M. Shanks, 'Public policy and the ministry of labour', in B. Roberts, *Industrial Relations – Contemporary Problems and Perspectives* (London, Methuen, 1962).

80 The Department for Enterprise *The Department of Trade for Industry* (London, HMSO, 1988).

81 Broadberry and Crafts, op. cit.

82 Barnett, op. cit. Barnett provides only limited reference to the actual presence or damaging effects of restrictive practices and provides no examination of what management wanted to do (see pp.300–1). See also C. Barnett, *The Audit of War – The Illusion and Reality of Britain as a Great Nation* (London, Macmillan, 1986).

83 F. Zweig, *Productivity and Trade Unions* (Oxford, Blackwell, 1951); Clark, op. cit.

84 Clark, op. cit.

85 A. Kilpatrick and T. Lawson, 'On the nature of industrial decline in the UK', *Cambridge Journal of Economics* (1980) 4: 84–102.

86 S. Kessler and F. Bayliss, *Contemporary British Industrial Relations* (London, Macmillan, 1998), see Chapter 3, Table 3.1, p. 41, and Table 3.6, p. 47.

87 Millward, op. cit.; Cully *et al.*, op. cit.

88 D. Gallie, M. White, Y. Cheng and M. Tomlinson, *Restructuring the Employment Relationship* (Oxford, Oxford University Press, 1998).

89 Keep and Rainbird, op. cit.

90 Clegg, op. cit.

6 The industrial relations system and post-war recovery

1 Modern Records Centre MSS 200F/3T/328/1 note on inaugural meeting of AACP UK Section. See also AACP, Final Report 1952, and G. Hutton, *We Too Can Prosper* (London, Allen and Unwin, 1953).

2 See A. Dulles, *The Marshall Plan* (Providence Rhode Island, Berg, 1993); M Hogan, *The Marshall Plan, American Britain and the Reconstruction of Western Europe, 1947–1952* (Cambridge, Cambridge University Press, 1987). For a more specific discussion of this view, see M. Hogan, 'American Marshall planners and the search for a European neo-capitalism' *American Historical Review* (1985) 90(1): 44–73.

3 I. Wexler, *The Marshall Plan Re-Visited* (Connecticut, Greenwood Press, 1983), Chapter 6, pp. 73–4. Wexler lists the primary sources on p. 271.

4 Hogan (1987), op. cit.; A. Dulles, op. cit. This is a useful source; as Dulles was involved in the recovery programme, it was written in 1948 but not published until much later.

5 See A. Milward, *The Reconstruction of Western Europe 1945–1951* (London, Methuen, 1984).

6 Milward, op. cit., pp. 94–7.

7 Milward, op. cit.; F. Northedge, *Descent from Power – British Foreign Policy 1945–1973* (London, Allen and Unwin, 1974); A. Milward, *The European Rescue of the Nation State* (London, Routledge, 1992), Chapter 7.

8 See A. Cairncross, *The Years of Recovery 1945–1951* (London, Methuen, 1985), Table 4.1, p. 66; S. Broadberry, *The Productivity Race* (Cambridge, Cambridge, Cambridge University Press, 1997), p. 97, Tables 7.2 and 7.3.

9 A. Carew, *Labour Under the Marshall Plan* (Manchester, Manchester University Press, 1987).

10 See material in Chapter 3.

11 AACP reports 1–66. Available in Leicester University Library. Original and some draft versions available in the MRC.

12 AACP Final Report 1952 (London, AACP, 1952). For secondary source accounts, see J Tomlinson and N. Tiratsoo, *Industrial Efficiency and State Intervention 1939–1951* (London, Routledge, 1993); for an earlier airing of this view; see G. Hutton, *We Too Can Prosper* (London, Allen and Unwin, 1953).

13 See AACP Final Report, op. cit., pp. 31–6; Simplification in Industry Report 1949; Materials Handling Report 1949, p. 9; and Management Education Report 1951 pp. 5, 19–20. For secondary source commentary, see Carew, op. cit.; Tomlinson and Tiratsoo, op. cit.; Hutton, op. cit. .

14 I Clark, 'Institutional stability in management practice and industrial relations: the influence of the Anglo-American Council for Productivity, 1948–1952', *Business History* (1999) 41(3): 64–92; Tomlinson and Tiratsoo, op. cit., pp. 133–5.

15 MRC MSS 200F/3T/328/1. For secondary source interpretation, see K. Middlemas, *Power , Competition and the State*, Vol. 1 (Macmillan, London, 1986), Chapter 3.

16 See C. Newton, 'The sterling crisis of 1947 and the British response to the Marshall Plan', *Economic History Review* (1984): s391–408. Sterling convertibility was a condition of a previously negotiated loan. For specific details, see R. Clarke, *Anglo-American Collaboration in War and Peace 1942–1949* (Oxford, Oxford University Press,1982). For a general treatment of both issues, see A. Cairncross, *The Years of Recovery* (London, Methuen, 1985), Chapters 1, 2 and 6.

17 The BOT was in conflict with the MLNS and the Treasury over particularly aspects of industrial policy and industrial relations policy. It appears that the BOT initially favoured an interventionary policy in both areas. For example, industrial policy based around removing 'inefficiency' deriving from cartel attitudes to production, particularly in relation to Empire markets. In terms of industrial relations policy, the BOT proposed more intervention to make collective bargaining work 'efficiently', whereas the MLNS and the Treasury both favoured a return to free collective bargaining. See L. Johnman, 'The Labour party and industrial policy 1940–1945', in N. Tiratsoo (ed.), *The Atlee Years* (London, Pinter, 1991). Also see K. Middlemas, *Power, Competition and the State*, Vol. 1 (London, Macmillan, 1986),

in particular Chapter 3, pp. 87–105. Summary views of BOT policy are in the Board of Trade journal; copies of wartime and immediate post-war years in LUSC OFF PUBS UK/ TRA B4096

18 Middlemas, op. cit.
19 C. Crouch, *Industrial Relations and European State Traditions* (Oxford, Oxford University Press, 1994), p. 179.
20 MRC MSS 200F/3T/328/1 25/8/48 Kipping to UK panel 'no US inquisition' 'put our programme to the Americans, our programme in the context of our manufacturing industry'. For a more conceptually based comparative and historical assessment of US production systems and their application and suitability to the UK economy, see J. Zeitlin, 'Americanization and its implications' *Business and Economic History* (1995) 24: 277–86.
21 MRC MSS 200 F/3T/328/1 Notes and memo to Trade Associations 16/4/48.
22 MRC MSS200F/3T/328/1 1 AACP S/3 26/10/48.
23 MRC MSS 200 F/3T/26/3 White (FBI technical Officer, London) to Kipping 6/11/50 *re* planning of AACP conference in Nottingham 'no joint union management discussions'; Kipping to Spencer (Spence Ltd, Basford, Nottingham) 23/11/50 *re* productivity exhibitions and conferences 'keep management problems and interests on productivity away from trade unions'.
24 MRC MSS 200 F/3T/328/1 AACP October 1948 Industrial Standardization in the UK.
25 AACP October 1948 Industrial Standardization in the UK, op. cit.
26 Ibid.
27 AACP October 1948 Industrial Standardization in the UK, op. cit., 14/9/48 AACP Size of UK Manufacturing Plants.
28 MRC MSS 200F/3T/3/26/3 White to Kipping 11/8/50.
29 MRC MSS 200F/3T/328/1 Kipping to White 11/8/50 and Herbert [Viyella (Nottingham) to Houghton (regional officer, central office of information, Nottingham, 8/9/50) *re* TUC (Leicester)]. Herbert indicates initial support for TUC suggestions for greater worker involvement in the conferences. The FBI response was unfavourable. White to G. White (FBI, Leicester) TUC (Leicester) and Herbert are 'jumping the gun' 'we don't want this'. Eventually, Dearing (TUC, Leicester) and Herbert concur with the FBI/AACP view, see Dearing to G. White 10/11/50.
30 See Tables 2.8 and 2.9 and Ian Clark, unpublished Ph.D. thesis, (Leeds, The University of Leeds, May 1996), Tables 8 and 9, pp. 56 and 57.
31 MRC MSS 292/552/32/2 Draft Document 5th session 21/4/52.
32 Middlemas, op. cit.
33 AACP Final Report 1952, see appendix 2, p. 31, 'Impact of the Reports on Industry'; the main benefits that are highlighted here concentrate on improvements to factory layout, and in the seven industry groups reviewed there is little mention of management techniques or management practice. However, there is an assumption that engagement with and the take-up of US management techniques is now the norm.
34 Carew, op. cit.
35 MRC MSS 200 F/3/T/328/1 AACP General Council 9 7/10/48 TUC submission and views on AACP rubric and mission 'The AACP should be a joint management–labour effort' to incorporate joint industrial councils and joint industrial committees, i.e. labour relations issues should be handled through existing collective bargaining machinery (as indicated by AACP chairman 25/8/48/).
36 MRC MSS 292/552/32/2 internal memo dated 9/5/48.
37 MRC MSS 200 F/3T/328/1 October 1948 AACP Industrial Capital Investment; for full details, see 'The re-equipping of industry', *The Times*, 15 and 16 October 1948; 'British plans for the first year of Marshall Aid', 22 October 1948; 'The Chancellor's Dilemma', 23 October 1948; all three articles are generally supportive if sceptical of the suggestion that output increases over the pre-war years are not as significant as the need to maintain improvement in productivity. The articles also refer to the AACP not as the productivity council but as the 'output council'.

38 MRC MSS 292/552 373/2B TUC correspondence. TUC (Leicester) to Hutton 1/9/50, Kipping to White 6/11/50. In addition, see TUC correspondence on the Hutton book on the AACP. The TUC were unhappy with the manner and format of the book, particularly the fact that it contained too much author opinion, was too journalistic and did not refer to the actual reports in any detail, yet overall the book made simple comparisons with the USA. See Fletcher to Tewson 22/7/52 and Fletcher to Williamson 28/8/52, where it is highlighted that restrictive practices receive much negative interpretation without full consideration as to why they might be necessary. Equally, there is much criticism of the later chapters and a suggestion that they need to be rewritten, e.g. 'British worker lethargy as a form of psychological sickness'. The TUC production department remained unhappy with the revised version of the book , see Fletcher to Williamson 9/1/53 'OK but not as we'd have written it'.

39 MRC MSS 292/557 91/5 'Productivity: The Next Step' draft details of TUC conferences on the question; equally, documents from individual trade unions on the issue of restrictive practices, see final version in 'Productivity' report to the General Council special conference of the Trade Union Executive Councils, November 1948.

40 MRC MSS 200 F/3T 328/1, see notes by Fletcher (TUC production department) on US productivity statistics. The material indicates that in the USA productivity is measured in terms of man–hours per unit of output, a practice not used in the UK. See also MRC MSS 200 E/3/T328/13 AACP correspondence on reports from US Bureau of Labour Statistics – this information was sent for industry to comment on. Representatives from British Sugar responded, saying they were unable to understand the figures, in particular 'Trends in man hours per unit of output'.

41 MRC MSS 200F/3T328/1.

42 Ibid.

43 MRC MSS 200F/3T/328/1 ES0/1.

44 C. Maier, *In Search of Stability* (Cambridge, Cambridge University Press, 1987).

45 P. Hoffman, *Peace Can be Won* (New York, Joseph, 1951), pp. 95–6 and 125–6.

46 Phillip Reed, Head of the US section, shared this view. Maier documents the development of 'a political' approach to productivity in US production policy by tracing it back to the 1918 War production board and Herbert Hoover's 'Business Associationism' through to the inter-war committee on Economic Development organized by progressive members of the business community including Hoffman. Thus, it appears safe to conclude that what Maier means by 'a political' is that the ideas came not from the US government but US businessmen. They were then appropriated by the US government and positioned within their wider foreign policy concerns in the immediate post-war years. See C. Maier, op. cit., Chapter 3, pp. 127–30.

47 For a supportive view of regulation, see B. Jessop, 'Regulation theory', in P. Arestis and M. Sawyer (eds), *The Elgar Companion to Radical Political Economy* (Aldershot, Elgar, 1994). For a more sceptical view, see R. Hyman, 'Economic re-structuring, market liberalism and the foundations of national industrial relations systems', in R. Hyman and A. Ferner (eds), *New Frontiers in European Industrial Relations* (Oxford, Blackwell, 1994).

48 See R. Edwards, *Contested Terrain: The Transformation of the Workplace in the Twentieth Century* (London, Heinemann, 1979).

49 Ibid.

50 AACP Iron and Steel Report, 1952, pp. 16–17; Steel Construction Report, 1952, pp. 17–19; and Internal Combustion Engines Report, 1950, pp. 18–19.

51 G. Hutton, op. cit.; Broadberry, op. cit., Chapters 12 and 13. In addition, see Chapter 2

52 Carew, op. cit., Chapter 9. See also H. Harris, 'The snares of liberalism? Politicians, bureaucrats and the shaping of federal labour relations in the United States 1915–1947', in S. Tolliday and J. Zeitlin (eds), *Shop Floor Bargaining and the State: Historical and Comparative Perspectives* (Cambridge, Cambridge University Press, 1985).

53 MRC MSS 292/557 91/5 National Federation of Building Trade Operatives report on AACP trip to USA.

54 See Carew, op. cit., Chapter 9. MRC MSS 292/557 91/5 National Federation of Building Operatives responses to TUC productivity inquiries and the AACP Buildings report.

55 See Tomlinson and Tiratsoo, op. cit., for the definitive study of this process.

56 See AACP Final Report, 1952, pp. 31–6; Simplification in Industry Report, 1949; Materials Handling Report, 1949, p. 9; and Management Education Report, 1951, pp. 5 and 19–20. This position is commented upon generally, i.e. beyond the confines of the AACP, by B. Elbaum and W. Lazonick (eds), *The Decline of the British Economy* (Oxford, Clarendon Press, 1986), opening chapter by the editors.

57 See Hoffman, op. cit.; H. Phelps Brown, *Britain and the Marshall Plan* (London, Macmillan, 1988), Chapters 5–7.

58 Wexler, op. cit., p. 94.

59 MRC MSS 200f/3T/328/1 AACP first meeting 25/8/48.

60 Ibid. TUC members of the AACP were unhappy with the inclusion of the BEC because industrial relations matters were not a central area of concern, see AACP General Council memo 7/10/48, however the BEC was admitted on 14/10/48.

61 Ibid.

62 MRC MSS 200 F/3T/26/3 correspondence and memos on the management of productivity conferences and exhibitions in the UK, November 1950.

63 See W. McCarthy, 'The role of shop steward in British industrial relations', 1966 Donovan Research Paper no. 1, HMSO; see pp. 12–13 for discussion of the situation in engineering.

64 F. Zweig, *Trade Unions and Productivity* (Oxford, Blackwell, 1951); N. Tiratsoo and J. Tomlinson, 'Restrictive practices on the shop floor in Britain: 1945–1960', *Business History* (1993) 36(2): 65–84.

65 There is only passing mention of this in the Donovan report itself, see p. 38. HMSO Cmnd. 3623. However, it is detailed in McCarthy's paper, op. cit. Neither considers the influence of external factors in this development.

66 McCarthy, op. cit.; J. Goodman and T. Whittingham, *Shop Stewards* (London, Pan Books, 1973); Donovan Report, pp. 29–35 . It has been pointed out that the Donovan research was biased towards particular industries, notably engineering and shipbuilding, in which the role of the steward was particularly developed. See H. Turner, 'The Royal Commission's research papers', *British Journal of Industrial Relations* (1968) 6(3): 346–59.

67 For a specific case study, see S. Tolliday, 'Government, employers and shop floor organization in the British motor industry', in Tolliday and Zeitlin, op. cit.

68 See G. Reid, 'An economic comment on the Donovan Report', *The British Journal of Industrial Relations* (1968) 6930: 303–15; H. Turner, 'The Donovan Report', *The Economic Journal* (1969) LXXIX: 1–10.

69 Broadberry and Crafts, 'Industrial performance in the early post-war period', *Business History* Volume (1996) 38: 65–91; C. Barnett, *The Audit of War: The Illusion and Reality of Britain as a Great Nation* (London, Macmillan, 1986); C. Barnett, *The Lost Victory: British Dreams British Realities, 1945–1950,* (London, Macmillan, 1995); Broadberry, op. cit.

70 Broadberry and Crafts (1996), op. cit., p. 87.

71 See TUC references to growth potential of the UK economy MRC MSS 200 F/3T/328/1 October 1948 AACP Industrial Capital Investment.

72 Broadberry and Crafts (1996), op. cit., p. 87.

73 MRC MSS 200F/3T/328/1, AACP/FBI Papers AACP 'Size of British manufacturing plants', October 1948.

74 Broadberry and Crafts, op. cit., 1996, pp. 80–5.

75 H. Clegg, *The Changing System of Industrial Relations* (Oxford, Blackwell, 1979), p. 5.

76 S. Prais, *The Evolution of Giant Firms in Britain 1909–1970* (Cambridge, Cambridge University Press, 1976); S. Prais, *Productivity and Industrial Structure: A Statistical Study of Manufacturing Industry in Britain, Germany and the United States* (Cambridge, Cambridge University Press, 1981).

77 K. Williams, J. Williams and D. Thomas, *Why are the British Bad at Manufacturing?* (London, Routledge, 1983).

78 See Chapter 3 for detailed analysis of these points.

79 MRC MSS 292/557 91/5, full details of TUC conferences and the responses of a large number of trade unions to TUC inquiries on restrictive practices. For example, National Society of Pottery Workers 11/3/49, the TGWU 2/5/49, the Iron and Steel Trade Confederation 12/9/49 and the Printing and Kindred Trades Association 18/10/49. These and many other responses either fail to cite restrictive practices as a serious issues or concede that management are only pushing on restrictive practices that seek to restrict overtime, especially if the latter is compulsory.

80 Ibid.

81 MRC MSS 292/557 91/5, TUC notes on the Productivity: The Next Step Programme. The TUC policy on restrictive practices had two main aims. The first aim was to clarify definitions, e.g. apprenticeship regulations were often inaccurately termed restrictive practices and, in addition, the TUC argued that many management restrictive practices were not recorded or accepted as being present, e.g. output restrictions and restrictive pricing arrangements. The second aim was to promote 'democratic' practices that served the interests of workers. 'Democratic' was defined in the context of collective bargaining. If a practice was no longer necessary, it would be removed from the bargaining agenda, e.g. restrictions on compulsory overtime or dilution of the skill level by the entry of unqualified workers. In many cases, practices in these areas had been relaxed during the war and had not significantly weakened the position of the skilled workforce.

82 F. Zweig, *Trade Unions and Productivity* (Oxford, Blackwell, 1951). Broadberry and Crafts cite Zweig in one footnote (no. 51) but do not engage specifically with his argument and data; equally, they appear to use his survey material in support of their criticism of Tiratsoo and Tomlinson, see below. The central point in Zweig's work is that management did not appear to be excessively concerned with restrictive practices. Further, Zweig demonstrates that the term was used without accurate definition. It would appear that this was part of a larger problem; management fell back on the term 'restrictive practice' to describe anything that inhibited production, yet restrictive practices operated within the wider pattern of management practice.

83 A. Marsh, E. Evans and P. Garcia, *Workplace Industrial Relations in Engineering* (London, Kogan Page, 1971).

84 W. Brown (ed.), *The Changing Contours of British Industrial Relations* (Oxford, Blackwell, 1981).

85 D. Cannadine, *Class in Britain* (New Haven, Yale University Press, 1998), p. 91.

86 S. Broadberry and N. Crafts, 'The post-war settlement: not such a good bargain after all', *Business History* (1998) 40(2): 76.

87 H. Clegg, 'Restrictive practices', *Socialist Commentary* (1964) December: 9–11. Cited by Broadberry and Crafts (1998), op. cit., p. 75.

88 'The Royal Commission on Trade Unions and Employers' Associations 1965–1968' Cmnd. 3623 (HMSO, 1968).

89 Broadberry and Crafts (1998), op. cit., pp. 73–4.

90 Barnett (1986), op. cit.; but more particularly Barnett (1995), op. cit.

91 W. Brown and R. Opie, *American Foreign Assistance* (Washington DC, Brookings Institute, 1954), p. 244. For a specific discussion of the UK's deployment of Marshall Aid counterpart funds, see J. Tomlinson, 'Corellie Barnett's history: the case of Marshall Aid', *Twentieth Century History* (1997) 8(2): 222–38.

92 J. Tomlinson, 'Economic planning: debate and policy in the 1940's', *Twentieth Century History* (1992) 3(2): 154–74,.

93 A. Kilpatrick and T. Lawson, 'The strength of the working class', *The Cambridge Journal of Economics* (1980) 4: 85–102.

94 This is more evident in Barnett (1995), op. cit., see pp. 34–8 and 299–303.

95 MRC MSS200/C3/C1//3/2 British Productivity Council Conference report, March 1953, pp. 4–7.

96 G. Maxby and A. Silberton, *The Motor Industry* (London, Allen and Unwin, 1959). However, as Nichols, op. cit., p. 46, illustrates, later studies did document the effects of labour restrictive practices in the workplace.

97 Broadberry, op. cit.

98 Broadberry, op. cit., p. 398.

99 Broadberry, op. cit., Chapter 1, pp. 1–4, Figure 1.1, Chapter 4, Table 4.1.

100 MRC MSS 292/557 91/5 TUC Registry Files, TUC notes on the Productivity: The Next Step Programme. There were two themes in TUC and union policy on restrictive practices. First, definitional, e.g. apprenticeship regulations were often erroneously referred to by employers as restrictive practices. In addition, the TUC argued that there were many management restrictive practices that were not recorded or accepted as present, e.g. output restrictions and restrictive pricing arrangements. Second, the TUC was only interested in democratic restrictive practices that served the interests of workers. Democratic was defined in the context of collective bargaining. If a practice was no longer necessary, it would be removed from the bargaining agenda, e.g. restrictions on overtime and dilution agreements.

101 For an account of this process, see B. Tew, *International Monetary Cooperation 1945–1965* (London, Hutchinson, 1965).

102 See Tables 2.10–2.12; and M. Kirby, 'The economic record since 1945', in T. Gourvish and A. O'Day (eds), *Britain Since 1945* (London, Macmillan, 1991). Also, National Institute Economic Review, February 1972, and C. Brown and T. Sherrif, 'De-industrialization: a Background Paper', in F. Blackably (ed.), *Deindustrialisation* (London, Heinneman, 1978).

103 Report of the Donovan Commission, op cit.; Royal Warrant, p. iii.

104 For elaboration of this issue, see Clark (1996), op. cit., pp. 43–5; Tomlinson and Tiratsoo (1998), op. cit., pp. 64–5 and 69.

105 See C. Bean and N. Crafts, 'British economic growth since 1945', in N. Crafts and G. Toniolo (eds), *Economic Growth in Europe Since 1945* (Cambridge, Cambridge University Press, 1996); Broadberry and Crafts (1998), op. cit., p. 77; Broadberry, op. cit., pp. 3 and 16.

106 C. Pratten, *Productivity Differentials within International Companies* (Cambridge, Cambridge University Press, 1976).

107 See for example Crafts's treatment of this study. Crafts concentrates solely on the impact of behavioural factors. N. Crafts, 'Economic growth', in N. Crafts and N. Woodward (eds), *The British Economy Since 1945* (Oxford, Oxford University Press, 1991).

108 R. Caves and L. Krause (eds), *Britain's Economic Performance* (Washington DC, The Brookings Institute, 1980).

109 D. Smith, 'Trade union growth and industrial disputes', in Caves and Krause, op. cit.

110 R. Caves, 'Productivity differences among industries', in Caves and Krause, op. cit.

111 D. Metcalf, 'Water notes dry up: the impact of Donovan reform proposals and Thatcherism at work on labour productivity in British manufacturing industry', *British Journal of Industrial Relations* (1989) 27(1): 1–31.

112 P. Nolan, 'Walking on water: performance and industrial relation under Thatcher', *Industrial Relations Journal* (1989) 20(2): 81–92.

7 Reform of the industrial relations system and economic restructuring since 1980

1 For definitive treatments of Thatcherism, see A. Gamble, *The Free Economy and the Strong State The Politics of Thatcherism* (London, Macmillan, 1988); B. Jessop, K. Bonnett, S. Bromley and T. Ling, *Thatcherism* (Cambridge, Polity, 1988).

2 Central Statistical Office, *Economic Trends Annual Supplement* (London, HMSO, 1993); S. Kessler and F. Bayliss, *Contemporary British Industrial Relations*, third edition (London, Macmillan, 1998), Table 3.1, p. 41.

3   D. Cannadine, *Class in Britain* (New Haven, Yale University Press, 1998), p. 135.

4   Kessler and Bayliss, op. cit., Tables 3.1 and 3.6, pp. 41 and 47.

5   P. Nolan and K. O'Donnell, 'Industrial relations and productivity', in P. Edwards (ed.), *Industrial Relations* (Oxford, Blackwell, 1995); J. Monks, 'Trade unions, enterprise and the future', in P. Sparrow and M. Marchington (eds), *Human Resource Management* (London, Financial Times Books, 1998); B. Towers, *The Representation Gap* (Oxford, Oxford University Press, 1997), Chapter 5, pp. 140–2.

6   R. Boyer, 'Capital–labour relations in OECD countries: from Fordist golden age to contrasted national trajectories', in J. Schor (ed.), *Capital, The State and Labour.* (Aldershot, Elgar, 1996).

7   I. Clark, 'The state and new industrial relations', in I. Beardwell (ed.), *Contemporary Industrial Relations A Critical Analysis* (Oxford, Oxford University Press, 1996).

8   Clark, op. cit.; B. Jessop, 'Post-Fordism and the state', in A. Amin (ed.), *Post-Fordism: A Reader* (Oxford, Blackwell, 1994).

9   D. Gallie, M. White, Y. Cheng and M. Tomlinson, *Restructuring The Employment Relationship* (Oxford University Press, 1998).

10 C. Crouch, 'The United Kingdom: the rejection of compromise', in G. Baglioni and C. Crouch (eds), *European Industrial Relations the Challenge of Flexibility.* (London, Sage, 1990).

11 S. Broadberry, *The Productivity Race* (Cambridge University Press, 1997).

12 Ibid.

13 Broadberry, op. cit., Table 8.5, p. 111; apprenticeships as a share of employment in manufacturing were 2.29 per cent in 1980 and 1.08 per cent in 1989. Figures for engineering were 3.35 per cent in 1980 and 1.60 per cent in 1989. See Table 8.7, p. 114, for comparative German figures.

14 H. Steadman, 'Vocational training in France and Britain: mechanical and electrical craftsmen', *National Institute Economic Review* (1988) 126: 57–70.

15 M. O'Mahoney and K. Wagner, 'Changing fortunes: an industry study of British and German productivity growth over three decades', *Report Series 7 National Institute of Economic and Social Research* (1994).

16 Gallie *et al.*, op. cit.

17 E. Keep and H. Rainbird, 'Training', in P. Edwards (ed.), *Industrial Relations* (Oxford, Blackwell, 1995).

18 Gallie *et al.*, op. cit.

19 H. Kriegbuam, A. Uhlig and Hans-Gunther Vieweg, *The EU Mechanical Engineering Industry Monitoring the Evolution of Competitiveness* (Munich, Ifo Institut, 1997).

20 *Labour Market Survey of the Engineering Industry* (London, The Engineering and Marine Training Authority, 1998).

21 'International benchmarking of the food and drink manufacturing industry', *The Food and Drink National Training Organization* (London, Food and Drink Association, June 1999).

22 *Employment Outlook* (Paris, The OECD, 1994), pp. 75–8.

23 M. Cully, A. O'Reilly, N. Millward, J. Forth. S. Woodland, G. Dix and A. Bryson, *The 1998 Workplace Employee Relations Survey – First Findings* (DTI, ESRC, ACAS, PSI, London, 1998), pp. 7–10.

24 N. Millward, M. Stevens, D. Smart and W. Hawes, *Workplace Industrial Relations in Transition* (Aldershot, Dartmouth, 1992).

25 N. Millward, *The New Industrial Relations?* (London, The Policy Studies Institute, 1994), pp. 125–30.

26 Cully *et al.*, op. cit., p. 10.

27 J. Storey, *New Developments in the Management of Human Resources* (Oxford, Blackwell, 1992); I. Clark, 'Competitive pressures and engineering process plant contracting', *Human Resource Management Journal* (1998) 8(2): 14–29; S. Wood and M. Albanese, 'Can we speak of high commitment management on the shop floor?', *Journal of Management Studies* (1995) 33(1): 53–77.

28 A. Pollert (ed.), *Farewell to Flexibility* (Oxford, Blackwell, 1991).

29 It appears that Harold Wilson was ready to reject many of the voluntary recommendations in the Donovan Commission Report. He favoured the more interventionary and legislative approach suggested by Barbara Castle in the 1969 White Paper *In Place of Strife*. In addition to this, it appears that all members of the Cabinet, except Callaghan, supported Castle's approach. Callaghan managed to bring the Cabinet round to the idea of continuing with voluntary arrangements. See M. Stewart, *The Jekyll and Hyde Years, Politics and Economic Policy Since 1964* (London, Dent, 1977), pp. 92–4; D. Healey, *The Time of My Life* (London, Penguin, 1989), p. 341; B. Pimlott, *Harold Wilson* (London, Harper Collins, 1992).

30 'Newspapers plot to circumvent union law', *Guardian*, 27 July, 1999.

31 For example, the TUC argue that these concessions breach EU regulations and threatened to complain to the European Commission. See 'TUC Confronts government over working hours', *Financial Times*, 10 September 1999, p. 8. In the light of this threat, Trade and Industry Secretary Stephen Byers attempted to clarify the government's position, suggesting that it was never the intention of the government to exclude an estimated 9 million white collar workers, only senior executives. See 'Unions and Employers should "reach a consensus" ', *Financial Times*, 13 September 1999, p. 14.

32 G. Watson, 'The flexible workforce and patterns of work in the UK', *Employment Gazette* (London), July, pp. 239–48.

33 *Social Trends, 1998* (London, The Stationery Office, 1998).

34 'The impact of labour market arrangements in the machinery, electrical and electronic industries', *The International Labour Organization* (Geneva, ILO, 1998).

35 *Measuring Flexibility in the Labour Market* (London, CBI, May 1999).

36 Cully *et al.*, op. cit., Table 2, pp. 7, 10 and 11.

37 P. Robinson, 'Explaining the relationship between flexible employment and labour market regulation', in A. Felstead and N. Jewson, *Global Trends in Flexible Labour* (London, Macmillan, 1999), pp. 93–9, Figures 5.5 and 5.6, page 95. Scandinavian figure incidence of temporary employment averaged from Denmark, Sweden and Finland.

38 'Our Competitive Future – Building the Knowledge Driven Economy', Cm 4176 (London, DTI/The Stationery Office, December 1998).

39 W. Hutton, *The State We're In* (London, Jonathan Cape, 1995).

40 Clark (1996), op. cit.

41 G. Brown and T. Sheriff, 'De-industrialization', in F. Blackably (ed.), *De-Industrialization* (London, Heinneman, 1979); see also Chapter 3.

42 N. Kaldor, *The Causes of the Slow Rate of Growth of the United Kingdom* (Cambridge University Press, 1966); N. Kaldor, 'Conflicts in national economic objectives', *The Economic Journal* (1971) March; N. Kaldor, 'Capitalism and industrial development: some lessons from Britain's experience', *The Cambridge Journal of Economics* (1977) 1: 193–204.

43 Kessler and Bayliss, op. cit., Table 3.1.

44 N. Crafts. 'Reversing economic decline: the 1980s in historical perspective', *Oxford Review of Economic Policy* (1991) 7(3): 81–98; N. Crafts, *The Conservative Government's Economic Record: An End of Term Report* (London, The Institute of Economic Affairs Occasional Paper 104, 1998).

45 'Our Competitive Future – Building the Knowledge Driven Economy', Cm 4176 (London, DTI/The Stationery Office, December 1998).

46 'Labour productivity levels in OECD countries – estimates for manufacturing and selected service sectors', *The Organization for Economic Co-operation and Development, Paris* (1997) April.

47 'Our Competitive Future – Building the Knowledge Driven Economy', Cm 4176 (London, DTI/The Stationery Office, December 1998), p. 11, paragraph 1.10.

48 'International benchmarking of the food and drink manufacturing industry', *The Food and Drink National Training Organization* (London, June 1999), Executive Summary.

49 Ibid.

50 Source of data, *Economist Intelligence Unit*. For summary discussion of data, see 'Productivity and over-capacity fears lurk behind the celebrations at Ford', *Financial Times*, 22 April 1999.

51 *Economist Intelligence Unit*, op. cit. The Economist Intelligence Unit calculated that Nissan's UK plant is the most efficient in Europe, producing ninety-eight vehicles per person per year, followed by General Motors Eisenach plant in Germany, producing seventy-seven vehicles per person per year. In addition, other General Motors plants in Spain and those owned by Seat and Volkswagen and Fiat plants in Italy all produce more than seventy vehicles per person per year.

52 Ibid.

53 Kessler and Bayliss, op. cit., pp. 236–7, Table 10.6.

54 P. Nolan, 'Walking on water: performance and industrial relations under Thatcher', *Industrial Relations Journal* (1989) 20(2): 81–92; H. Kriegbaum, A. Uhlig and H. Vieweg, *The European Union Mechanical Engineering Industry – Monitoring the Evolution of Competitiveness* (Munich, Ifo Institut, 1997).

55 For a summary of the study, see 'Now Schroder and Germany must face the 1990s productivity test', *Financial Times*, 1 October 1998.

56 T. Nichols, *The British Worker Problem* (London, Routledge, 1986), p. 128; Clark, op. cit., p. 61.

57 Kriegbaum *et al.*, op. cit.

58 Confederation of British Industry Pay Bank Report 17/9/98 (CBI, London).

59 Kriegbaum *et al.*, op. cit., pp. 10–17 and 173–4.

60 The 1998 Capex Scoreboard (London, DTI Innovation Unit, November 1998).

61 Ibid.

62 The 1998 Capex Scoreboard, op. cit., p. 70.

63 Kriegbaum *et al.*, op. cit.

64 W. Cooke and D. Noble, 'Industrial relations systems and US foreign direct investment abroad', *British Journal of Industrial Relations* (1998) 36(4): 581–611.

65 J. Coakley and L. Harris, 'Financial globalization and deregulation', in J. Mitchie (ed.), *The Economic Legacy 1979–1992* (London, Academic Press, 1992).

66 For a full discussion of this issue, see W. Hutton, op. cit.

67 'International benchmarking of the food and drink manufacturing industry', *The Food and Drink National Training Organization*, op. cit.

68 M. Tam, *Part-Time Work: Bridge or Trap?* (Aldershot, Averbury, 1997).

69 The Department for Education and Employment, *Labour Market and Skill Trends 1996–7* (London, The Department for Education and Employment, 1995).

70 The Confederation of British Industry, *Flexible Labour Markets – Who Pays?* (London, CBI, 1994).

71 The Department of Trade and Industry, 'Fairness at Work' White Paper, Cm 3936 (London, The Stationery Office, 1998).

72 The Department of Trade and Industry, op. cit., foreword by Prime Minister, p. 3.

73 'Our Competitive Future – Building the Knowledge Driven Economy', op. cit., p. 11, point 1.12.

74 'Our Competitive Future – Building the Knowledge Driven Economy', op. cit., pp. 47 and 66.

75 See *Financial Times*, 20 April 1999, p. 1.

76 Employment Trends Survey 1999, *Measuring Flexibility in the Labour Market* (London, CBI, May 1999).

77 Gallie *et al.*, op. cit.

78 A. Ferner and R. Hyman (eds), *Changing Industrial Relations in Europe*, second edition (Oxford, Blackwell, 1998), preface by the editors, p. xxxiii.

79 Kriegbaum *et al.*, op. cit., p. 285.

80 Cannadine, op. cit., p. 125.

8 Economic decline: the state, regulation and industrial relations?

1   W. Hutton, *The State We're In* (London, Jonathan Cape, 1995), p. 319.
2   E. H. Carr, *What is History?*, second edition (London, Penguin, 1987), p. 21.
3   B. Jessop, 'Post-Fordism and the state', in A. Amin (ed.), *Post-Fordism: A Reader* (Oxford, Blackwell, 1994).

Subject index

Author index